CW00943672

fuLfiL

ment

© Neo,

. co-uic

Racing Horses

About My Father's Business

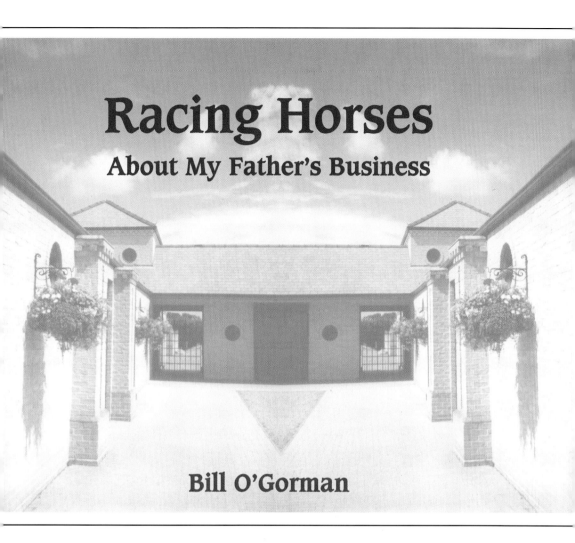

Bill O'Gorman

*I would like to thank Michael McDonnell for his
help with this production*

Romney Publications

⟫⟫◆◀⟪

For all fathers and sons separated by the generation gap

⟫⟫◆◀⟪

ISBN 0-9528566-7-0

ISBN 0-9528566-8-9 (Leatherbound)

Published by:

Romney Publications, UK.

Romney Publications: 351 Exning Rd, Newmarket, Suffolk CB8 0AU, UK.

First published 2000

© Romney Publications. All rights reserved.

No part of this publication may be reproduced by any means without the prior permission of the publishers. Every effort has been made to obtain permission to reproduce the illustrations in this book, but this has not been possible in every case. The publishers apologise if rights have accidentally been infringed.

Designed and typeset by:

Equine Veterinary Journal Ltd., UK.

Printed by:

Geerings of Ashford Ltd., Kent, UK.

Contents

Foreword by Peter Rossdale

*L*ike father, like son is my impression having known Bill for most of his life; a chip off the old block. I was privileged to serve as veterinary clinician to Bill's father, Paddy. He had just started training at Harraton Lodge in Exning and included in his string a number of horses belonging to Jack Gerber, the South African millionaire who had bred and raced the redoubtable Bebe Grande who finished second in the 2000 Guineas (to Nearula) and third in the 1000 Guineas, in the same week, to Happy Laughter. Gerber had a 2-year-old filly, Palm Court, that suffered a severe fracture of the pelvis and required to be put in slings. I remember Paddy sitting all night in the box alongside the filly, over a period of several days. It was this dedication to his charges that distinguished Paddy, along with his depth of knowledge of and insight into the needs, behavioural quirks and factors involving health and disease of horses. Palm Court eventually won a maiden race at Newmarket and, I believe, Jack Gerber told the jockey, Willie Snaith, before the race that if he won he would give him the stake money. Whether or not he ever received this, I do not know.

Paddy came from a farming background in County Cork, moving to England in 1934 and taking various jobs including schooling polo ponies. He also worked with Bertram Mills' Circus, which probably influenced his future approach to horsemanship. Whilst working for the Ministry of Agriculture in Scotland, he married Marie McLeod. When they moved to Burwell he worked at Marshalls and she taught at Soham Village College. Paddy returned to working with horses when he joined Jack Colling at Newmarket and was put in charge of Scaltback Stud. He received his first training licence in 1953 and had considerable success with a small string of inexpensive animals, including Majority Rule, Golden Horus and Drumbeat.

Paddy's son, Bill, was born in 1948 and attended the local Grammar School. He rode as an amateur on the Flat and was twice successful in the Amateur Derby over the Epsom Derby course. He rode Henry Cecil's first winner as a trainer, Celestial Cloud. On his father's death, he was granted his training licence at the age of 21. He trained a small string with moderate success for some years until applying for a jockey's licence, being the first person in the UK to be licensed both as a jockey and a trainer concurrently. He concentrated on precocious and inexpensive yearlings with notable successes, including Provideo and Timeless Times (USA) who both won 16 races at 2-year-olds to equal the record set by The Bard in 1885. Superpower and Mac's Imp (USA) were both champion 2-year-olds in Ireland trained by Bill.

Raymond Hopes, my colleague, who was veterinary advisor to Bill for many years, recounts the background to Bill's first big race winner. Royal Smoke, owned by Irving Allen, the American film producer who owned the Derisley Wood Studfarm, Newmarket, won the Stewards' Cup at Goodwood shortly after Bill's father died. The horse had been returned to Irving's studfarm by his trainer in Epsom as being too lame to train for the cup. Raymond was asked to examine him and could not find him to be lame. He was therefore sent to Bill and, having worked and not gone lame, ran in the cup 5 days later ridden by Taffy Thomas. Bill lavished praise on his previous trainer, but Bill's name is in the record book.

In *Racing Horses*, Bill O'Gorman sets down the techniques of racehorse training that have stood his family in such good stead over the past 50 years. Concerned by what he sees as the gradual demise of good old-fashioned horsemanship, he was anxious to record for posterity the philosophies handed down to him by his late father, who in turn had been the beneficiary of centuries of horse wisdom when growing up in Ireland. As Bill relates, there is no great mystique to the art of training horses;

commonsense attributes such as hard work, patience and empathy with your subject will take you a long way. His sadness is that these days, with racing increasingly a numbers game and its staff crisis growing year by year, those fundamental qualities seem to be in decline.

Of course, Bill O'Gorman's success as a trainer was based on more than old-school values. He was shrewd enough to ally these methods to a commercial awareness, appreciating that in modern-day British racing, with its relatively poor prize money, the best hope of turning a profit was to invest primarily in speed and precocity. It is no coincidence that his best horses were 2-year-olds and sprinters. The fact that within these pages he advocates concentrating on this type of animal to the exclusion of more classically-bred sorts may not please the traditionalists, but his coherently-put reasoning is that the contemporary trainer cannot afford to waste time and his owners' money producing late-developing stayers with little resale value and no prospect of recouping their cost through prize money. It is not an argument that can be lightly dismissed.

Sadly, Bill has all but retired from training, but now perhaps racing's loss will be publishing's gain. At times wise, contentious and instructive, this book is a unique contribution to the literature of the subject and deserves to be read by anyone with an interest in British horse racing in the 21st century.

It is a privilege and pleasure to write this Foreword to Bill's book which highlights the potential for success and failure for those brave enough to take on the task of training racehorses. Bill is, as they say, his own man; and this is reflected in the text through which his spirit shines. "*We stand upon the shoulders of giants*", as Isaac Newton and others have noted; and both Paddy and Bill were giants in their chosen profession.

Outline Of Theory For Equine And Human Survival In Racing

"Prove all things, hold fast to that which is true." Thessalonians 5:21

*D*epending *on one's frame of mind, training racehorses might variously be described as a vocation, a livelihood or an affliction. In fact, it is a fascinating combination of all three. Few professions provide a similar sense of euphoria when things are going well, but the many frustrations involved can often seem a heavy price to pay. Strangely enough, most trainers actually seem to feel that the highs still outweigh the lows. However, they also tend to lose sight of that vital middle element, which is that the exercise is supposed to generate at least enough money, on a regular basis, to enable the stable to be run in a proper manner.*

It is proposed to examine closely the process of training both the racehorse and those who attend to him. As we shall be following certain basic precepts of horsemanship, these notes may also prove of interest to readers who do not necessarily come from a racing background. In an acknowledgement of the fact that the text may at times appear a little long-winded, and does occasionally go off at a tangent, the oral tradition of this subject is pleaded in mitigation. The deviations may prove of general interest and may also be thought to lighten the overall tone. The use of the term 'we' throughout is intended to emphasise the widely ignored fact that both trainer and owner of a racehorse, not to mention lad and jockey, are supposed to share a common goal - success!

A professional trainer should be as aware of all expenditure as if he were spending his own money. Unfortunately, this approach is not, in many cases, welcomed by the very people whose money is at risk. The widely repeated notion that an owner would appreciate an accurate estimate of his animal's ability, or lack of it, is in most cases extremely inaccurate. Many owners will go to great lengths to avoid confronting the fact that their Pegasus cannot in fact fly. Small wonder, then, that the 'Treat owners like mushrooms: keep them in the dark and smother them with bullshit' theory has been so widely and enthusiastically adopted by trainers and owners alike.

Someone has famously said that racing is a game where the trainer has the experience and the owner has all the money, with the game being over when the trainer has all the money and the owner has the experience! Most owners do sail through their racing lives losing money hand over fist and fail to absorb even the most elementary understanding of why that is happening. Indeed, very many owners enter and soon depart the sport with little understanding of what racing is, or at least should be, all about. This sorry state of affairs is so prevalent as to be accepted as the norm. It can hardly be an ideal philosophy in recruiting for long-term participation in the sport, as the ultimate disenchantment factor is predictably high. Fortunately, it is relatively simple to implement a more practical and no-nonsense approach, and it is proposed to explore such a course of action here.

Horse racing, particularly in Britain (because of the low prize money), must be regarded as a very high-risk undertaking, but that risk can be considerably reduced if owner and trainer agree to embark upon a joint strategy of exploiting each and every horse to

Daylami, arguably Godolphin's best runner, was bought from his breeder, The Aga Khan. Frankie Dettori up.
(Photo courtesy of Leslie Sampson)

his maximum potential, and eventually disposing of him to the greatest possible advantage. To have any chance of doing this, they must adhere strictly to a predetermined plan of damage limitation and should never attempt to justify lost causes, either to themselves or to each other. For this seemingly simple plan to work, the trainer needs also to be able to assume that his early recognition of those members of the string not likely to make the grade will be appreciated and that the gaps in the stable strength will be soon filled. Sensible culling must not leave the trainer too short of horses to make a living, or there is little incentive for him to recommend it.

A realistic owner will recognise that, in most cases, a great deal of his loss is made up of training fees. Those fees are far better spent on fresh prospects with some chance of success than on further confirming the fall in capital value of failures. Enormous amounts of money are wasted simply because very many owners seem unable to grasp this basic precept. This irrational approach seems particularly likely when a homebreeding programme is involved and, for this reason, such ventures should never be allowed to become numerically too significant a part of the stable if we hope for above average success.

Anyone advocating a homebreeding scheme as a basis for a competitive racing stable need only examine briefly the workings of the world leader amongst owners, the Dubai-funded Godolphin operation. Although they have access to the produce of the most expensive stud operation ever known, their predominance as a racing stable depends to a very great extent on their continually buying 'made' horses in from outside, with the added consideration that this also effectively removes those athletically proven purchases from the ranks of opposition. If the Maktoum band of excellent broodmares cannot apparently produce enough classy runners to keep Godolphin at the forefront of the sport, there seems little sense in any ordinary breeding programme. The homebreeding-to-race experiment has been carried out repeatedly and, as the results are freely available, we can accept that it is very unlikely to prove effective.

The Aga Khan might be the exception to prove the rule, but the strength of his organisation did not come about overnight. Rather, it evolved over several human and many equine generations.

Perhaps it may be as well at this point to deal with the obvious argument put forward by breeders, that every successful runner was, in fact, bred by someone. However, if there was any sure way of predicting that horse's success, his breeders would have kept him to race themselves, whether they were a commercial operation or not! Homebreds would be exactly as viable as yearling purchases if they were approached in the same way, that is if something like 75% of them were rejected at the yearling stage as physically unlikely to succeed. Taking into account the wastage that will have taken place even before that point, breeding to race is a statistically senseless exercise. It can easily be imagined what the total expense over a long period of time might be of trying properly to implement such a plan, and many exponents delude themselves sadly over the real price of their fantasy. The true cost involved in training unproductive siblings, added to an unwillingness to sell at the optimum time those animals that do show some ability, is astronomical in terms of both finance

and frustration. Quite apart from the cost to the owner, any trainer accepting a disproportionate number of homebreds should resign himself to the fact that, however healthy his monthly cash flow might appear, his chances of major success are severely compromised, purely because the quality of the intake has not been determined by physical examination.

Harry Hieover, in his 1851 publication *The Pocket And The Stud*, scathingly compares homebred horses to homemade sausages and homebrewed ale, remarking that, "The chances are that those who partake of either delicacy will wish they had been made a thousand miles from home!" This writer is well worth seeking out for his humorous and practical slant on many equine matters.

In fact, not only should we take this hint seriously as far as homebreds are concerned, but there is also a strong argument for adopting, albeit at a more modest level, the Godolphin policy of acquiring made horses after someone else has done all the spadework and buried the casualties. It is always well worth paying a premium to get the right item. A stable that believes in its own ability to produce runners should never be afraid to take on selected horses that have already proven their ability.

Buying foals in the expectation of their becoming productive racehorses is safer than breeding, in that we can at least see what we are getting. Although my brother Dick O'Gorman did select the smart trio On Stage, Fayruz and Pacific King for the stable as foals, such young animals are very much liable to change radically for the worse in the ensuing 12 months. Judging foals is a specialist and high-risk area and, as a general rule, the nearer to his actually entering competition that we commit ourselves to owning a racehorse, the greater should be our expectation of success.

It is unrealistic for any owner to set out with the expectation of actually making money in racing. However great his success in his own field and however much business acumen he may

Ascot, winner's enclosure scene - the object of the exercise. Mac's Imp (USA) led by George Aitken and accompanied by jubilant connections Tom Mohan and Michael McDonnell after The Coventry Stakes. Alan Munro up. (Photo courtesy of Kenneth Bright)

bring to bear, the Sport of Kings has many pitfalls. The naïvety of many owners leads to a distinct suspicion among racing professionals that Big Business may not, in fact, be particularly cerebral. A more realistic aim is to play this exciting and challenging game for the long haul, to accept the inevitable lows and to hope to prevent these from becoming disasters by applying a sensible policy based on the laws of probability. Although a serious and professional approach is essential, that does not imply the need completely to abandon basic sporting principles. Scattergun attacks and running horses with a view to their future handicap mark seem currently to be the most commonly adopted

procedures, in spite of the fact that both policies have serious financial drawbacks if properly examined. We should actually expect to achieve a more satisfactory outcome by adopting more traditional values than by following the procedures currently adopted by the majority of the opposition. The satisfaction resulting from being competitive in Group races and at Royal Ascot with inexpensive animals will far outshine the inevitable low spots. Major successes are not an unrealistic aim and, as long as all eyes are kept firmly on the long-term objective and the laws of probability used to advantage, it should be possible to generate enough income from sales to remain in the game with that end in mind.

Physical Examination And Auction Strategy

"Ye have not chosen me, but I have chosen you." St John 15:11

It is difficult to define a set of concrete objectives for a racing stable, as we must deal with many variables. However, it is vital that all inmates should be evaluated as quickly as is reasonably possible. With practice, it will be seen that a fairly accurate prediction of the potential of most horses should have been made by, at the latest, August of their two-year-old year. There may be some exceptions, mainly those who have been injured or sick, but overall culling at this stage will very probably prove cost-effective, even though it may initially be quite unpopular with owners. This policy can only be applied if all purchases are strictly selected as being likely two-year-old runners, although they should also possess the physical scope to give hope of an extended career. It definitely does not pay to purchase the type of horse that will obviously need a lot of time, as the percentage of these big backward horses that do eventually make the grade is not high enough to finance an extra year of training for the whole group whilst they are sorting themselves out. Some of these animals may make handicap campaigners as they get older, but will not have any great resale value in many cases. The same type of horse can easily be purchased after someone else has wasted their money getting him handicapped.

Most eventual top-class horses do not look particularly backward as yearlings, and could show speed as two-year-olds. They may never be called on to do so simply because they enter stables where they will be given time as there is no sense of financial pressure. The better examples of well-bred but obviously physically backward yearlings are very expensive at auction and yet an alarming percentage of them will still wind up in 1³/4 mile maidens at Yarmouth as back-end three-year-olds. 'Backward' can be another way of saying 'slow'! It is much safer to concentrate on those horses that look as if they may come to hand quickly and may be suited by distances up to a mile, because if these horses don't show any early potential it is psychologically much easier for owners to abandon them without worrying unduly that they might come to life for someone else.

Having adopted this approach based on precocity, it might be reasonable, over a period of years, to anticipate 75% of the intake making it to the track, with about half of those winning a race within a reasonable period. Obviously, with prize money lamentably low in Britain, the key to the system's viability must be the resale of the horses, but it is also important to aim at a total of races won that approaches the number of horses we run in any given year. Obviously, wins at the lowest level, whether in selling races or from very low handicap ratings, are useless from the point of view of either earnings, stable prestige or of improving the capital value of the horses. The total income from sales of horses by the yard can be made to equal the cost of buying in yearlings only so long as a high percentage of the stable inmates enhance their resale value by becoming Allowance class runners, or, better still, are officially rated as amongst the leading 5% in the end of year two-year-old standings. All this will, of course, be far easier said than done. However, in the words of the late Newmarket trainer Jack Waugh, "It is vital to have a plan; it may not actually work, but if there is no plan then it can't work!"

"The day you buy is the day you sell" is an excellent maxim for horse buyers to keep before them at all times. The simplest interpretation of this tried and tested precept is that the eventual realistic resale prospects of every animal should be borne in mind even at the time of purchase. Reasonably correct and athletic horses can usually be sold, albeit at reduced prices, after they have been tried, always assuming that their lack of ability has not been too much highlighted in public. A very incorrect horse is unlikely to be helped from an athletic point of view by his defects and, when he has eventually been weighed in the balance and found wanting, it can often be difficult to give him away - in fact, give him away is exactly what we should do. An outstanding French owner/breeder the late Marcel Boussac reputedly employed a rather arbitrary system in which the two-year-olds were formally tried and those appearing to lack ability were summarily shot. Another ancient formula for disposal of an unproductive team member is to "Swap him for a dog, and shoot the dog"!

Most yearlings will be bought at public auction and it is as well to give some thought to the advantages and pitfalls to be encountered at the sales. The greatest advantages of the auction system are that far greater choice is available than with any other method, and the fact that comparisons can readily be made with other animals of similar age. The biggest drawback is the possibility of political and financial intrigue.

One method very popular with many owners is the production of a list of potential purchases before the sale. This approach is used by the majority of those considered to be the most serious players. However, it has little to recommend it to anyone intending to put together a stable of runners at reasonable cost, for the simple reason that the numbers on a list compiled from the catalogue will appear on similar lists supplied to all the opposing buyers. There is no point in making lists unless we are financially in a position to apply the simplest of all formulas for success at auction, which is just to bid last!

One of the problems that can arise when too much soul-searching goes into the proposed purchase of one particular animal is that, as there is no guarantee that the most suitable lots will be evenly distributed throughout the sale, it is very easy to miss the next suitable purchase purely because we are still fretting about the loss of a previous lot. This is far less likely to happen if we are trawling the whole of the sale for suitable purchases without the constraints of any list.

Another drawback to the lists method is the clear and present danger of the vendor, heaven forbid, being able to divine enough of our intentions to formulate a sales ring strategy that may not be to our advantage. As a basic rule, no one should be aware of our plans, something that will be even more important when we have proved ourselves a discerning buyer. In the event of our achieving better than average results with our selections over a period of time, it is as well to be wary of doing the leg work for the opposition. Some people may be aware enough, and uncharitable enough, to observe for which horses we are bidding and, without bothering to do their own research, outbid us.

It is vital to bid quickly and decisively and to give rival bidders the distinct impression that resistance is useless. The only time less aggressive tactics are indicated is if we have any suspicion that the vendor could be, probably indirectly, taking a hand in the proceedings. Obviously, if that were the case it would be more constructive to give a strong impression that we might walk away at any second. However, as long as the price is around our estimate, it is usually better to get the job done in the ring, even if we may suspect a little vendor support. The situation often gets confused when trying to buy an unsold yearling after the auction, especially if he is an attractive type; and if he isn't a nice horse we shouldn't have been trying to buy him in the first place. The ludicrous recent decision of the racing authorities in Britain to consider animals that have been bought-in at auction to be qualified for Auction races has obviously given at least tacit acceptance to the questionable practice of vendors bidding for their own horses.

The best method of buying yearlings, in fact probably of buying anything, is to see as many examples as possible and to be prepared to make quick decisions. We must have the judgement and the knowledge to bid confidently on a horse that we may have seen for only two or three minutes. This is obviously not a technique that can be acquired overnight, but it can be learnt in time. It is not practical when using this system to have the horses examined by a vet; however, once we have mastered this way of operating this will cause few problems. We could probably inspect several yearlings during the time spent discussing the veterinary report on one. This does not imply a dismissal of veterinary opinion, but a recognition of the fact that vets must always err on the side of caution, for professional reasons. If we were to involve them then we should logically give credence to their opinions which would make the system advocated here unworkable.

If we do buy a yearling with a serious wind problem then we can return him. If he has something that shows up on an x-ray but is invisible to our naked eye and is not apparently bothering him, we are probably better off not knowing. Many good horses have been rejected under these circumstances. In fact, there is some argument for saying the old system, which did not even guarantee the wind of yearlings, was better than the one we have now. Once the hammer fell they used to be sold, for better or worse, and there was no comeback or soul-searching.

Of course, the ideal situation would be getting an iron horse like recent American champion Skip Away and then having his price discounted by the vendor because of a minor defect!

For the purpose of argument, unless we are spending a lot of money, we should forget about routine vetting of yearlings and concentrate on refining our own ability to sum up horses quickly. This is definitely a technique that can be learned, but it does require discipline and concentration. Implementing it may be easier said than done when there are a succession of moderate individuals to be examined and, in this situation, it is always better to err on the side of ruthlessness than to attempt to make a case for poor individuals that may appear acceptable because they are the best of a bad lot.

It is essential to record basic conformation notes on all yearlings examined whilst honing these skills; the very fact of summing up any horse in writing concentrates the mind on the business in hand. The description of each horse will necessarily be brief, virtually in shorthand, but it will serve to enable us to describe each yearling to members of our team. This procedure for evaluating every sales yearling may have been originally applied in England by Richard Galpin, and was passed to me by my brother Dick who spent his early career with Galpin at the Newmarket Bloodstock Agency. Obviously, it is essential to use the same parameters when describing every animal. It is an excellent proof of the effectiveness of this system if we can confidently use our yearling description as a snapshot of horses we may be selling at a later date, subject to adding any blemishes sustained during their racing career.

As we will, by and large, be working within a small group of people, it can also be helpful in some cases to refer to past horses known to our group. This can be very useful if we have seen a yearling that should probably fail a strict inspection but which we feel has something to recommend him. However, we must bear in mind that the benchmark horse mentioned was good in spite of his faults, not because of them!

Just as the method of working from a preselected list can cause problems, there is a drawback to this snap decision method in that if one of us is unable or unwilling to take the time to attend the sale he must either give carte blanche to those who do attend, or risk missing horses that fit our requirements. It is because prospective owners quite naturally wish to feel involved in how their money is spent, without necessarily investing the time to inspect the large numbers of animals, that the list system has evolved. It is greatly valued by both vendors and bloodstock agents as an aid to their forward planning.

Now that we have, more or less, determined our approach, it is time to discuss the actual basis for the selection of yearlings to race. The guiding principle is still that "the day we buy is the day we sell", and if we adhere to this we cannot go far astray.

It is not intended for this to be a technical or complicated work on equine conformation, as there exist many excellent offerings elsewhere for detailed study. However, these notes may prove the equivalent of the popular no-nonsense guide books now in vogue in other fields. The excitement at which both media and public greet those who have revived an awareness of training and schooling practices which were well recognised a century ago is clear evidence of how widespread the loss of basic equine awareness has become in a mechanical age.

Whilst on the subject of magic, reference should be made to those farm horsemen of an earlier era, particularly those in East Anglia and Scotland, the ablest of whom were at great pains to protect their personal horse knowledge through the ritual of secret societies which mystified and even demonised it. Theirs was a purely oral tradition of passing on that knowledge, the Horseman's

Word, to selected followers who were sworn to secrecy. Written records were so encoded as to be uninformative to the layman. The tradition of these men having made a pact with the Devil added to the potency of their influence in their community. Secret ceremonies involved blood oaths, sometimes sealed by shaking hands with the Satanic cloven hoof, and a form of Black Mass. Visits to lonely streams at midnight and at full moon were made in order to select a toad's bone talisman; the selected bone being that which would float upstream against the current, and which would invest its possessor with great power over all horses. These practices naturally set members apart from their contemporaries, maintained their mystique and also guaranteed their social and financial supremacy in the working hierarchy. Obviously, in order to maintain this state of affairs such men had to demonstrate in their daily lives a superior 'power' over horses; however, the shield of perceived magic very effectively protected their copyright of advanced equine behavioural knowledge from challenge by uninitiated rivals. They seem to have relied on the horse's sense of smell to perform some of their more spectacular achievements. The ability to fix a horse on the spot by use of a scent as an arresting agent is well authenticated, and was a favourite method of demonstrating the Horseman's uncanny power. Once so halted the animal could only be moved if the smell was neutralised by whoever had fixed it - or by someone else who shared the secret. A certain awareness of the horse's sense of smell survives in the application of 'Vick's vapour rub' to the nostrils of colts who share transport with fillies. On a more basic level, it is likely that many of them relied on various forms of war bridle as a training aid, although they may have tended to fashion such equipment from a cord sufficiently light to have been unobtrusive beneath a working horse's harness. Like many talented specialists, those horsemen were at pains to develop their knowledge and observation of their subject continuously, but they also adopted a little showmanship, not to say shamanship, as a commercial safeguard of the time that they had invested.

Suffolk was heavily represented in the early emigrations to the New World, with some of the earliest Pilgrim Father arrivals hailing from Groton in deepest Suffolk. The Senate House in Washington was built with bricks from Woolpit, which is only a few miles from Newmarket. Great similarities in archaic speech patterns, and even in accent, between some less progressive or less outward-looking populations in America and East Anglia still exist today, and many instances reflect 17th century English rather than incorrect usage. A prime example is the universal American remark that a horse "win", rather than "won", when referring to his past exploits. This would be quite normal in the villages in Suffolk as a shortening of the old past tense "winned". "Good ol' boy" and "neighbour" are very common terms in the Newmarket area, and the very ancient form "yeah" was the normal term of agreement amongst the older rural population long before they had enjoyed any exposure to transatlantic speech. Reinforcement of an idea by the use of a double negative is another throwback to a more naive age, both in East Anglia and in America. Two words are perceived as reinforcing the point, rather than nullifying each other. As the doyen of American jockeys, Eddie Arcaro observed - "Don't get beat no noses!" Those American horsemen currently gaining global acclaim in the equine behavioural field may after all prove to be part of a tradition quite local to Newmarket.

George Ewart Evans touches frequently on such matters in an excellent series of works on East Anglian rural life in the 19th century, published by Faber from 1960 onwards. Most of the successful practitioners of public horsetaming did publish books, or at least pamphlets, advocating their methods. Unfortunately, many have not survived the Internal Combustion Revolution and they are no longer easy to find. The most comprehensive recent work may be a series of four books first published in the 1970s and 80s by Tom Roberts in Australia. There are also one or two recent anthologies giving brief details of the leaders in this field, although these works tend to dismiss or even ignore some previously acclaimed exponents of the art altogether, presumably due to the difficulties encountered in properly researching the subject.

Revenons a ces moutons! No racehorse was ever helped by being incorrect. That is to say, by being made in a way that compromised his athletic efficiency, even though many horses have achieved great things in spite of seemingly serious defects. Bearing in mind that it is not unknown for people to get struck by lightning or to win the lottery, but that both are very unusual, we must confine our buying to those yearlings which appear, mechanically, to stand a reasonable chance of surviving rigorous training and of emerging sound enough to be sold on as a racehorse at the end of that training.

To define in a few words the ideal type of racehorse is not easy. In fact, one of the most repeated sayings is that they run in all shapes and sizes. However, careful analysis of successful runners, whilst it will definitely show a wide range of differing physiques and, indeed, of defects, will also reveal many essential qualities that have enabled those animals at least partially to overcome any structural handicaps. We must remember that however good an incorrect horse may appear he must, by definition, be compromised by his physical faults. He cannot run as fast as he would have done as a correct individual, he probably will not stand the preparation he needs to show his best possible form, and his career may well be cut short due to predictable injury. Traditionally, those colts which were best received as stallions were animals which had completed fairly long and arduous careers on the turf. Sadly that is no longer the case. The fact that a short (and frequently medication-assisted) career has become acceptable in a stallion prospect is not, however, likely to be of much assistance to us when we are readjusting our portfolio, as we will normally be selling second-hand racehorses, which must still be sound to race at the point of resale.

The single most important asset in the racehorse is athleticism and, if it comes to a straight choice between an athletic and precocious, but slightly incorrect, individual and an absolutely correct, but inactive and stolid-looking one, the athlete should be selected. In making this choice, we would weigh the prospect of being in and out of our ownership of the athletic one, having hopefully won a race or two, against the alternative of eventually having to sell the less athletic one as a correct riding horse. With this in mind, we should make our first requirement that any yearling we buy carries himself at the walk as if he means business. The best indication of an athletic stride is obtained when the subject is viewed from the side. The hind foot should easily clear the print left by the forefoot and the whole body, from head to the tail, should demonstrate an easy and rhythmical swing. If, which is not the case, we were to make our selection based on only one requirement, this might well be it. This pattern of walking initially indicates that the horse may cover the ground in an efficient manner. Unfortunately, it would appear to have become a more common accomplishment and is presumably, in some cases, acquired rather than natural, since the use of walking machines in yearling sales preparation has become widespread. It is essential to view the horse from the front and, to a lesser extent, from the back, in order to discover whether the flight of his feet is straight enough to allow him to move efficiently at

speed. There are no walking races. A horse that overstrides but forges, catching the ground surface of the toe of his front shoe with his hind foot as he walks, should be avoided.

A word of caution is needed here about the overstride theory as an indicator of speed. Although this is a most effective indicator of likely speed, there can be situations where the reverse is true. Horses that demonstrate an extreme overstride of around 18 inches should be viewed with some suspicion. These animals are often not absolutely positive and controlled in their hind action. We should have these ones turned round and round very sharply, in both directions, to observe their coordination. If they appear to get their legs tangled up then they may have coordination problems. The same applies to horses that tend to kick the dirt or gravel up with their hind feet when they walk. Experience shows that an appreciable percentage of the very exaggerated overstriders will not have complete control of their movements. We want a good loose walk, but not too loose. With practice, the potential disasters are easy enough to recognise.

If we like the way the yearling moves in the walking ring we next need to examine him at rest. At Keeneland the reverse procedure must be employed, because the horses are standing still when we first see them. In actual fact, it is much easier to look at a large number of horses at Keeneland because they are standing in line, approximately 20 at a time. It is relatively easy to determine those correct enough to be followed up to the presale walking ring in order to see them walk for a few strides. Remember, this method of purchasing calls for very quick decisions and considerable self-belief, but once we have mastered it the system does work very well.

At rest, the horse is first viewed from the side and, with practice, an overall impression can quickly be formed. The very same opinion could probably be formed, after lengthy measuring procedures and at considerable

The ideal sprinting physique - Paranoide (Arg), brilliantly speedy and a durable weight-carrier.
(Photo courtesy of Caroline Fyffe and Yearsley Bloodstock)

expense, by various specialist commercial organisations. The basic requirements of good conformation are not disputed by the majority of successful buyers, but unless our eye has been trained to observe the important facts swiftly and accurately it is impossible to review any large number of horses in the time available. This is the rationale behind a refined version of the list theory based on pre-examination by a third party. We can only use this method if we have absolute faith in the third party's judgement, as horses once left off a list are unlikely to be seen in time to examine them. Those on the list may tend to include some animals with which the list provider already has some financial or political connection. A successful racing enterprise cannot afford to become a clearing ground for other people's mistakes, and all horses added to the stable strength should be selected on their own merit.

Opinions vary as to the right size for a yearling. Any auction provides an impression of what is the average size at any particular stage of the sales season. There is a great difference between July yearlings and December yearlings. We should prefer an individual of medium size but for the overall purposes of our programme it is safer to err on the side of too small rather than too big. We should not buy a small horse unless he is strong and well-muscled and looks as though he will come to hand quickly. We need to think in terms of being in and out of our involvement with him, having won a race or two, before the better class opposition appears and, hopefully, before there are any other two-year-olds for sale. It is often possible to obtain an excellent price for an early season two-year-old with form, purely because it is a seller's market. Big yearlings carry the additional risk of tending to be more backward, which makes it much more difficult to form a confident early opinion of their eventual worth. Meanwhile they can eat us out of house and home. A possible exception to this rule is the taller sprint type of yearling who already looks quite mature. This stamp of horse, although at first glance too big, may be seen on closer examination to have a level top line, with his withers well developed and clear of his shoulder; he may have done most of his growing already. Should this horse pass the other aspects of our inspection, then we should buy him; early next year he will probably have a distinct physical advantage, which his contemporaries will be unable to challenge.

These horses are just more mature than the rest and all else being equal, may be too strong for their rivals early in the season. Sometimes this type can look very good as early two-year-olds, and can realise excellent resale prices, without actually being tremendously talented. The ideal situation here is if they have something close up in a sprinting pedigree that makes staying a mile look feasible to the next purchaser, enabling us to charge a premium price. It is not recommended to buy this physical type unless they are speedily bred; they will tend to be more expensive if they have a stouter pedigree and in that case will probably still need plenty of time.

After checking the basic size, we are looking for symmetry. Whether we seek it from a mechanical or an aesthetic point of view scarcely matters, but without it no horse can deliver optimum performance. As noted elsewhere, racehorses might run with defects,

but not because of them. Good-looking horses are always easier to dispose of than ugly ones. Basically what we want to see first are a well-sloped shoulder and a good length from the point of the hip to the tail and to the hock. Study of the equine skeleton will probably demonstrate the reasons for this, but we need only keep it before us as a benchmark. The impression that the shoulder, as indicated by the withers, goes well into the middle of the back is very desirable. Actually what we are looking for is a horse that appears to have a relatively short back although his overall length is good. As a very general rule, horses with a longer back and a short hip will tend to be stayers, although many of them do seem to lack speed without even being true stayers! These horses will not tend to do well when viewed for overstride at the walk.

In viewing mature horses, a level top line is desirable, but in yearlings, because they tend to grow in fits and starts, this is not always the case. Often a yearling will be an inch or two higher behind than in front and most of them will have levelled up by the time they are ready to run. Occasionally, particularly with sprinters, including some pretty smart ones, they never do level up. Sayyaf and to a lesser degree Group One winner Sayf El Arab were high-class sprinters with this conformation.

As we are really selecting for likely two-year-old ability it is as well to favour those that already show better than average strength and development across their loins. This is particularly important in a small yearling.

The neck should look in proportion to the size of the animal. Opinions seem to differ on the optimum length, but as a general rule it seems reasonable to suppose that if it looks right it is right. A very stallion-like neck is not desirable, and may be an indication that the presale diet has included other than grain and hay. It is not uncommon for very impressive-looking sales yearlings to fall away badly once the steroids and growth

Sayyaf, a high class performer until the age of five despite having sizeable splints as a yearling

a) Defeating champion sprinter Sharpo, Tony Ives up

b) Getting a well deserved pat from Elaine O'Gorman afterwards, with brother Dick in background.
(Photo courtesy of Wallis)

promoters get out of their systems. The opposite extreme, a ewe neck that looks as if it is put on upside down, is not recommended either. These horses can tend to be awkward to restrain, particularly when they have had a little speed introduced into their training; they also give the impression that should they wish not to go through with their effort in a race then they will be difficult to ride.

The head can be a very emotive subject, and whilst horses do, without doubt, run with all sorts of heads there are certain points we can bear in mind. Obviously we would prefer a horse with a handsome head, in proportion to the rest of him, with big, bold eyes, medium-sized ears and a proud expression, and the nearer we can get to that ideal the better horse we are likely to have. Lop-eared horses are uncommon nowadays, but were traditionally supposed to be very honest; on the other hand even in Shakespearean times a "prick-eared rogue" was considered less than ideal. It is possible that prick ears might indicate over-reliance on hearing due to defective eyesight, which might well explain behavioural problems with these animals. Experience seems to show that deviation from the ideal, although often unavoidable, does bring various more or less

Superlative returns after the July Stakes - The Look Of Eagles. Tony Ives up, David Lowry at his horse's head. Milk of the Barley's lad Eddie Cuthbert, in dark glasses, and a youthful Newmarket Heath gallops manager John Taylor follow him in.

serious problems with astonishing regularity. Horses with a prominent bump between their eyes are virtually certain to be difficult to deal with once they start to feel the pressure of training. Horses showing distinct white around their eyes tend to be flighty, probably because the eye is not set in the head correctly and vision may be distorted.

A more positive observation is that those few horses that do turn out to be talented runners may very often exhibit a confident, rather distant, expression, even as yearlings. This has been referred to by horsemen as the 'Look of Eagles' and, all else being equal between two horses, we should definitely favour the one who shows this trait. A haughty demeanour will not, of course, protect him from the many risks he will encounter in training.

We have now completed the basic examination of the body and must move on to the forelegs, which are the most common source of problems in the racehorse. This is basically a mechanical examination and there are certain basic precepts that should be adhered to as closely as possible, although the ideal situation of complete balance and strength is depressingly rare. This is where experience in making serious and immediate decisions about the likely viability, or otherwise, of yearlings as racing prospects is essential. We do need a reasonably sound, if basic, appreciation of the structures of the leg. This must be coupled with a working knowledge, based on experience and observation, of what constitutes an acceptable deviation from the ideal.

Moving away from the body we first examine the forearm. This is not an area that causes many problems, as although it will occasionally be subject to stress fractures these will probably heal unaided, sometimes even undiagnosed. It is desirable to have a strong and well-muscled forearm and this seems usually to be the case in fast horses; it is a very noticeable feature of Quarter Horse conformation.

Most leg trouble in Thoroughbreds occurs in the front legs from the knee down, because at some point in each stride the total weight of the body plus that of the rider will be passing over each foreleg in turn. Obviously, a simple calculation combining this weight with the speed involved will give an idea of the enormous stress to which this relatively delicate structure is subject, and confirm the need to keep as close as possible to an architecturally, for want of a better word, sound construction of the limbs.

Viewed from the side, the forelegs should ideally be quite perpendicular through the knee, that is to say the horse should neither be 'over at the knee' with the knee appearing to sag forward, nor 'back at the knee', also called 'calf-kneed', with the knee appearing to be bent backwards. The former is very uncommon now, and although it always looks as if it would make stumbling more likely, the older generation in Newmarket used to say that horses never got a tendon strain when they had this conformation. A degree of back at the knee conformation seems to be virtually unavoidable nowadays, and our inspection will, in most cases, be determining levels of acceptability on this score. Most slightly afflicted horses seem to show few ill effects, particularly if their pastern set-up is normal. There may be additional stress to the tendon area in more serious cases and there is greater risk of all injuries caused by backward deviation of the knee. This is demonstrated in the alarming photos sometimes seen, usually taken near the end of a race, where the knee of the supporting foreleg seems to be displaced backwards into a grossly exaggerated version of the original conformation defect, whilst the fetlock has dropped right onto the track surface. These injuries tend to involve both soft tissue strains at the rear of the limb and crushing injuries to the front surfaces in both knee and fetlock areas.

There is some difference of opinion on the importance or otherwise of a horse having plenty of bone below the knee. The point at which the theoretical measurement is taken includes soft tissues, and the value of checking this area is to be sure that the horse is not 'tied in' below the knee, that the line of the rear of the tendon is perpendicular to the ground. The side-on view of the leg below the knee must not give the impression of being narrower just below the knee than just above the fetlock as this tied-in conformation does seem to predispose to tendon injury. As far as the bone itself is concerned there seems to be every possibility that the rather coarser types of seemingly heavy-boned horses remain less sound than the light-boned ones. We should feel the tendons and joints, but it is most unlikely that at this young age any damage will be felt. However, we will occasionally see a yearling with a tendon that is not quite straight. Some of these are not very noticeable from the side-on inspection and we must always look down the leg whilst positioned at the horse's shoulder to check for any deviation. Even though these may not be true tendon injuries (possibly being what is known as a 'bandage bow' or resulting from carelessly fitted lunging boots) we should reject these horses.

The fetlock joints should look and feel tight and firm, not fleshy or gummy, as after all

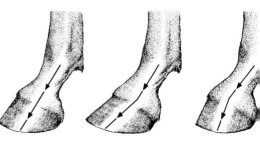

| Ideal | Axis broken back
- long toe
(or v. straight pastern) | Axis broke forward
- club foo
(or v. slac pastern) |

they are supposed to be virtually new. We occasionally notice a slight gristly appearance on the front of the joint, which does not appear to cause problems. It is very important to check the rear inside area of the joint for damage due to interference in the sesamoid area, and this can be confirmed visually from another angle when we observe the horse obliquely from behind.

The angle of the front pastern should probably be in the region of 50° to the ground. This is obviously not an exact specification, and if it looks all right it usually is. In areas like this, the auction situation does provide ample scope for comparison with the apparent norm. The angle of the centre line of the pastern should agree with the angle of the front face of the foot. If the foot is markedly steeper than the pastern the axis is said to be 'broken forward', while if the reverse is true, as is typical of 'long toe, low heel' shoeing, then the axis is 'broken back'. The pastern must not be too long, and this can easily be checked as the yearling walks. A long pastern shows too much slackness, and in this case the axis tends to be broken forward. Even at a walk it is obvious that the fetlock joint is descending too far towards the ground and it can be imagined what might happen at speed. If in doubt, comparisons are readily available. Too short or

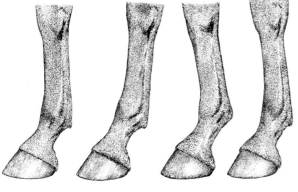

Ideal   Back at knee   Over at knee   Tied in

too upright a pastern is not acceptable either, as this causes a different (though in fact less disastrous) set of problems due to the failure to absorb the shock of hitting the racing surface; once again, if in doubt, compare. There seems to have been a distinct change over the last 30 years, in that very straight in front or upright yearlings are now uncommon, whereas the number with very long, slack pasterns seems to be increasing. It would be interesting to determine whether this is due to genetic or dietary factors. There may be some confusion amongst beginners as to whether a horse should or should not be straight-legged! The front legs should appear as straight as possible when viewed from the front but not when viewed from the side.

Ideally, the knees should appear flat when viewed from the side. However, they will sometimes appear concave in profile, in which case they are called 'open' knees and may indicate that the horse will require a little more time for the knees to mature. This conformation should probably not deter us from buying an otherwise suitable animal and, in fact, they may well lower his price. The reverse, which is a convex profile or any protruding irregularity of the knees, or more likely, of one knee, should be regarded with grave suspicion. If there is evidence of a superficial injury to account for the swelling, and if there are also x-rays to demonstrate that the joint itself is not involved, then this too may indicate an opportunity to buy at a discounted price.

We are now ready to give some thought to the feet of our subject. Everyone has heard of the saying "No fut, no 'oss". Fortunately this is not quite true, in view of some of the offerings we are about to witness. However, there is no doubt that a good-footed horse is easier to train than a bad-footed one. The front face of the forefoot, viewed from the side should again, ideally, rise at an angle of around 50° or so to the ground. This does not need to be precise, and yet again there is every opportunity to make a judgement based on what seems to be the norm amongst the sale entries. It is, however, important that an imaginary line drawn through the middle of the pastern shows an angle virtually identical with the angle of the front face of the hoof. Fortunately, at this age there is every chance of this still being the case, but we need to be sure that long toe, low heel shoeing, even in the short time he will have been shod, has not altered this hoof-pastern axis from normal to broken back.

The feet of yearlings, particularly in Britain, have been much altered for the worse in the last relatively few years. The causes of this are an ever-increasing paranoia on the part of vendors about apparent correctness in their consignments. This in many cases involves quite severe dressing of the feet on one side or the other from an early age to give the impression of the animal standing straight on his legs. If we add to this many vendors' predeliction for a big foot and further add the fact that it is impossible to keep a properly full-fitted shoe on a yearling that is doing considerable work on the lunge, it will not surprise us to observe many lots with their heels already destroyed, and with feet very flat. Fortunately we can usually improve this flat-footedness and the foot pastern axis in moderate cases. It is difficult to predict the likely outcome of subjecting many of the more severely corrected horses to a strenuous athletic regime. This should theoretically be one area where a homebred programme could be an advantage, but even studs breeding to race seem to delight in trying to improve on nature. Correction is now the general order of the day. We may not always spot moderately collapsed heels, even by picking up the foot, as the final shoeing before the sale will be a little more full at the heels, thus hiding the true position of the heel itself. If the underside of the foot seems to have little arch to the sole, and if the impression is that it seems a big foot for the size of horse we can anticipate some problems. However, this situation is now prevalent, and we have to live with it; how to address it will be dealt with elsewhere.

Although it is not yet clear exactly what the problem may be, there should be definite scepticism about the overall training prospects of any yearlings that demonstrate patches of white horn on a black foot which has no white hair at the coronet. The same thing applies to those white-footed horses showing a great deal of red bruising in the walls of their feet. Unfortunately, these animals are often virtually impossible to spot due to the thick hoof dressing in general use. Severe fever rings on the feet of a yearling are often a sign of some episode of illness, but may also be associated with dietary changes in the sale preparation; in general they may give less cause for suspicion than do the red or white marks on the feet. The latter often seem to predict reduced racing success from these animals, whose systems may be so undermined as to prevent their standing the rigours of training. Were any of our purchases to exhibit such marks once the dressing had worn off his feet we would be well-advised to immediately initiate an extended course of treatment with a broad spectrum antibiotic. It is as well to start the treatment without waiting to discover whatever bizarre symptoms might emerge should, as is likely, the marks result from a laminitic episode connected with a systemic disease which might have invaded the central nervous system. This subject will be discussed more fully at a later point.

We must now examine our prospect from head on, and once more we will look at him from an engineering point of view. What we would hope to see first is a fairly wide chest indicating sufficient space for what is, basically, the engine room, and to allow reasonable clearance between the forelegs.

Our next wish is for a leg in which a vertical line, viewed from the front, passes through the middle of the forearm and continues through the middle of the knee, the cannon bone, the fetlock, the pastern and the hoof in turn. Unfortunately, in most cases we will be disappointed. The purpose of our examination is to decide which horses are likely to live with any minor shortcomings and emerge relatively unscathed, and saleable, after strenuous training and racing. If a horse has good form, and his x-rays are clean, minor incorrectness will probably be accepted by whomever we happen to sell him to next year. This applies only to minor deviations from the ideal; a very incorrect individual will always be regarded as an accident waiting to happen, and we may well find ourselves unable to sell him. Once again, degrees of deformity can easily be compared in the sales paddock, but with practice the decision-making process becomes largely intuitive.

The condition in which the knee does not sit directly above the fetlock and squarely between the forearm and the cannon bone we will call 'offset knee'. It is quite often present in only one leg. Simple observation shows that this condition vastly increases the forces at work both in the knee itself, leading to fractures, and below it, leading to splints. There will also be an effect on the flight of the foot. The animal must at every stride, in order to proceed forward, swing the offending foot into the direction of the body's progress and away from the direction in which it faces at rest. The variation can be either in or out, relative to the horse's mid-line. Offset knee is due to different rates of growth in the small bones of the knee as a foal and may be related to diet. This is not intended to be a technical discussion, and we will not attempt to distinguish between carpus valgus, where the leg goes out from the knee, or the reverse conformation, carpus varus. Nor will we bother to remark on 'base wide' and 'base narrow' stance since both in most cases merely reflect an irregularity higher up the

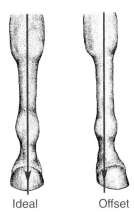

Ideal   Offset

leg. For the purposes of our shorthand, every variation of this common affliction will be referred to as 'offset'; if we do wish to record the direction of the deviation we can add the self-explanatory 'knock-kneed' or 'bow-legged' to our description. When viewing large numbers of horses at a sale it will be obvious that a high proportion of them are slightly afflicted. We should not bid unless our comment is 'slightly offset' at worst, and the horse otherwise appears attractive. Anything more than minor affliction with this condition will still count against a horse when he is being resold, particularly to America, however good his form might be. If we wished to avoid confusing purists by blanket use of this terminology we might consider substituting some other general adjective, such as 'crooked knees'. Although it is not unheard of to see useful racehorses with even a considerable degree of offset knee conformation, it is very common to see it in bad horses.

Obviously, all yearlings will wear boots for breaking. It may be advisable for those that turn their front feet out slightly, and which will therefore swing them inwards as they move, to continue to wear boots at exercise as even very minor regular contact, though not serious enough to cause lameness, may easily result in a blemish. Apart from being unsightly, any fullness caused by hitting on the inside of the joint will of course further increase the danger

of interference and injury. If the horse is normally protected in this way, and does not seem to mark the boots, we will probably dispense with the weight of the boots on race day. If he does regularly touch the boots, greater caution is called for.

The various descriptions applied to limb and gait deviations can prove confusing. An easy aide-memoire is that when used to describe either the direction of the leg below the joint or the direction of foot in flight then the shorter words 'varus' and 'dish' refer to the shorter preposition in, and the longer words 'valgus' and 'paddle' refer to the longer preposition out. For embryonic sailors the same formula should be used to remember the directions for port and starboard!

Any splints that are already present at this stage are obviously cause for comment. Often they may be a matching pair. As long as they do not seem to result from stress apparently attributable to a deviation at the knee, splints can provide an opportunity to purchase an otherwise attractive horse at a discounted price. In many cases they will cause no further problems and they will not be held too much against a horse with good form when he is resold. There may also be a possibility of reducing, if not removing, them in some cases. Both Sayyaf and Reesh had two big splints as yearlings. They had originally been purchased to go to other trainers, but eventually came into my stable largely because their purchasers became concerned on closer examination of these blemishes that the horses' prospects were likely to be compromised. Both proved to be very sound horses and won many races at the highest level.

Deviation of the pastern and the hoof relative to the fetlock is simply referred to as 'toe-out' or 'toe-in', and, as in other points of conformation, degrees of affliction can be easily compared. We may also notice situations where the leg goes out from the knee and again from the fetlock but the foot

 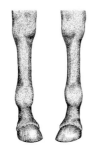 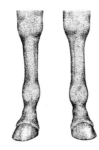

Offset - corrected; still out from knee, but now in from pastern. Foot flight can be unpredictable

Toe in - foot flight paddles out

Toe in - foot flight wings in

Toe out
Axis broken in

Ideal
All near fore

Toe in
Axis broken out

appears to be towards the inside of the pastern when viewed from the front. On viewing the ground surface of the foot, the frog will tend to point inwards.

It is a good idea to look at every horse obliquely from the rear, in order to spot better the rather bulldog-like stance of this condition. The oblique angle of examination can also serve to highlight any irregularity in the sesamoid area, which should be investigated.

Ideally the forefeet should resemble each other as closely as possible in size, shape and angles. Feet that do not appear to be a pair may indicate considerable correction having taken place, although difference in size may be somewhat disguised by a clever shoer. When the foot is picked up, the bulbs of the heels should be level, as if they are not the horse may suffer a 'sheared heel' and this can prove difficult to deal with. It can be taken as evidence of quite severe correction in a horse of this age. Although big, flat feet are

itself tends to turn in. These horses may have been inclined to exaggerate their splay-footed stance when reaching for the grass as foals. As the foal's neck grows longer this problem tends to resolve itself and so the trimming designed to correct the condition may often be unnecessary. The natural decrease in the straddled stance allows the horse's legs to straighten up naturally as he gets older and so greatly exaggerates the effect of any trimming designed to achieve the same result. The fact that the reverse condition occurs rarely tends to reinforce this explanation. This is far from an ideal situation from the point of view of future soundness, but can sometimes look fairly acceptable on quick examination from the front, as the foot may appear to be in line with the body and roughly below the knee joint, although the plumbline will not pass through the centre of the cannon bone and pastern. The foot-pastern axis is now broken out and the bulk of the foot

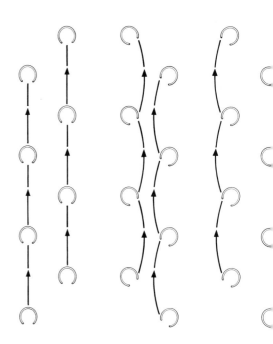

Ideal
Foot travels straight

Splayfooted
Toe out
Wings in

Pigeon to●
Toe in
Paddles o●

The oblique view is an essential part of the examination, demonstrated here by Thoroughbred and Quarter Horse sire Apollo (USA). (Photo courtesy of Vessels Stallion Farm)

undesirable, very small and contracted feet may indicate disease of some description, or may result from lengthy box-rest following a serious skeletal injury.

The uneven stresses that occur in incorrect legs are not the only problem to be faced. Every deviation from the perpendicular will result in a foot flight that cannot be straight. If the foot turns in the flight must tend to be out, known as 'paddling', and vice versa, which is called 'dishing'. The most severe form of dishing is referred to as 'plaiting', which is self-explanatory, and to be avoided. The use of the term 'winging' is acceptable but should be qualified as either 'winging in' or 'winging out'.

Minor degrees of one or other defect may have to be accepted, purely because they are so widespread. Traditionally, toe-in conformation has been generally less abhorred by horsemen than toe-out, simply because pigeon-toed horses do not tend to interfere in front. However, toe-in racehorses can be prone to hitting themselves behind with their front feet due to the path the front foot is obliged to follow coinciding with that of the hind leg. This seems to occur most often in speedy horses, which tend to overstride at the walk, because their hind legs do reach further under the body at each stride. This hazard can often be overcome by careful shoeing. On balance the old horsemen are probably right to prefer toe-in as the lesser of the two evils. There is a possibility of an even more bizarre foot flight with the more severely corrected horses, which often leads to both structural damage and insurmountable interference problems.

We can now turn to the hind leg inspection. Fortunately this is not usually such a danger area as the forelimb in flat racers. Ideally, a vertical line from the point of the buttock should follow the line of the hind leg from the point of the hock down to the rear of the fetlock. Viewed from the side the point of the hock should be level with the chestnut on the foreleg, according to Ben K. Green in his excellent, but hard-to-find, 1969 work *Horse Conformation as to Soundness and Performance*. This will provide the most efficient set-up for the driving mechanism for the whole machine. Obviously, once again, comparisons may be helpful in initially establishing what degree of deviation from this ideal seems to be commonplace. We will in fact be seeing a high proportion of horses in which the hock is placed further behind the body than our favoured position. We can refer to this as 'hocks behind', and should confine ourselves to, at worst, those animals we record as only slightly affected.

The area above the hock is not one that needs particular scrutiny; it should be well muscled and there should be no evidence of swelling or soreness in the stifle area. We should be alert to any slight stiffness or awkwardness behind as a possible indication of stifle lameness, usually caused by bone cysts or OCD lesions. This is unlikely to be causing soreness at this stage, unless we do see the animal when he first leaves his box, but a percentage of horses will have a problem with this in the early stages of training. This is an area where x-ray definitely aids diagnosis and would enable us to avoid the problem. However, given that OCD afflictions seem increasingly common,

and that most horses are either minimally affected or do recover quite well, it does not at the present seem worth disrupting our present system. It is not clear what the true relevance of these lesions, either in the stifle or elsewhere, is to the long-term prospects of the horse, but it is quite clear that they can greatly confuse things at point of purchase. A fairly large-scale survey has recently shown the afflicted animals in a group to have raced more productively than those which did not show the lesions as yearlings!

The repository system of x-rays for presale inspection that is being adopted by American auction companies does make much more information available to purchasers. However, there is no reason to suppose that the introduction of these presale x-rays has altered the percentage of any given foal crop carrying career-threatening injuries invisible to the naked eye, or succeeding at the track. The primary decision on purchase has to be made on the basis of personal examination if we are to have time to go through the majority of the horses in the sale. It will be sufficient to check any certificates lodged in the repository and put a line through the catalogue page of any lot number with a certified fracture or similarly compromising defect that we cannot see on personal inspection in the flesh and evaluate. There just is not time to look at the x-rays of a large enough number of horses. If we are, occasionally, spending a large sum on a particular animal it might be sensible to make an exception and review all available information.

The other problem above the hock that seems to have become more commonplace is a fracture of the tibia. This may merely be because of improved x-ray techniques! These injuries normally heal well on their own.

The hock itself should now be closely examined for blemishes or any deviations from a normal appearance. A curb, if not too unsightly, is not normally reason to reject an otherwise suitable horse, as these rarely give trouble once they are established. Any soft swelling on the hock must be regarded as serious unless it is associated with an active wound. As with the knees, a blemish that does not appear to compromise full flexion can sometimes be overlooked as long as it is the subject of a vet's report and of x-rays showing that the mechanics of the joint are unaffected.

The cannon bone and the fetlock in the hind leg tend to be fairly trouble-free and should appear strong and clean. There are often various minor blemishes due to paddock and transit accidents but these are clearly of no significance in most cases.

The hind feet and pasterns, again, give relatively little trouble in the Thoroughbred. They should be examined in the same way as those of the forelimbs, although the natural angle of the hind foot should be higher, around 55°, than that of the forefoot. It is also important that the angle of the pastern is similarly higher. Weak or slack pasterns are undesirable due to the danger of the animal running down and making the underside of his fetlock joints sore. This happens more frequently behind, and is much more common on artificial surfaces.

Until quite recently all yearlings went barefoot behind, and they still tend not to have been subjected to much correction or alteration to their stance even if they are shod. We should still inspect for deviation of the feet from the direction of the body at rest as the hind feet will be equally subject to erratic flight; however, this is often easier to control in the hind limb by careful shoeing, and at any rate does not normally present problems as severe as when it occurs in front.

If we stand directly behind our subject we can confirm our impression of where both fore and hind feet are positioned and also take note of whether he is very close, which we refer to as 'cow-hocked', or wide and appearing to be bow-legged at the level of his hocks. The

former, because the feet are naturally turned out at rest and so will tend to travel inwards in flight, may cause interference to the other hind leg at a later stage. The latter can give an impression of lack of control, with the hock sometimes appearing to rotate at every stride, although Reesh was a pretty good horse despite being markedly affected in this way.

Having made our inspection of the yearling at rest we will now have him walked about 50 feet straight away from us, and straight back towards us. We should have him continue a few steps past us on the return trip, so as to see him from another angle. This procedure is followed wherever possible, even with the horses we have previously seen in the walking ring, although unfortunately at Keeneland there is no real opportunity to see horses walk far in a straight line without previous visits to the barn area so we must pay extra close attention.

Many horsemen will want to check the airway of each lot, in fact they may well commence their examination on that basis, by determining the width of each horse between his jaw. Obviously, due to varying hand size in different people, each must adopt his own set of values, and as yearlings will tend to be smaller than old horses, presumably further allowances must be made. If we felt the need to adopt this test it would be relatively simple to identify the norm by comparison. However, although it is obvious that a large airway should be an advantage, it is doubtful if anything other than a disastrously small one should be considered undesirable, particularly in horses racing relatively short distances.

Another test, not seen so often in recent years, is the testing of the yearling's tail strength as an indicator of his overall strength. On page 591 of that excellent publication *The New Care and Training of the Trotter and Pacer*, Dr Kenneth P. Seeber says, "When all else checks out normally, a decrease in tail tone seems to be a finding fairly consistent with

Brondesbury posing on Newmarket Heath in June as a 2-year-old. A brilliantly speedy colt.
(Photo courtesy of Rouch & Co.)

EPM." The old horsemen were probably aware of an unacceptable degree of failure in weak-tailed animals in recommending this test and we should certainly give it some thought, particularly if any yearling during our short inspection should show other suspicious signs such as sloppy gait, erratic or very dull or stupid behaviour, or discoloured feet.

EPM, or certainly awareness of it, has increased rapidly in the past several years. The disease is far from completely understood. Possibly it is one of many infections that were inadvertently subdued by the general use of antibiotics throughout society in the last few decades, even to the extent that everyone largely forgot how devastating some of them were. Some of them are presently recurring in more virulent form. Tuberculosis in humans is an example supporting this theory.

The total time we need to spend looking at each yearling to evaluate him on this basis should be less than two minutes. This can only be achieved with practice, and a speedy examination is recommended even when more time is available, in order to remain comfortable with this method. Although it is difficult to explain, it seems that some experienced yearling buyers may develop, over many years, the ability actually to see speed, in the same way that a cattle buyer might predict the better of two beasts. This is probably the ability to perceive a difference in muscle tone, which may in fact be indicative of the ratio of fast-twitch fibres, or something similar. Whatever it is, it takes practice, but results in some successful buyers being able to glance at two yearlings which might measure the same and accurately predict the superior runner.

It is extremely inadvisable to allow a situation to develop at an auction where anyone feels able to ask us to stand back from any particular lot so that they can buy it, and we should not expect to do it to anyone else. This sort of tit-for-tat arrangement invariably causes trouble somewhere along the line. It is also true that no vendor should influence in any way the selection of our purchases, unless he does so indirectly in that he has previously provided us with an above-average number of animals that far exceeded the call of duty in their racing careers. We should actively avoid yearlings from those drafts that have previously shown us below-average results. Stallions whose offspring have on previous ventures repeatedly flattered only to deceive should also be spurned, as such sires may well have some unsuspected but transmissible failing that might account for their regularly getting offspring that fail to fulfil initial promise.

As far as price is concerned, the method detailed here has proved effective in securing runners at very reasonable prices, but to ensure success we should be prepared for an outlay per horse of more than the median for the sale. For instance, if the median (which is normally fairly predictable) is 50% up from the bottom we should be prepared for our own purchases to average around whatever figure is likely to be 66% up from the bottom. This will, based on all past experience, enable us to buy horses both reasonably correct and with a little pedigree to aid the resale prices. If we can pay somewhat above the median we should buy plenty of the type of animals we want, assuming that the sale does contain reasonable specimens. We do not have to spend all the money allotted just for the sake of it, but it is as well to have our budget properly prepared beforehand, so as not to be trying to work it out whilst a prospective purchase is in the ring.

Pedigree

"Fables, and endless geneologies." Timothy 1:4

On the pedigree front we should be very flexible. There is an enormous amount of pedigree expertise available, but it is noticeable that much of it seems to be provided by those who have not themselves been outstandingly successful as owners or breeders. We need to remember that basically our purchase will be unable to call on his relatives in his hour of need, and we should select those whose own physique gives hope of success. In fact we really abandoned the pedigree experts when we abandoned the presale list. Even if we go to a sale where none of the pedigrees convey anything to us, we should be confident of buying able runners using our approach, despite any doubts shed by the established pedigree buffs.

There seems some logic in the theory that it is better to select our purchases on the basis that they are both by and out of successful runners. It is obvious that the actual racing merit of the mares will tend to be much lower than that of the sires; however, that will usually remain true of everyone's selections. The surest recipe for racing ability must logically be racing ability in both parents, preferably demonstrated over an extended career. This is an ideal situation, but if this can be found in a yearling whose own physical attributes are above average, then the expectation of his racing success may be well above average. It may previously have been the case that some major breeders, particularly of harness racers, did retain well-bred unraced fillies for stud (in what is now seen to be illogical expectation that their 'nervous energies' would not have been wasted in competition and so would be passed to their offspring), but we can nowadays assume that any unraced mare failed in some way in her training. Statistically, stakes-winning mares do breed more stakes winners than nonstakes-winning mares, and their offspring, if attractive, will tend to be more expensive.

The most important time for some fashionable aspect in a pedigree is not on the racecourse but when we are fortunate enough to have a stallion prospect to sell, as at that stage pedigree will definitely command a premium. Animals that have close relatives running well in America might attract a higher price for us on resale, but this attraction, which is not always common knowledge, should not be allowed to influence our purchase of an otherwise unsuitable horse.

Mares that have failed to produce successful runners after several attempts should be avoided. The only exceptions might be if the yearling before us is physically outstanding, and either the very low recorded sale prices of his elder brothers and sisters indicate that they were probably moderate individuals, or they were all by stallions which are acknowledged disasters. Brondesbury's pedigree was the proverbial white page, but his own appearance gave every indication of speed. In similar cases we can, to a degree, back our judgement and perhaps benefit from a price that will be depressed by the probably predictable failures of his siblings.

There is no reason to discriminate against old, successful sires. In fact, they can represent excellent value, as even though they may be out of fashion their genetic make up remains, of course, unchanged. First-season sires, on the other hand, can be poor value, since there is a strong tendency for their lots to be protected by their connections, and there is as yet no evidence of their ability to sire winners. A hard-knocking but very unfashionable handicap horse will occasionally present a very good looking yearling, having passed on some of his own attributes. We need to accept that the mares this type of horse attracts are often of very moderate quality and that the stallion's contribution to the total make-up of even a good-looking offspring may not be sufficient to provide a useful runner.

The produce of old mares should be viewed with distinct caution unless the yearling looks exceptionally well forward and unless there is currently a useful two-year-old out of them to indicate that there is still reasonable prospect of success. Mares obviously have much more than a purely genetic input into their offspring, and elderly matrons tend not to have provided for their foal so well, either before or after birth as a younger mare would have done; in these circumstances many yearlings will never catch up.

As soon as we have signed the ticket, we must arrange for the new purchase to be scoped to check that he has no impairment of his airway which will make him returnable. In fact, to be eligible to go back he must both fail the scope and convince a panel of vets that he makes a noise on the lunge. Most people seem to lunge their purchases first, but given that the process involves some risk and stress to the horse, and that he may well be unreturnable anyway on the scope, it makes far more sense to do the scope examination first.

To have realistic hopes of making some sort of impact on the racing scene we must constantly be aware of the laws of probability, and we must equally constantly attempt to weight them in our favour. It is unrealistic to expect to discover high-class runners immediately or regularly. By focusing on the purchase of horses that will have reasonable prospects of resale on a physical basis, we will at least give ourselves a better prospect of generating cash flow. If this ensures a longer turn at bat, it should also increase our chances of hitting a home run.

Breaking In Process

"Let your yea be yea, and your nay, nay." James 5:12

*T*he next part of the process is the breaking of the yearlings to ride, with a view to turning them into racehorses. It has become unfashionable of late to use the word 'breaking', with terms such as 'starting' being adopted instead. However, breaking has been normal usage for centuries, and we will stick with it, though obviously we try our best not to, in any negative sense, break our new investment. What we do want to achieve is a horse capable of showing the very best form of which he is capable whilst being handled by people with a less than perfect grasp of the plot. The Old Man, as we addressed my father in his absence, always said that he made a mistake with the first yearlings he broke in forgetting that they were to be ridden by stable lads and trying to make them into show hacks. That was 50 years ago when the lads were a lot better trained than those we have now; we should always remember the parameters within which we have to operate.

The success of our plan to survive in the racing business will hinge on the viability of our purchases as frequent and productive competitors. This can best be achieved if they are trained for racing in all senses of that word. As well as being fit, they must also learn how to conduct themselves well both in their races and throughout every aspect of their daily routine. If it were possible to enlist the help of some riders with a basic understanding of collection and impulsion for the early stages of our horses' ridden career then that might prove very beneficial in teaching them to carry themselves to the best advantage before their serious training began.

The breaking period is certainly one of the most important stages of a racehorse's career, although the ease with which the process is completed may bear little relation to ultimate success on the racecourse. In fact, many horses that sail through this part of the proceedings without a murmur will spend their whole lives simply going through the motions in the same way if we are not constantly alive to that possibility. This may be even more likely in a big yard and it demonstrates the sometimes fairly close resemblance between equine and human behaviour. This is not anthropomorphism; a horse is naturally not human in his thought processes, but all young things seem to share a tendency to identify quickly the easiest way to get along.

Experienced horsemen will recognise the syndrome whereby an animal that has been allowed to take things too easy becomes resentful if that regime changes. This is very evident in many small ponies, most of which must presumably have started off quite normal, otherwise they would never have been selected as suitable for children, but which often become quite evil in their attitude after being allowed too much leeway. In a similar way, many lads from the bigger stables have become virtually institutionalised and this can hardly avoid affecting their charges. If any assumedly quiet horse is seen to become troublesome with a weaker rider then that rider should be changed immediately, even if only for a few days, in order to prevent the bad behaviour becoming established.

Most of the yearlings we get today are far

easier to deal with than they used to be. Unfortunately, this is often not the case with the homebreds. The sales preparation today is in most cases so well managed that many youngsters are nowadays virtually broken when trainers receive them, certainly by the standards of 30 or 40 years ago. Unfortunately, the skill of the lads who will have to ride them has been decreasing at a very similar rate. What would happen were today's riders faced with the almost untouched intake that was then the norm is anybody's guess. Happily that is not the case, although we are now suffering the effects of a benign, rather than a vicious, circle in that because awkward horses are now uncommon the necessary procedures that allowed them to be handled relatively easily have been dropped and very quickly forgotten.

We will try to describe here a basic traditional method based on the assumption that the subject is virtually untouched, in the hope that it may prove of interest and instruction. Obviously this does not mean untouched in the sense of wild, but it does imply that the youngster's education has not yet started. Although many of the procedures described may seem time-consuming they were actually designed to be time-saving originally, and it will do no harm for a (not necessarily the) correct system to be adopted. If these procedures are implemented without fail we should not only have a sensible racehorse, but will also have benefited from the fact that this year's assistant breaker should have sufficiently absorbed the theory to be able to take over the breaking himself after a couple of seasons. We are hoping to describe a method that should prove equal to any foreseeable situation, but the need for these procedures to be adhered to closely cannot be overstressed. Any changes that may prove necessary are not to be made by staff without discussion and instructions. Using these methods, a really experienced man will handle most situations comfortably even without an assistant. What

we advocate here is a belt and braces approach, aimed at producing both well-mannered horses and creating trained and competent personnel.

All yearlings should have their teeth attended by the vet or by an equine dentist as soon as they are quiet enough to be handled easily. All vaccinations should also be reviewed and put in order, and a worming programme initiated.

The safest and most efficient way to approach the breaking process is for an experienced lad, with a helper, to be delegated to handle all new yearlings for the first few days. He can then observe their characters and start them off in the correct manner. This is much safer than allocating yearlings to all and sundry as spares before we know anything about them. Two novices together always used to be regarded as a recipe for disaster. Under our system the yearling will have some basic stable sense before he gets his own lad, although the new groom must be made aware of the routine he is to follow if the foundation is not to be quickly undermined. To this end we can strongly convey to all staff that there are only two basic ways of doing things, these being number one, "All the other ways", and number two, "The way you will do it if you want to stay here!"

The team leader will be aware of the vital part played by voice in these proceedings and must impress this on his assistant. The actual words used make little difference, as unlike in some other disciplines a racehorse will not be routinely required to recognise very specific verbal commands, but the tone and inflection of the voice are important. Many excellent yearling men will keep up a constant conversation with their pupil, rather like a mother with a baby, and although it is rather one-sided the horse is obviously listening and taking confidence from his teacher's voice. It is very apparent too that the horse is well aware of displeasure, as indicated by a dramatic roughness of tone when he is wilful; however, this correction must always be directly connected in the horse's mind to an unacceptable act on his part. He will also be encouraged to greater efforts to please, in the same way as a dog or a small child, by being addressed in a very hearty and enthusiastic manner. Like a child, his attention can often be distracted from a potential problem in this way, as long as the handler is thinking ahead. Unfortunately, it can be extremely hard to make the average stable lad accept this as they seem afraid of sounding silly and so tend to operate in silence unless frequently reminded otherwise. For handlers who are not particularly aware of the finer points of equine body language the adoption of constant spoken contact along these lines is a viable alternative; in fact, their own body language may tend to reflect, and so to reinforce, their verbal communications, and vice versa.

With luck, however little has been done with him the horse will be wearing a head collar when he arrives. It is not uncommon, though, for whoever delivers him to remove this when they drop him off, sometimes leaving us with a distinct impression that our new inmate has had very little human contact when we try to fit a replacement. As a general rule, all yearlings should wear their head collars constantly at this stage; adopting this policy is much easier than wasting time on the odd horse that is hard to catch.

All work with yearlings must be done in a calm and reassuring manner. We must give an impression that there is nothing to worry about; however, it must also be quite clear that we are in control of the situation. An experienced man will be able to do this with a minimum of fuss, but the presence of an assistant for the first day or two can make things go that much more smoothly, as well as reinforcing safe procedures in the assistant's mind. Horses much prefer to know where they stand, and are better off not learning any bad habits that may be prevented by the presence of the helper. As a matter of course both should always be on the same side

of the horse in order to avoid it jumping away from one and on to the other.

Initially we will not attempt to tie up a yearling, as he will often have been used to having a holder whenever anything was done to them. If we assume this to be so when we commence, we will soon form an impression of whether or not he is nervous of anyone working with him. It is quite common for a yearling never to have had his stable cleaned or tidied when he was in it, and if he has also never been tied up we can run into a problem straight away. With the helper holding, preferably with a shank, it is simple enough to shake up the bedding quietly and generally straighten his box without starting any great commotion. Yearlings tend to make a mess of their beds anyway, so we need only get him used to the idea of the fork and the bedding moving around his legs as we roughly clean the stable. If new shavings need to be added to the bed this should be done with care as this often causes alarm initially. The water can also be changed, if necessary, while a holder is present as this too may well be outside the horse's experience and frighten him.

When his stable is tidy we can see how he responds to a gentle wipe over with a soft dandy brush and a rubber. The sale yearlings should all be quite happy with this. If we find one that objects, we don't need to make an issue of it, but we should simply complete a token effort with the minimum of excitement. In many cases the improvement overnight will be considerable, and this will be found to apply to many other aspects of his education. The next step might be to see how he is as regards his feet. We must be quiet but firm; even though he may have been shod it is no guarantee that he will be perfect to handle. If he is at all difficult in front we can ignore his hind feet for today.

It might be as well to introduce a couple of little mottos here. The first is adapted from a gambling system: "Always stop when you are winning." This might be the most important single thing to remember when dealing with young horses, particularly with any difficult animals. We must always part on a successful note, even if we have not achieved all that we had hoped for. The second maxim is borrowed from Aesop: "More haste, less speed." Every time we forget either of these mottos when working with young horses we are inviting difficulties.

A true horseman will often recognise the need for a minor change of plan in order to finish the lesson on a positive note if he sees an approaching difficulty, and he will instinctively make that change. Actually he will take pride in knowing that no audience, and quite probably not even the horse, would notice there was in fact a potential problem. He will also avoid putting himself in situations where adequate time is unavailable to complete the task in hand safely. This fine judgement, however, is not learned easily, but only by working with many different animals. Any opportunity to observe a top horseman/showman, or indeed sheepdog or gundog trainer, at work can be very instructive, although the performance may need careful analysis in order to obtain maximum instruction from it. The one thing all the top animal handlers do have in common is that they never ever become flustered. They may often, by distracting the attention of both their subject and any onlookers from potential difficulties, appear to proceed with great ease in situations that threatened to go amiss. The more yearlings we handle using this system, whether they need all its safeguards or not, the less likely we are to encounter any problems, and the easier we will find it to deal equally smoothly with anything untoward that does arise.

The use of the term 'horseman' is not meant to imply a specific gender but is used to denote any person who, by their acquired skill and knowledge, may be capable of selecting, caring for, and training the horse to a high level. In a male-dominated sport, many females will never have been instructed in breaking procedures, but, generally speaking, girls may tend to be more conscientious than lads in faithfully applying specified procedures and are well worth educating in this area.

As the horse settles in to his new surroundings we constantly assess to what degree we can safely move on to the next stage. In most cases he will be unafraid of having his litter done in a day or two and can then be tied up. A loop of bale string should be attached to the back ring of the head collar, to receive the chain and to prevent the head collar being broken by the chain if he does fly back in alarm. The string must not, as is sometimes seen, go on the wall ring for the obvious reason that the chain will then be flying around his head if he does get loose. It is essential to have everything likely to be required to hand before tying him up. He must not be left tied up and unattended for an instant at this stage, and if we do find we need anything he is to be loosed whilst we fetch it. Only having left a yearling for a few seconds at this stage is not an excuse if he should get loose. The horse need only be tied on a long chain at first, so that he doesn't panic. Initially we must always keep towards the rear of the box so that if he is inclined to pull back we can hustle him back up to the front wall. If we are paying attention this is quite easy, as long as we remain behind his girth. The fact that the front half of the box may not get much attention for a day or two is far less of a problem than a horse that knows he can get loose. After a couple of days, most will be fairly comfortable with us moving around the box and will move themselves about as required. If he does have a problem with moving across, and if he does tend to crowd into the corner looking back at us, then it is best to get the helper back to resolve the problem quietly rather than fluster him. We never get in front of a yearling when alone with him until we are confident he won't take fright and fly back, and initially we never ever leave him alone when he is tied up. Assuming that he soon settles on the chain, which he should as he has had no reason to do anything else, we can continue to wipe him over and handle his feet, again calling on a holder if necessary. When wiping his face he should always be untied at this stage to avoid alarm. After a couple of weeks we may judge him ready to be left alone when tied up, but this should at first be for a few minutes only and we should stand silently outside the closed door. After a short time he may become restless and as soon as he shows any inclination to lean back on the chain we must immediately hustle him up vocally, preferably without him actually seeing us. If we do this a couple of times he will probably think we are always watching and will settle down. He should then be loosed and this procedure should be repeated for two or three days. It is time well spent to have a horse that goes through his life without getting loose in the stable or breaking a head collar. Yearlings should never have their hay in the stable whilst they are being taught to tie up, so as not to tempt them into scraping or getting loose. There is no point in chastising an animal on returning to the stable and finding that he is loose or has been scraping his bed. Any correction will only be effective if applied when the offence is actually in progress. The success of many of the horse-tamers of the 19th century was largely based on various devices which were designed to cause the subject some inconvenience or discomfort, automatically and immediately as soon as he erred. Without realising that the man was even involved in the matter, the horse assumed that his own action had caused an unpleasant reaction, and eventually decided not to provoke it. The fact that such procedures fell into disrepute and disuse was probably because the appliances did more harm than good in the hands of those who had failed to grasp completely the basic theory.

We may occasionally come across a subject that has already formed the habit of getting loose from his tie. Rather than make too much of the situation, a lunge rein should be run from his head collar through the ring on the wall so that even when he does run back he has not actually escaped when he reaches the back wall and he can soon be manoeuvred back into position without any fuss. He should not be left unattended even using this method. After a few days he will normally accept matters quite happily, and will eventually become quite trustworthy in this respect.

It is now time to consider the handling of our yearling outside, which may in fact be considered the actual breaking process, the previous notes having covered stable manners. It is a good idea in most cases to remove the shoes before we start, for the simple reason that there is a great tendency to lose them anyway. Most yearlings should have enough growth of foot to go barefoot as the early exercise will all take place on a soft surface. Although soft ground tends to make all horses pull off their shoes by delaying breakover, it causes no damage to the bare foot. Apart from the disruption of continually waiting for a farrier to refit the shoe, there is great danger of breaking the foot and some danger of serious injury through a shoe that doesn't come off cleanly if we persist in keeping the yearlings shod at this stage. After removing the shoes, the foot should have the edges rounded, in the same way as would a horse being turned out to grass, to prevent them from splitting.

The whole breaking process is much simplified by having a properly constructed fenced arena with a suitable surface, and serious consideration should be given to achieving this, preferably at reasonable expense. The main requirements might be a lunging pen of about 45 feet diameter and an adjacent area to do very basic ridden work. Both should have safe surfaces with some degree of weather resistance. If there is easy access to the gallops, so much the better. It is important to monitor the condition of the lunging area regularly as the cushion will tend to be thrown continually to the outside. This drawback will be largely avoided if horses being lunged are continuously moved around the arena so as not to make a track, rather than being confined to the single circle, as soon as they are well enough behaved to do so. The drainage should be as good as possible, with some mix of sand and rubber or plastic the best footing. This can be reasonably achieved on a self-help basis with a local contractor rather than involving specialist schemes. The addition of coarsely chopped car tyres seems a great help in frosty conditions, and some form of oil or jelly will improve frost resistance although it will greatly increase the cost. Obviously a covered arena takes a lot of the pressure off the surface, and extremely competitive quotes are available for steel buildings.

To begin at the beginning is the most sensible approach to breaking, whatever the history of a new arrival is said to be. Over a large number of yearlings much time will be saved by not cutting corners, despite assurances that others may have already completed various stages satisfactorily with some arrivals. It will soon be obvious if a horse is in fact well versed in his education up to a certain point. We can much more easily press on after ensuring for ourselves that a lesson has been taught and learned than we can resolve a disaster caused by our making erroneous assumptions.

The first step is the fitting of the bridle and in most cases this is no problem. As in everything we will adopt a procedure which assumes an unhandled subject. The type of bridle to be used needs to be considered. Traditionally, British racehorses have started their education in a ball cheek jointed snaffle with keys to encourage a wet mouth. However, these tend to come in a size that may be too much of a mouthful for some yearlings and there can be a tendency for a horse to get these bits through his mouth to the extent that the keys are out at one side, usually the left. An alternative may be one of the sweet-mouth bits

now available. These do not have keys but the different metal is supposed to produce the same effect and as these bits tend to come in smaller sizes they do appear more comfortable for smaller horses. Many standard breaking bridles are also too large and have the alteration holes too far apart for small yearlings.

When putting bridles on yearlings we should always let them well down to avoid difficulty in getting over the ears. This takes 20 seconds, but it can often save 20 minutes straight away and will also avoid creating the ongoing problem of a horse being nervous about the ears. Once on, the bridle should be adjusted so that the bit barely wrinkles the corner of the mouth. Because of the unsuitable size of the traditional bits, the keys are often hanging too low in a small horse's mouth, which is far from ideal. The adjustment should be even on both sides. If the holes are too far apart for correct fitting then extra intermediate holes can easily be added. The traditional bridle has a loop to hold the side bar close to the cheek-piece and some horses appear to find this too rigid, but the loop can easily be dispensed with. If fitting the bridle does prove difficult, it should be accomplished with the aid of our helper and if possible without becoming a major confrontation. It is better to use a humane twitch or sedation rather than have a prolonged battle and in this situation the bridle should not be removed after exercise, and sometimes not for several days. The bit can be unbuckled and removed, with the ends of the cheek-pieces left buckled onto the bottom ring of the head collar until the horse has gradually learned to accept having his head and ears handled. It is not generally appreciated how often this problem can be created when taking the bridle off, and for the first few days we should always let it down before we take it off as well. As previously noted, the head collar stays on at all times, except on the rare occasion when some soreness may occur behind the ears.

Yearlings should always wear boots in front for exercise in the early stages since they may

(All breaking photos courtesy of 'Titch' D. Coombes.)

be prone to sudden and erratic movements when fresh and are likely to become careless when tired. Occasionally we find one that brushes behind, in which case a double thickness of tubular elastic stocking, kept up with tape, can be used. The tape should not be too tight and should be fitted close above the joint. The stockings can easily be washed out and will last a few days. Extra protection can be gained by inserting Gamgee between the two layers of stocking. These cases are often due to weakness, but the balance of the feet should be checked. The ideal front boot is a simple neoprene one with Velcro straps incorporating some elastic. The elastic seems to have virtually eliminated the problem of lost boots, but it may need renewing occasionally. When fitting the boots it is essential to be aware of the possibility of causing a blemish to the tendon as this will definitely not enhance any horse's value, even though it usually has no effect on his soundness. The way to avoid this is to secure the bottom strap snugly, with the boot at the correct height on the leg, and then make sure the top strap is slightly more loosely fastened.

The boots must be rigorously brushed, inside and out, between horses to avoid chafing and should be dried each night and brushed again to soften them in the morning.

We are at last ready to commence! The lunge rein should initially be attached to both the bit and to the back strap of the head collar to prevent too severe an impact on the mouth [1]. The head collar should be adjusted so as not to pinch the corners of the mouth between it and the bit. This method allows some of the pressure to be transferred to the nose and the arguable slight loss of control is not a problem in an enclosed space. The fact that the pressure, should he attempt to get away, is not straight on the yearling's mouth will be much less alarming for him.

Once in the arena we can quietly lead the horse around to let him get his bearings. If he is a little green, whether flighty or reluctant to walk, we can call on our helper to do a little gentle chasing as required until the horse is leading quietly. When the yearling does get the hang of it we can call it a day. A very flighty horse should be kept almost pressed against the fence until he relaxes. Very occasionally we will get one that will not lead at any price, and rather than have a major row it might pay to get a pony to walk in front of him which should prove a quick and painless solution.

On the second day we can make a start on actually lunging in the round pen with a helper. It is a good idea to have on hand one of the long but very light lunging whips which are quite inoffensive, but which greatly extend our range of pursuit. This will do away with much rushing about by the helper. We select the area to be used and lead him around it a few times following the circle we intend to describe. If the whip is used it is only to give the horse the sense that he is being pursued, not particularly aggressively, but just enough that he feels that he should keep moving. Gradually we can give him a little more rein and the assistant can gently pressurise him to keep walking rather than allow him to wonder why we have to some extent left him. A natural progression will normally see him jogging round fairly happily in a few minutes, although there may be one or two fits and starts which we will do our best to ignore. Of course we keep up a constant rhetorical conversation with the horse the whole time we have him out, and that is always to be taken as read throughout the whole breaking process. There should be as little charging about as possible, and if the horse doesn't settle down to a jog after a little while we should resume leading him, so that the lesson finishes happily. Funnily enough, some of the sales yearlings are actually much more difficult to lunge than the untouched ones because they often think they can do what they like based on their experiences before the sale. With these we may need our helper to join us on the rein sometimes with a horse that may have become accustomed to getting his head straight and getting away. With these animals we might prefer to put the rein straight onto the ring of the bit. They can't actually get away from us in a round pen, even though many seem to have been accustomed to doing so in their previous home, and they normally soon settle down.

If the yearling seems to accept things quite readily we may try him going round clockwise, and we first need to change the rein to the offside. To accomplish this we first take several feet of the end of the lunge and slip it through the ring [2] before we unbuckle it to transfer it to the other

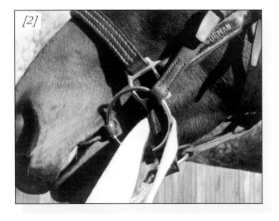

[2]

side, so as to have hold of the horse should he become startled during the changeover.

It will save time to repeat the leading process around the reverse circle before we start as, possibly because of the equine optical mechanism by which each eye sees a different picture, there is every chance that he will view this very similar task with extreme suspicion. We simply repeat the procedure, but we must be prepared for at least a repeat of any difficulties we encountered going anticlockwise. The yearlings that have been previously lunged by others may frequently be very troublesome going this way. As before, the object is to resist any excitement and to finish on a positive note.

Depending on the yearling's reactions we should now press on with his education as quickly as we can without at all alarming him and causing a setback. The reason for this is that we cannot absolutely predict the attitudes of those horses still to come, and if there is a difficult one we may need more time to spend on him. The riding lads will also be more relaxed about their task as soon as the first ones are ridden away successfully. The weather can also be unpredictable, and it is not ideal to have many horses still to break if we do get frozen in.

As soon as he is lunging calmly it is time to get some tack on our pupil. Opinions vary as to the best method, but this one has been found safe and effective. On his return to his box after exercise we can carefully fit him with a light roller with a breast girth, such as is worn over paddock clothing at the races. As this is very insubstantial it causes very little objection in most cases. We keep the bridle on and we first allow the horse to smell and examine the roller. Next we place the roller, which is folded in half, gently over the withers. When he seems comfortable with feeling it moving and touching him, the breast girth can be carefully secured. There is no need to tuck the strap ends into the billets at this point. Once the breast girth is fastened we can lift the doubled up belly band up and down a few times to let him see

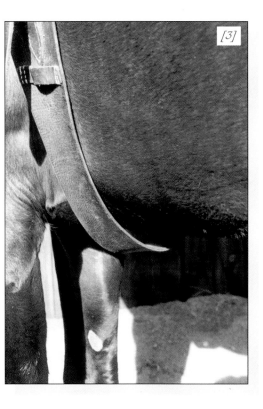

[3]

up too quickly, from the angles both of safety and of trust which is vital to the learning process. The less crashing and banging the prospective riding lads hear, the better for their morale! Once we are satisfied that the roller has been accepted, we can tuck in the ends of all straps, ensure that the breast girth is reasonably tight but that the belly band is about half an inch or so from touching him when he is standing relaxed, and leave him in soak. We can check now and again that everything is still in place and we may by evening stable time find he has somehow or other got out of it, but, as long as he hasn't destroyed it or eaten it, he should not object to having it carefully refitted. Horses that do flinch when the roller is put on or off for grooming should continue to wear it in the stable, even though they may have progressed to the saddle for exercise. Of course, many yearlings will have worn stable rugs before the sale and will be unconcerned by the roller; however, these procedures assume that the horse has never worn anything about his body. Always do the breast girth up first and undo it last; this is an absolute rule, which also applies to all rugs in all stables at all times.

With most yearlings we can quite easily upgrade from the paddock roller to the breaking roller, which is much more substantial. As we already have the light roller fitted we can take him out to lunge with it on, keeping his attention so that he does not attempt to plunge when he comes out into the open. He may also be inclined to plunge at first when we start to lunge, but we should avoid this if we let the belly band out a hole or two for the first few turns and then quietly take it up, and repeat the procedure. If this goes smoothly it is time to substitute the heavy breaking roller, and again we take a few turns with it quite loose before gradually tightening it. This roller feels much more restrictive to him but we still wish to avoid him having a go if at all possible. As the change of rollers takes place with virtually no

and feel it before carefully passing the buckle end over to the off side. We do not throw it over and we try to ensure it does not flap against the off knee causing him to jump. Whilst keeping the horse occupied both with voice and by moving the bit in his mouth, we can reach down and do up the belly band extremely loosely [3]; it should not initially come within three inches of the horse. With a big horse we may need a longer roller as we do not want him to plunge and try to get it off if he suddenly becomes aware of it because there are not enough holes to fit him loosely to start with. We give him a turn around the stable and then take the roller up a hole, and repeat this one hole at a time. This will occupy a little time, but he should soon be quite content with the roller secured, so that it is just touching him but without feeling tight, and nothing worse will have been done than putting his back up a little. This is a far better system than one that risks alarming the animal by pulling the roller

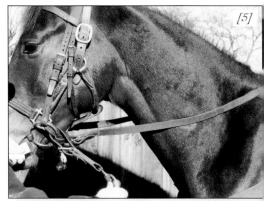

time lag it is normally easily accomplished.

One of the old theories that has stuck in people's minds is that horses should be encouraged to struggle and fight in order to "get it out of their system". This is almost certainly based on a faulty recollection of an old theory of correcting spoiled horses through the use of some self-punishing appliance. However, particularly in the absence of anyone competent to apply such a theory, it seems reasonable to assume that if we don't teach our pupil to buck he may in fact never buck, which will obviously be an advantage to all concerned. Trainers need to be aware of their ever-increasing responsibilities under the Safety At Work legislation, and to implement the safest possible procedures.

Once we have the big roller on and have gradually tightened it to the extent that it is quite stable although not yet squeezing him, it is time to add the side reins. Again these will be introduced in such a way that he will scarcely notice them at first. Both side reins should be attached to the roller at a length that we judge will be too long for him to feel them at all even with his head right down [4]. They are crossed over the withers and fastened to the bit below the lunge rein. After a few turns we can shorten them slightly, and we repeat this until he is conscious that he has them on, in that he can no longer get his head right down, but not to where he feels he wants to fight them [5]. An approximate measurement might be that the

side rein should hang three or four inches below an imaginary line from the cross on the withers to the bit when the horse is standing normally. After he has become accustomed to them and has been round both ways a few times we can call it a day. We should, as always in the early stages, take care that the clockwise circle is not allowed to become an excuse for excitement.

The horse should if possible be given his exercise without getting black with sweat and if this proves difficult he should be trace clipped. Funnily enough, most yearlings are quite simple to clip at this stage. To save time and trouble if they do show a tendency to kick whist being clipped, we need trace clip only as far as the stifle. This will save us from trying to make sure the rear view matches whilst also trying to avoid getting kicked. As long as the neck and belly are done, that is sufficient. Difficult cases can, of course, be sedated. The fact that, on average, most yearlings prove easier than most older horses to clip is indicative of how easily they tend to accept things of which they have no previous experience, as long as they do not become alarmed. This is the prime reason for not wasting time on the breaking process with those animals that progress normally, as familiarity does tend to breed contempt if too much time is spent without progressing to the next stage.

It is a good idea to ensure that all yearlings are quiet with the hose pipe at this stage, in order to save time in the summer when they will be bathed daily after exercise. Obviously we will not bathe them in the cold weather, but they should become accustomed to having their legs and feet washed. The hose pipe should be carefully introduced, initially at low pressure, to the feet and then to the legs and to the girth area. We must always have an assistant and be prepared to waste a little time at first; however, learning this lesson properly will save hours over the course of the animal's career. This procedure should be learnt with a minimum of fuss, so as to avoid accidents such as the horse slipping over. In difficult cases two assistants may be necessary and sensible use of one of the more humane twitches, a war bridle or comealong halter, or even of sedation, might be indicated. Once a horse has accepted the hose pipe he is normally sensible with it for life, and in fact it can prove an important lesson in overall obedience for certain rebellious types. Actually, many old horsemen relied heavily on desensitising their pupils by obliging them to accept distasteful situations, thereby emphasising the fact that the horse could not resist the instructions of his handler. As remarked elsewhere, these practices fell from grace because they came to be badly applied by those who failed to understand their reasoning properly. The troublesome subjects will invariably be those horses that have been accustomed to resisting their handlers generally before we get them, rather than the completely unhandled ones.

A common injury to horses being lunged, even if they are barefoot, is an overreach on the bulb of the front heel caused by a blow from the hind foot. Any minor flap of skin should be removed, and the wound should be cleaned thoroughly. Either the ubiquitous blue spray or an antibiotic cream such as Dermobion will normally prove effective, and the wound should be left open to the air in most cases. The spray is alarming to some horses as the hissing sound it makes is swiftly followed by a severe stinging sensation, and this can cause much apprehension at the follow-up treatment. Yearlings seem to take very little notice of these wounds, although the same thing might render an older horse quite lame. There will sometimes be chafes caused by the boots, although these will be kept to a minimum if the boots are religiously cleaned. Dermobion is normally effective in dealing with them, although a piece of clean lint should be worn under the boot until the leg heals. If a horse should ever sustain a very serious cut it is well worth treating it with honey, although it is obviously a very messy remedy; veterinary advice should, of course, also be sought.

Although the horse will normally continue to wear the roller 24 hours a day at this stage we must ensure that it does not cause him to chafe, and his girth mark should be removed as well as possible before the roller is refitted and he is loosed. The roller should be just loose enough to admit a couple of fingers, about half an inch from his body when he is standing normally [6].

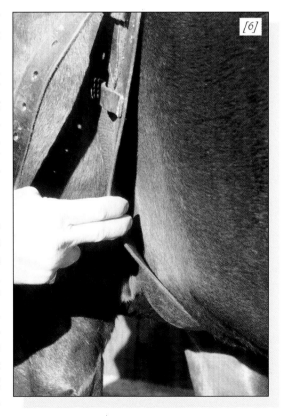

[6]

As long as we are quite confident that our pupil has accepted his lessons so far with good grace, we should proceed to the next step, which is the saddle. However, we must always remember that more haste often means less speed. There is no point in rushing if it will mean we lose time in the end. The only point of trying to make this fairly rapid progress is to allow more time for any difficult horses so it is obviously vital that we do not create an additional problem by overtaxing our current pupil.

When we do decide to put the saddle on it is important to know beforehand exactly how we intend to go about it. We should do this in the stable, not in the open. The bridle and boots are fitted as usual. We should always put the boots on before fitting any tack on yearlings, as it can save them jumping on us when we are bending over their legs should they suddenly feel the tack and have a momentary fit of panic. If this happens when we are standing up it is unlikely that we will be hurt, but if we are bending down it could easily lead to an injury. This is a reminder that no horse should ever have his legs attended to without first being tied up; accidents from this cause may be infrequent but they can be extremely serious. As a boy I had four or five square inches of bone removed from the top of my skull by a very quiet horse called Dan Somers, purely by ignoring this simple standing instruction and letting him down to eat his evening feed before attending to his knees.

Next, we put on a standing martingale, at a long adjustment, and fasten it to the bottom ring of the head collar. With the assistant holding the yearling, or with the lunge attached to the bridle and either held or in a neat coil on the floor below the horse's head – that is to say the horse should not be tied up for this first saddling – we can let him inspect and smell the saddle and pad in the same way we did with the roller. Using an assistant is safer. The side reins should be attached to the saddle and again should initially be left very long and must obviously be level. They should be tied in a loose knot in front of the saddle and the buckle ends tucked through the near side stirrup, while the other ends should be under the second girth strap and pointing back out of the way [7]. Both stirrups must be tied up, not just run up on the leathers. It is important to insist that the saddle is also arranged like this every time it is taken off a yearling in order to prevent problems with putting it on the next horse. Throughout the yearling season, all keepers for attaching side reins to the girth straps should be securely tied to the top of the girth straps with string, in order to avoid time wasted searching for any those that fall off when the saddle is being used for an old horse (which would obviously not require the side reins themselves). The best type of pad or numnah is a soft one that is well worn and pliable. The mock sheepskin ones in the shape of the saddle do very well. After the horse has

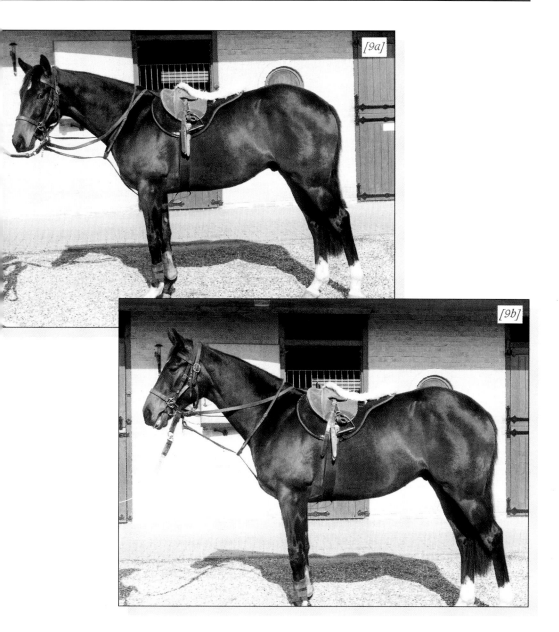

been allowed to examine the tack with his nose, we first place the pad on the horse's withers and let him feel and see that it will not harm him. When we are sure he is quite happy we let him feel the saddle as well, making sure that the girths are folded over the seat and that they will not alarm him. We now, quickly but without rushing, sit the saddle in place on the pad, gently take down the girths, making sure they don't touch his legs, pass both girths through

the martingale, and do the girths up loosely. If the old practice of poling young horses, or gently but repeatedly touching them all over with a light pole, were implemented at the commencement of breaking they would obviously be less sensitive to everything that touched them subsequently – including the starting stalls. This is something that is worthy of cautious investigation. If we have an assistant, he attracts the horse's attention by gently moving the bit; if not, we should have the dangling rein over our left arm so as to get hold of him easily if he jumps. Again there must be constant verbal communication with the yearling, especially at every fresh stage of his education. We now gradually tighten the girths to the degree that he is used to from his all-day roller, and we can then give him a turn or two around the box. The side reins can now be untied and secured to the bit, below the lunge as before. They are to be crossed over the withers and this cross is under the neck strap of the martingale. It is best to make sure that the saddle pad is further forward than normal, although the saddle obviously sits in its usual position, because the pad may tend to work back until the girths are quite tight, causing unwanted hold-ups for readjustment [8].

We are now ready to make a start on the mouthing and educating of the horse, both of which may have great bearing on the success or otherwise of his career, and we take him again into the arena. When he begins to go round this time he may tend to be aware of the new equipment, but it is not going to restrict him at the present adjustment and any jumpiness will pass quickly. We want to avoid him trying to fight his way out of the tack due to feeling trapped. When he has settled down we gradually take up the side reins as before, at the same time making sure that the girth is reasonably tight so as to avoid losing the pad [9a and 9b]. Then we can shorten the martingale to the point where he cannot quite feel it when holding his head normally but will be prevented from raising his head too high. Assuming that all goes smoothly and that he lunges quietly in both directions, we will now pass a second lunge rein over his neck and fix it to the offside of the bit, above the side rein and also through the back strap of the head collar. It is quite possible to put the second rein around most yearlings at an earlier stage, but by waiting until all the tack is on before doing so we will have much more control over the occasional objector.

The process of physically putting the rein round him for the first time is an important stage and needs careful handling. Once again a helper can prove beneficial, although an expert may feel that things can become too crowded as initially two men and a horse will be occupying a circle of only 10 or 15 feet in diameter. We gently work the offside lunge back until it falls behind the horse's quarters, but we must keep his head towards us as he will probably panic to some degree when he feels it [10, 10a, 10b]. If he does start to run, as long as we keep him tight to us and speak to him, no harm will occur and he will soon relax. More difficult are those horses that try to sit down on the lunge and are afraid to go forward as these often tend to keep turning in towards us. The assistant may initially need to chase them round but once they are going forward the problem is soon resolved. As always, we try to avoid the horse charging about, and the steadier they go the better. To change direction we merely repeat the procedure from the off side but we must expect at least the same degree of difficulty. Once he is going both ways we begin to teach him to turn from one direction to the other [10c, 10d ,10e] without us having to stop him and actually change sides. This is relatively easy in a round pen but at first we may need to face him up the fence to stop him [11]. We can then walk across behind him before setting him off in the reverse direction. After a few times he will realise what is required and will turn easily due to the change of pressure from the front to the back rein. When the horse has grasped this we can untie the knots in the stirrup leathers in order that the irons gradually come down and start banging against his sides [12]. It may needlessly alarm him and distract his attention from the business in hand if we do it any earlier. Once this stage is reached we can alter the attachment of the lunges so that they are buckled directly onto the bit. We should realise that this set-up is more severe, but he will be ridden straight off the bit

[10]

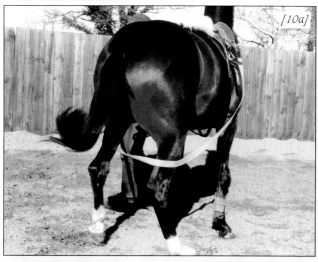

[10a]

[10b]

[10c]

[10d]

[10e]

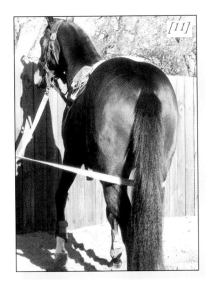

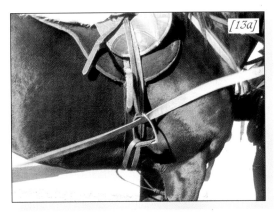

and he must get used to it beforehand. We now have more control should the horse tend to be heavy-headed, which does occur in some that have previously been lunged. Working straight off the bit requires a lighter touch because none of the pressure is absorbed by the head collar, and some horses may be a little sensitive to the change at first.

There are two difficult situations which often arise at this stage. The first is the horse that will not stop running away from the back lunge; with him we initially have to use the outside fence as a brake and if that does not soon work we can use it to stop him completely and then have the assistant lead him around until he relaxes. The second is when the horse continually kicks the back rein up and over his back. If we cannot prevent this by trapping the rein under his tail (low down, not under the bone where he can clamp down on it), we may have to run the outside rein through the stirrup [13]. The stirrups are let down and a strap is run from one iron to the other on top of the girth [13a]. This will stop him getting the rein over his back. Unfortunately, if we don't stop and reverse the attachments of the reins whenever we want to change direction then some horses will find the indirect pull on the inside rein [13b] very severe.

Very occasionally, and almost always with a filly, we will get a yearling that will not accept this back rein procedure at all. The best thing to do is to move on without too much confrontation. This will mean she cannot be driven, but many horses are successfully broken by other handlers without ever being driven. Prolonged struggling with this type does not normally produce a happy ending, and we should avoid it. If we are determined that a pupil that really objects must have the rein around, then it is best to let her desensitise herself by wearing a piece of lunge rein firmly attached to a roller or in place of the tail string of her rug constantly, until she accepts that she cannot get rid of it but that she will not be hurt by it. She should have plenty of bedding in her stable so as to avoid slipping over before she accepts that it will not come off. This attachment should initially be left in place whilst the second rein is used at exercise, in the hope that the second lunge rein itself (which is purely to enable her to be mouthed) is scarcely noticed.

Our yearling has now progressed to the stage of lunging in both directions as required and next we want to teach him to drive, so as to educate his mouth. This is an extremely important stage as it will greatly influence the way he conducts himself when ridden. The purpose of this part of his education is to teach him to follow the instructions he receives through the bit, to be steady with other horses and with traffic, and to stop and stand still as required. If he learns these lessons well, life will be easier for all of us. We will also teach him to back, not because that is a common

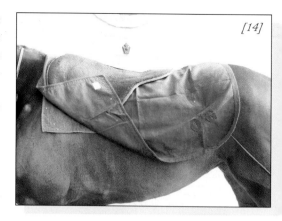

[14]

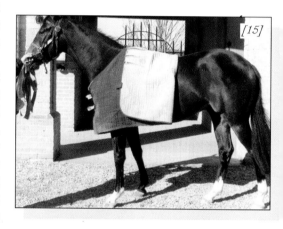

[15]

requirement normally, but because it is an effective form of painless correction occasionally useful for horses that rear or otherwise misbehave.

As soon as the yearling is used to the saddle, a light exercise sheet should be added, which should always have a tail string. This avoids the problems caused by his first wearing one on a wet and windy day and becoming alarmed by it flapping. Care should always be taken that whenever an exercise sheet or rug has the corners turned up, these are placed on top of the pad [14]. Now and again we can get a blemish on a horse's back caused by the weight coming on top of the area where the corners overlap if they are straight on the back. This is unsightly, uncomfortable, and difficult to get rid of, but it will never happen as long as the sheet is turned up on top of the pad and the

[16]

[16a]

[16b]

saddle without alarming him and this careful method should always be used for a few days. It is quite simple to unfold the rug over his back, but the breast strap must always be secured first. The same procedure for the girths is followed as before but the flank strap should not come within two or three inches of touching his belly. The rug should have a tail string and some antichew preparation should be applied. Occasionally a particularly nervous horse that has not had any handling may have to be desensitised by wearing a rug in order to avoid wasting too much time because he is unusually frightened of the tack. Great care should be taken in fitting and removing the rug initially in such circumstances, and there must be plenty of bedding to avoid accidents.

The driving process evolves easily from the change of direction on the lunge. We simply let the horse walk in the circle whilst initially walking level with his hindquarters but a few feet to the side [16,16a,16b]. This is very similar to what we have been doing when we lunged him, and the only problem is to let him know we want to walk rather than trot. Again we can do this by use of the outside fence as a brake; but he will quickly realise what is required. As soon as he seems ready to walk we can leave the round pen for the adjacent open arena, but it is safer to remain in a fairly enclosed area until we are quite confident that our student is relaxed and is responding to the bit. When teaching him to stop we again make use of the fence. Initially we let him approach it at 90° so that he has to stop, which makes him associate the stop with the positive but fairly gentle pressure on the bit and the request, "Whoa". Immediately he stops the pressure on the bit is relaxed and the horse is warmly praised for his cooperation in the tone used to praise dogs and small children. The success of our whole racing enterprise will largely depend on the degree of cooperation we get from our horses.

When driving, the horse should walk on freely and boldly and should be encouraged if

saddle has a proper central channel.

If we wish to put a rug on him in the stable we can basically use the same method as for putting on the saddle. The rug should of course be the right size and should initially be folded in half so that the back edge touches the withers [15]. Once the horse has been allowed to examine it we can slip it on as easily as the necessary with vigorous slaps on his sides with the lunges as well as a positive voice. The noise and the movement will have more effect than the discomfort, but he must absolutely learn to go purposefully forward on command. We should look ahead to anticipate all real or imagined terrors and encourage him to satisfy himself that there is no danger whenever we do encounter anything that may appear strange to him. The lunges should be neatly furled at all times to allow controlled adjustment, and their relative lengths should be subject to constant subtle change rather in the way the steering wheel of a car is fed through the hands. Basically, we do not send a left turn signal without completely relieving the tension on the right rein, and as soon as he responds to the left turn he is rewarded by the increased pressure being taken off the left rein. When walking straight there should be only very light physical contact on both reins, while constant verbal contact continues. It is recommended to walk slightly to one side of the yearling, normally to the left when travelling straight, but towards the outside, like a sheepdog, when turning. This is in order that he may see his driver, even though there is constant verbal contact, and so that he can be easily turned in a circle in an emergency. Should the latter occur, we have simply reverted to a lunging situation and can easily stop him and then set off driving once more.

Many people drive with the lunges through the irons as described previously for kickers, but this can cause serious problems if things do go wrong. Should the horse ever turn to face the driver through fear of something in his path, then the rein will be pulling him in the opposite direction and a complete tangle is the likely outcome. When the reins are not through the irons it is much easier to get out of such minor problems without their escalating. The driver is sometimes seen to be running behind a yearling, but this is extremely foolish as they will have no chance of stopping the horse if he does become startled and make a run for it.

The tone of voice is as important as the word and, although purists maintain that verbal commands should be absolutely specific, this does not happen in the racing environment. For example, "Whoa" is commonly used for both slowing down and for stopping by racing lads without seeming to cause any confusion; "No!" as a corrective does not seem to cause any confusion as the sound is so similar and the anticipated result is not dissimilar. The various requirements to walk on and trot on, and all acceleration commands are normally conveyed by a click of the tongue or a chirrup. With high rates of staff turnover, it would prove very difficult to implement a standard vocabulary. Racehorses are probably handled by more different people than any other horses except riding school inmates, and actually cope surprisingly well considering that they are also to some degree under constant pressure. Basically, all slow down requests are to be made in as quiet and as calm a voice as possible to inspire confidence, whereas speed up instructions are designed to create excitement. A brisk, no-nonsense tone should be employed when the horse seems to be undecided, and expressions of displeasure are gruff, sharp and instantaneous, so as to be obviously relevant to the offence. It might prove interesting, if the stable jockey were closely involved in riding the young horses, for him to experiment with the teaching of "Right" and "Left" to one or two of his mounts purely for his own benefit in races. This would only cause problems if attempted with the general run of lads!

When the horse has mastered the stop lesson we will teach him just two specific verbal instructions, "Stand" and "Back". Although this is not the usual racing practice they can both, on occasion, prove useful. These two lessons will both follow naturally from the stop lesson [17]. To teach the horse to stand we merely allow him to remain still after he has stopped, but we relax the pressure on the lunges whilst repeating the instruction, "Stand", and praising him [17a] until he

[17]

[17a]

lesson leads into the beginning of the stand lesson and this should be reinforced verbally. This lesson well learnt can be useful in some loading procedures and in manouevring in confined spaces, but that is not its primary purpose. It is most useful simply because horses do not like to go backwards and will only do so themselves if they wish to avoid an even less attractive alternative. If the reversing procedure is perfectly learnt, we can use it to tackle the situation when we have a horse that continually refuses to cooperate, simply by offering him the unpleasant option of backing up or of going quietly about his business. This can be amazingly effective, but success is absolutely dependent on the back lesson having been so well learned that the horse does not contemplate disobeying it. This method of correction should only be applied in serious cases and with a good rider. In fact we should always think in terms of offering an uncooperative horse a less attractive alternative rather than punishing him with a view to him thinking that the sensible thing to do is, in effect, be sensible!

After two or three days mastering these lessons, and becoming accustomed to driving around the yard and seeing everything there, the yearling is ready to see the outside world. This should not be attempted until we are sure he has a sound grasp of steering and stopping so as not to be a danger to himself or the rest of the world, and he should have his basic exercise on the lunge before he goes out for a drive. For the first trip off the premises an assistant is an advantage, as he can walk beside the horse in order to give him a little more confidence. He can also take hold of the horse's head should we meet anything too alarming and allow him to examine it and touch it with his nose. In most cases, the horse will not then take any notice of the same obstacle the next day, even without the helper. In the same way that we gradually worked away from the fence in the arena, we try not to take the yearling into a very open space too suddenly. It is much safer to stay by a hedge or a fence for the first day

accepts that he is not to move. Initially, we can make use of the fence to prevent his walking forward. If he moves we simply return him to where he was. When we do wish him to move away we must signal this by a brisk click and by restoring contact through the reins. There must be an obvious relaxation in our attitude when we are standing. If this lesson is properly learnt it may prevent difficulties when he is first ridden, and it may later prove useful when saddling at the races, or in the starting stalls.

The command "Back" is simply "Stand" taken one step further. Initially, it is probably easier to have an assistant to gently push the horse back whilst we exert gentle pressure on the lunges. Again, the command must be constantly repeated as he comes back, and the pressure on the bit must be relaxed as soon as he steps back; at first one or two steps are enough [18, 18a, 18b]. Obviously, the end of the back

until he gets his bearings, particularly as he is now likely to see strings of ridden horses, which he may regard as most exciting. We should remember that after so few lessons he may well suffer a relapse in his composure and we should always anticipate such a possibility. Obviously we will have selected an area with minimal traffic, and that traffic is probably aware of the horses, but we should exercise extreme caution in introducing him to cars and lorries. It is best to occupy the middle of the road so as to oblige traffic to stop and then to be effusive in our thanks rather than to depend upon their good sense. When passing an approaching vehicle or other horses, we always take the right-hand side. We practise the horse's new skills constantly during the course of the trip; in fact, if we do get tangled up with a string of racehorses, then the stand lesson may prove invaluable.

It is worth remembering that all horses, not just young ones, are often alarmed by the sight

even of what we would regard as objects familiar to them when such objects appear in an unaccustomed setting.

After the first day or two outside, it will be easy enough to take a more adventurous attitude and explore the various gates and railings he will encounter on and around the gallops. It is a good idea to drive him over various road markings and on and off any artificial gallops so he can become familiar with their different appearances and the steps up and down that they involve. If there is an opportunity for him to stand and watch other horses cantering, so much the better. This can prove a useful accomplishment in later life as he can be used as the trainer's hack when required.

Some methods will have acquainted the yearling with the starting stalls on the gallops at this point. This does involve some risk of getting into a confrontation without having the help on hand to resolve it successfully. Given

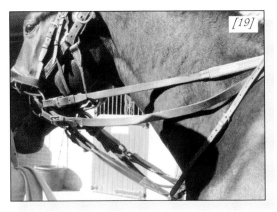

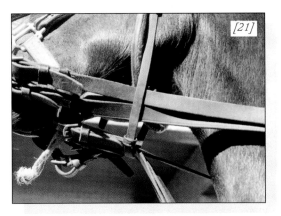

the long-term importance of stalls manners, we can hardly regard that as a sensible risk. If we do have stalls at the home premises, we can effect an early introduction with enough help available to ensure success.

This part of the curriculum should last about a week, which may mean we have now invested a total of two weeks in an averagely sensible animal. With reasonable luck, another week will see the yearling riding quietly and ready to commence his actual training as a racehorse.

As a general rule we always try to get any yearling ridden for the first time at the beginning of the week if possible. If, unavoidably, an individual does happen to first get backed at the end of the week then he should go out on Sunday, so as not to risk forgetting his lesson at an early stage. It is remarkable how well many horses seem to digest something new overnight, in the sense that they will appear much improved next day, but it is also true that to miss a day at any pivotal stage is inviting trouble.

We will make a start on the backing of our horse after he has done his full exercise so that he has already got his back down. We must fit a pair of riding reins to the bit, and when the horse is to be ridden they go above the side rein [19]. The main control rein always goes on top, so for lunging and driving the lunge should be on top. If possible, all breaking tack should be made to a standard pattern as various items are frequently broken or lost; if everything is interchangeable, two halves will make a whole. Because of other horses' exercise we may not immediately have a suitable rider available and we may have to leave our yearling in soak until we do have one. If we do this we must always be certain he cannot get in a tangle as we don't want to risk leaving him tied up for any length of time. The stirrups must be safely tied up and if the riding reins are fitted they should be crossed over the withers and their end placed under the back of the saddle [20]. Everything beneath the horse's neck, that is, reins, side reins and the martingale, should either be caught up inside the throat latch, if it is long enough, or else be gathered together with a short piece of string in order to prevent him getting a foot over them [21]. The hay should be taken out of the box so that he does not try to reach it.

When our riding lad does appear, we remove

the tie from the reins, take the reins from behind the saddle and reattach the lunge. The lad should introduce himself to the horse and should not be wearing a very bulky jacket or crackly waterproofs. He must wear his helmet. The top door should be closed to lessen distractions and there should be plenty of bedding in the middle of the stable.

Holding the horse's head towards the wall to prevent his jumping forward too violently, we gently lift the lad to lean across the saddle with his left elbow hooked over the horse's neck to give him a little purchase. If this results in a violent plunge, the lad simply slips down and we try again, talking positively and soothingly to the horse (and the lad!) all the time. In most cases, if the lad is willing and fairly supple there will be little difficulty, but the reason for the dress code is now obvious. We quietly persevere until we can take one or two turns around the box, then slip the rider off. This should be repeated until both going up and coming down are completely accepted. After four or five repeats we can normally get the lad astride, reminding him to make sure he goes up cleanly, and to keep his head down for a short time to avoid visually alarming the horse. After one or two laps crouched over he can gradually straighten up. Throughout this procedure the wall is to be used as a brake in the event of any charging about.

After a few minutes the lad can allow his new mount to feel his legs against his sides. He can then pick up the reins and shift his weight about in the saddle, although control is still through the lunge rein. If we give him a turn in the other direction without difficulty we can loose him and let the lad ride him, both ways, around the box for a few minutes whilst we watch from outside.

We always take hold of the horse's head before the lad dismounts as this can easily cause alarm, leading to an ongoing bad habit. It is best to reinforce the mounting lesson several times before we finish for the day. In fact, yearlings should always be carefully dismounted and then remounted a couple of times when they come in after exercise for the first few days.

We have to decide how well each yearling accepts the lad before going any further, as some will obviously do so quicker than others. A good, though not foolproof, guide is how much the horse has his back up. A back still raised normally foretells a possible explosion, but we cannot guarantee that a relaxed horse won't suddenly light up, so we should always hope for the best but be prepared for the worst.

A great disadvantage to yearling breakers nowadays is the virtual absence of anyone willing and able to ride anything remotely challenging. Previously, the younger lads used to be mad keen to show that they could do a man's job and far from being frightened they might have been too bold. Unfortunately, nowadays that particular age group seem to assume that they have nothing to prove, and tend to be very short of the necessary pluck when it is required. This does not imply that we should be looking for cannon fodder but it is indisputable that any horse can immediately pick up on nervousness. Many of the problems that do occur would be avoided if the riding lads were more confident, which in turn would naturally lead to the lads themselves being more competent. That is why an absolute and seemingly rather pedantic procedure is advised, in the hope of giving the lads and the horses more faith in themselves and in each other. The present fashion of riding with only the tips of the toes in the iron is not recommended and we should not allow it. A relatively minor plunge can very often produce a loose horse, when the foot being well home in the iron would have enabled an uneventful recovery. The argument that there is less likelihood of becoming hung up is indicative of a defeatist attitude which is of no use in a yearling rider.

As long as the backing went fairly smoothly, the following day should see the yearling ridden in the arena. He should be lunged for 10 or 15 minutes so as to take the edge off his natural freshness, and the previous day's backing procedure repeated exactly. When he has completed a few turns of the box with his rider we can take him out. The girths should be checked for security but should not be too tight, and the side reins can be shortened slightly. The lunge is attached and we lead him straight to the arena, making sure his attention is centred on the leader by voice and by jiggling the bit in his mouth. We will sometimes encounter a little excitability when first in the open, but we should do our best to reach the arena as quickly and quietly as possible. If a pony is outside the door when we come out we are virtually certain of getting to the arena without any fuss, as the yearling will be watching him with great interest. The pony referred to can, of course, be a horse in training, just as long as he is quiet and will not kick whatever happens. Obviously he must be a male, preferably a gelding. The object is to phase in the situation of tacking up the yearling and mounting him immediately like an old horse, but we should take care to progress gradually in a manner that does not create any unruly habits.

All yearlings should be ridden with one of the lad's fingers in the neck strap to avoid pulling on the horse's mouth in an emergency and to give extra security. However, as this can tend to produce one-sidedness in a horse's mouth, care must be taken to change the stationary hand regularly. This will need constant reminders, but will also prevent the riders from becoming one-sided in their use of their hands.

Once we get into the arena, assuming the yearling has not really got his back up, we can lead him round the perimeter behind the pony. After a lap or two we tell the pony to jog on and we follow, being careful not to allow the yearling to charge about, if possible. It is normally safe to undo the lunge almost immediately and most yearlings will continue trotting behind the pony without registering any change. The lad on the pony must always be aware of where the yearling is and should try to maintain an invisible contact of not more than one or two lengths, otherwise the pupil may fall behind and

get confused. He will then be very likely to stop. If, on the other hand, the yearling is tending to run all over the pony's heels, the pony boy must ensure that his mount is not provoked into kicking. He should also be on his guard against a cheeky colt jumping on the pony. In fact, he must always remember that the yearling rider does not yet have very sophisticated control and that his own job is to assist as much as possible without unduly risking the pony, which may be needed for many subsequent missions. The pony rider should also keep up a cheerful sing-song, both to keep his own mount's mind occupied and to reinforce the idea that the pony is something to follow.

If the yearling does have his back right up when we reach the arena it is best to lunge him with the lad on board for a few minutes before turning him loose. If yearlings miss exercise for two or three days for any reason, it is as well to do the same thing.

Occasionally the yearling will seem too confused to follow the pony, even if he has previously done everything perfectly. When this happens we must improvise. If we run beside him and the pony comes past from behind he may join in. If we lunge him and have the pony drop in in front of him he may get the idea, or if we chase him waving our arms and tossing clods of dirt he will probably, in running away from us, have lapped onto the pony before he realises it. The vocal encouragement should always sound cheerful, like a huntsman encouraging his hounds. The riding lad must be sure that the horse does have his head so that he can go forward. The side reins will prevent him from getting his head right down to plunge, and if he does shoot forward the rear of the pony will stop him. For the safety of the pony, the benefit of unshod yearlings in this situation is obvious. The lad on the yearling cannot be expected to take quite such a conscientious view of the pony's welfare and will probably have little regard for keeping his mount off that schoolmaster's back legs. In the unusual case of a yearling absolutely refusing to go, we should try to finish on a positive note in some way, even if it is back on the lead rein, and he should be put back on a purely lunging and driving routine with emphasis on teaching immediate start-up on verbal command. It is essential that yearlings are not overtired by too severe exercise at this stage, despite the wishes of the riders. The very sullen and defiant types at this stage will normally not prove to be satisfactory racehorses in the long term.

If the rider can be persuaded to take an attitude of benevolent aggression at this stage, it usually prevents problems in a few days' time when the yearling will have found his 'sea legs' and may be inclined to take his rider on and rebel to some degree. This does not imply any cruelty, but it does mean that the rider should have no hesitation in making free both with his heels and on occasion with the buckle end of the reins (whips should never be carried on yearlings, ever) to get his horse going freely on command. However, human nature being what it is, most of our riders will be extremely passive if we allow them to, being satisfied to settle for a quiet life presently even though they might be asking for trouble in the future. Although it may appear rather rough, a certain amount of rousting during the first couple of ridden sessions definitely produces the best long-term results in most horses. As it is currently almost impossible to find lads who do understand these matters, we hope our system may teach them as well as the horses. Obviously, we do not want to abuse any horse, even if only from a commercial point of view. However, experience proves that a yearling is far more receptive during the first lessons as everything is new to him, and it makes sense to teach him thoroughly the basics of going where we say and when we say so at this stage. While appreciating that many may find this offensive, it is a fact that the more passive the regime the higher the percentage of graduates that do eventually cause problems.

It is very important in educating young horses to observe logical processes, as perceived by the pupil. It is senseless to continue to punish in any way an animal once he is going forward. If the rider maintains a stranglehold through apprehension then a confusing signal is sent; the horse must always be given enough freedom of his head to enable him to go on when he is required to do so. It is also quite illogical, although not uncommon due to fear and apprehension in the rider, to pet a horse when he is refusing to go as directed. If any horse does get in a state of extreme excitement the stand lesson should be employed rather than seeming to praise the animal for disobedience.

Unusually nervous yearlings again call for a certain amount of improvisation and cannot always be subjected to all of our normal methods. In fact, they may take several extra days to accept each of the above stages. It is because we never know when we may have to invest an enormous amount of time in one of this type that we should get on as quickly as is reasonable with the quiet ones. The first rule with the nervous ones is always take your time and do not take any liberties at all as they can often explode. However, because of the extra trouble taken with them, these horses very often become the best rides in the end. The most difficult type of all is the nervous colt that is also cheeky and above himself, and this type does require extreme caution to achieve a good result.

Those yearlings that appear incapable of learning normally should be regarded with suspicion, particularly should similarly afflicted individuals share a common background either as regards breeding or the premises from which they were drawn. Any obsessive or erratic behaviour or apparent stupidity quite possibly indicates some impairment of their brain or central nervous system. These animals are unlikely to race consistently at a respectable level. Howard Beissinger confirms, in *The New Care And Training Of The Trotter And Pacer*, that to persevere in wasting time with slow learners is, overall, a sure recipe for disaster in a racing stable. The number of stupid ones that will eventually make the grade will not repay the extra time spent on these animals as a whole. Symptoms associated with Lyme disease in humans, as described by sufferer Angela Knight in *The Daily Telegraph* on 29 June 1999, include inability to concentrate and impairment of short-term memory, overacute hearing and jumpy vision. We may see some yearlings whose behaviour might be well explained were they suffering similar symptoms. If untreated, these problems can hardly do other than severely compromise any hope of meaningful athletic achievement in a racehorse.

It should be noted that certain diseases may well be transmittable to humans in a variety of ways, and in the light of some very unpleasant examples worldwide in recent years this fact should be borne in mind.

When the yearling will follow the pony happily around the arena, perhaps doing a few figures of eight, we can finish the first ridden lesson. We practise dismounting and mounting the rider three or four times before putting the horse away.

The next day our yearling should require only a brief lunge before being ridden and, if he has previously proved sensible to mount, the lad can be put on in the arena without going back to the stable. We place the horse's head against the fence as a precaution when mounting and the pony should be standing by.

When he has been going round for a few minutes with a lead we can send the pony out or to one corner and see how the yearling goes on his own. If he seems relaxed and steers well enough in the figures of eight, we can take him off the premises to see how he reacts. As he has been driven outside on several occasions he will probably behave well. We should not be too complacent, however, and unless we have complete faith in both the yearling rider and the pony rider we should go with them on the first trip. Once again it is advisable to remain close to any fence or hedge until we see how the land

lies, but as long as the yearling seems calm he will soon be able to venture into more open territory and jog in circles to practise steering. At first he should stick close to the pony but after a few minutes he may be taken a short distance away to learn to steer rather than follow. Care must be taken that he is close to the pony if they meet a string of horses at this stage, as although he may become excited and forget himself he will tend to follow the pony. Over the next days he will be taught to become self-reliant.

Any nearby artificial gallops can be walked on and off. If this is not practised, long delays can sometimes result when we have to cross one of these tracks, which might involve a step of over a foot high, on the way to some distant part of the gallops. The stand and back lessons should be practised before taking him home. As previously stated, it is important not to get yearlings too tired.

After a day or two, the yearling should be fit to be mounted straight away but as he is no longer being lunged it is advisable to ride him around the box a few times before going outside. The mounting and dismounting after exercise should continue for a week, or until he is perfect, and if there is ever any question of not being perfect the practice should be reinstated, as a horse that is difficult to mount is a nuisance at the races.

This general programme is continued for a few days and by the end of the third week we should have a fairly civilised embryonic racehorse. He will have had an introduction to hack cantering but this should initially be very steady, with the lad sitting in the saddle to avoid any danger of excitement. Hopefully he will have a decent mouth on him and will have learned his two verbal commands, although these should be reinforced daily for some time.

By now the yearling should be treated almost like an old horse in the stable but patience will still be required. He should not be left tied up for too long as yet and his hay should not be in the box when he is tied up so a not to tempt him to get loose. The method used to prevent him from getting loose should also be effective in preventing him from scraping his bed up when left tied up; he will soon form the impression that there is always someone outside watching him. However, there is absolutely no point in chastising him when he is not actually scraping, as often happens purely because the lad cannot be bothered to adopt the correct procedure. Twenty minutes teaching this lesson over three or four days will save hours straightening his bed over the course of the horse's career. He should be required to pick his feet up carefully whenever he gets across the stable, initially by having them gently tapped with the side, not the point, of the fork.

The turning and figure of eight period is now largely behind him and we may think about getting the yearling reshod in front as there will now be less danger of the shoes getting pulled off at exercise. There is no need for hind shoes at this point unless they are fitted for a specific purpose such as to prevent brushing, although attention should be given to keeping the hind feet balanced. We will deal with shoeing elsewhere.

The breaking tack can now be discarded for a plain, jointed snaffle with a bib-running martingale. If the sweet mouth was used for breaking there will be no change of bit. The martingale will normally be adjusted so that the ring almost touches the angle of the jaw and the throat when the horse is standing normally, but may be better slightly shorter for the first day or two. A bib presents less danger of a horse getting hold of his martingale, which can cause a panic. The side reins should be left on for a couple of days and should go outside the bib [22]. Martingales should not be used with buckle-on reins unless stops are fitted to prevent the ring lodging on the buckle which can cause a panic attack.

It is best not to allow yearlings much hard feed whilst they are being broken, although they should have good hay *ad lib*. A Timothy mixture is probably best, but it should be bright in colour and not too hard in texture. Top-class meadow hay of the type seen sometimes as feed for show goats would be ideal, but does not seem to be available; presumably it is carefully made in small quantities for a specialised market. If they also receive a small feed at night, about four pounds of good oats with some wet bran, or a similar amount of manufactured mix, it will be quite sufficient until they start to canter properly. In fact, even this small amount of hard food can add to the difficulty of breaking some particularly uncooperative yearlings, and these rebellious ones will come to no harm on hay and water until they are going quietly.

This breaking regime will not be regarded as fashionable nowadays, and indeed there may be much to be said for those systems that are based on total cooperation between man and horse. They are certainly refreshing in that they have resurrected knowledge of, and general interest in, equine behaviour worldwide. However they do tend to be reliant on personnel who are both knowledgeable and dedicated, and so are of limited use in a racing environment. The method described above may seem, particularly in its emphasis on minor detail, to be both old-fashioned in its recommendations and boring to read. It is offered as a basis for safely breaking the vast majority of yearlings under the prevailing conditions. It has produced the most prolific winning two-year-old in Britain on six occasions.

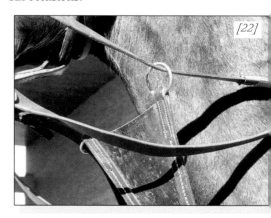
[22]

Basic Training Of The Two-Year-Old

"He being made perfect in a short time, fulfilled a long time." Wisdom of Solomon 4:13

This section will form the main body of this offering, and it may be as well to preface it with a quotation from Keene Daingerfield: *"There is no legerdemain connected with training horses, no sleight of hand, no magic words to change a bad horse into a good one. Anyone with ordinary common sense can win races with good horses; no one can win them with bad ones. There is however a proving ground; the great body of ordinary animals. The trainer who gets maximum results from average material is the good trainer. Luck, too plays a prominent part; but luck, as a substitute for brains, does not last forever."*

This sentiment can be adopted as our theme in what will be necessarily a rather long-winded section as unfortunately many of the basic rules we wish to discuss here have definite exceptions to them. If there is a trick, then it may be said to be knowing when those exceptions should be applied. If there is one rule that should never alter it is that every horse in the yard is for sale, as long as the price is right. To keep the show on the road it is essential to generate cash flow by selling horses continually and replacing them with fresh ones. To be able to do this we must keep our horses as sound as possible, and preserving soundness should be considered just as important as winning prize money.

Once the yearlings have been broken and ridden away they are ready to commence their training proper. It is as well if we can get them all going within four or five weeks, so as initially to train them as a group. As long as there is a relatively short time lapse the problem can be overcome by taking it easy with the first ones ridden for two or three weeks, allowing the stragglers to catch up. Yearlings will always learn to handle themselves better and to be more competitive in a group.

The exception is the very flighty horse that requires much more time to accept every new idea. This type of horse can prove very disruptive to the group as a whole and he can for a time be left to a more long and steady exercise routine, probably with the pony to accompany him. He must not, however, be allowed to get too fresh, even though we are not in a hurry with him, as fresh horses rarely learn anything except bad habits. After a while these erratic ones settle down and can gradually be introduced into the string, perhaps at first joining the others to walk home after they have done their work and are more amenable. Hay and water is the only diet a horse like this requires until he accepts the normal routine.

The main body of yearlings will follow a programme of steadily increasing work that they can normally all cope with at this stage, although as the pressure increases it will be obvious which ones do need a little more time. This training plan was formulated on the assumption that the weather remains reasonable and that the horses remain healthy. Unfortunately that is most unlikely always to be true, and various different scenarios will develop which necessitate minor improvisations. The other qualification to be made is that it is far from easy to find the riders to guarantee the successful application of these formulae, although we will expect to some degree to train our own riders as well as our horses. The basic plan is not particularly complicated.

The exercise regime does depend to some degree on the weather, which is obviously out of our control, and common sense should always be used regarding underfoot conditions when working with young horses. Slippery surfaces should be avoided, and also very rough and frozen ones. Yearlings should not be cantered on ground that is very heavy, nor on ground with frost in it. However they should actually miss as few days as possible, and it should normally be possible for them to have trotting exercise even in bad weather. Running racehorses should never trot fast for fear of pulled shoes and of damaged knees after stumbles. We should always remember, when tempted to miss a day in marginal conditions, that the next day the weather may well be even worse and that all youngsters soon learn bad habits when fresh. This is even more true once they start being fed a little more hard food. If any one day is particularly cold or wet there is no need to subject horses or lads to their full exercise; however, this cannot become a regular occurrence.

At this age there is no real need for most yearlings to be out more than 45 or 50 minutes, certainly not if they are behaving themselves well. We should also keep the exercise fairly near to home at this stage because many babies still walk very slowly and these slower walkers should not be constantly chivvied to keep up. Over the next few weeks they will all learn to walk at the pace of the older horses.

By now we assume that the yearlings are capable of going straight onto the gallops in a string. They should have a sensible older horse to lead them and if necessary his hard food ration can be slightly reduced to ensure his better behaviour. This will be a fairly relaxing task for a horse that has been hard trained and we should be able to find one that enjoys it.

However, he is doing a job and too much joie de vivre will not be constructive. In fact, leading yearlings can sometimes prove a dramatic revival process for any horse feeling the effects of a long campaign, but giving the young ones a good example is always the primary objective. A horse that misbehaves going on to the exercise ground should never be used to lead yearlings.

At this stage, yearlings should always have a good trot when they first get to the exercise ground in order to get any freshness out of their system before the serious business starts. They can do some circling and figures of eight to practise their steering skills, and for this they should split up rather than blindly follow the leader. The lads will need constant reminding to go their separate ways. They must also be warned not to turn sharply on those horses that have been reshod in front for fear of getting their shoes off, particularly if the ground is soft. It is a good idea for the horses to trot in and out of the string, crossing each other's path as if it were a musical ride, to trot tight upsides each other, and generally to simulate the bunching and interference of a race. This practice is very helpful in making horses accept that they need not worry about their classmates and it must therefore enable them to concentrate on the job in hand. There seems a widely held but erroneous opinion amongst racing people that upsides work implies purely speed work; this should not be so and in fact the majority of a racehorse's education should be complete before he ever does formal fast work. We may need to reiterate this fact constantly to the lads. Care should obviously be taken to identify any persistent kicker and therefore avoid unnecessary accidents; however, with care those animals that do initially kick at their workmates soon learn to relax and behave themselves in company.

The harness racing world is much more aware of the importance of teaching racing technique and racing manners to their horses. In a time-oriented sport they have concrete evidence of the difference total training can make. This approach should be more widely adopted in the Thoroughbred sport for best results. The fact that many Thoroughbred trainers, especially most of the more fashionable ones who tend to train the better horses, have had little or no experience of even riding work on young racehorses must explain this difference in philosophies.

After trotting for 15 minutes or so, and practising the two verbal commands once or twice, the yearlings can walk to the cantering ground. Although we do not want any horses to become too fresh, great care should be taken for the first few days that the latest recruits are allowed to get their breath back between stages. They are less fit than the first wave, and if overtired at first they may become resentful. These later arrivals catch up in a few days.

Initially the yearlings canter three or four furlongs. They have been used to hack cantering a furlong or two in the past weeks but it is important that they do go far enough to settle down and pay attention now that they are in a string. Even with the old horse in front there will be a certain amount of swerving and running about for the first day or two, but the yearlings will soon get the idea. It is a good idea to make them all walk along the cantering ground and allow them to trot and then canter away only when the back markers are ready, rather than set them off individually as soon as they get there.

The old horse should go up the middle of the cantering ground for the first few times to allow a clear passage between the discs or markers, as the yearlings will initially show a tendency to swerve away from these. This greenness will soon pass and the lads can gradually get closer to the discs over a few days, in fact the sooner the better because they will then be able to use the fresh ground opened by the markers' moving over one horse's width each day. To use the best ground is another subject for daily reminder to all lads on all horses, especially any older animals with leg problems.

The point at which the string are to pull up must be made clear before it sets off, but the lead rider must still loudly signal his intentions a furlong earlier in the hope of avoiding a pile-up. All yearlings (and in fact all racehorses) should always trot out for a few strides when they pull up. The all too common method of stopping dead from a canter to a walk with the attendant jarring and stumbling probably causes the start of many injuries, and we should absolutely not allow it. To make the pull-up smoother it should never, if this can possibly be avoided, be on a downhill section. Many yearlings, although otherwise well-mannered, do have a tendency to kick when pulling up on the first few occasions, but they soon grow out of it but initially great care should be taken not to get any horses, or riders, hurt.

Basically the yearlings will now do two canters on most days, with a short walk between, as long as the ground is suitable. After the first few days they will hopefully be cantering in a recognisable string and in an orderly fashion. They should be going just fast enough that they are not playing about and the lead horse should be careful to control the speed. As a rule they are not to pass the leader. There will be the odd yearling that drops himself out and falls well behind, and this trick must be quickly stopped before it becomes a habit. These horses must set off near the front of the string so that the others are chasing them up, or helping them along. The longer this habit of dropping out is tolerated, the harder it is to break.

As a general rule it is advisable for all young horses to be encouraged to conduct themselves as soberly as possible. Bad habits are all too easily formed, and resentment is very often caused in trying to resolve them if they are allowed to become confirmed. We might occasionally give a little leeway to an older horse, particularly a more able member of the team, as long as matters do not get out of hand. Knowing just what degree of tomfoolery is acceptable in order to keep an old horse happy in his work is one of the most important aspects of training; unfortunately, it has to be learnt by bitter experience.

Some of the colts may show a tendency to be either aggressive or amorous with their classmates when at close quarters, but as long as these horses are always ridden by fairly strong characters they normally realise quite quickly that this is unacceptable behaviour. We should remember that they have been used to establishing a pecking order when running out in the paddocks, and that some may now wish to declare their superiority. In most cases this does not seem to imply that these coltish individuals will be superior runners and their bad habits should certainly be corrected as soon as possible. Particular care should be taken not to allow them to jump up on another horse when they, for instance, may find themselves behind a very slow walker, or if the string stops for traffic. If by any chance a horse shows every sign of continuing with this cheekiness, or if he shows other distinct signs of having a mind of his own generally, we should give serious consideration to having him gelded straight away. The sooner the cutting is done, the sooner he can start to get over it, and the less confirmed any bad habits will have become. We would far rather have a decent runner, and be sorry to have cut him, than have a wastrel and regret not cutting him.

Yearlings in most cases recover very quickly from this operation, although all horses that have been cut should normally go out twice daily until the swelling subsides. Trotting exercise is normal for the first ten days or so, with a 30 minute lunge at evening stable time. Twenty minutes of hosing the wound is also helpful, as long as the weather is not too cold.

The insurance company must be informed of the operation. The decision of whether or not to insure racehorses needs some consideration, and is a matter of personal choice. The premiums are fairly high, and cover is normally limited to death or humane destruction, but when things are going wrong they often seem to go very wrong, and recovery of at least the capital value of the horse is very welcome. If we should buy any American yearlings, none should be put into quarantine on an aeroplane without being insured as we are then assuming additional risks outside of our direct control.

Castration should not be expected to act as if we had simply switched off a light and it may take some time to see any dramatic improvement. In fact, particularly in the case of older animals that are more set in their ways, the improvement may take so long and be so gradual as to be imperceptible. With a very rebellious old horse it is often advisable to give him a complete break once the wound has healed, and eventually start afresh with an established gelding, which may have a more relaxed attitude, rather than to battle on with his old attitudes still fresh in his mind. Some cases that do appear to have demonstrated fairly instant rehabilitation may involve the misbehaviour having been due to an illness which responded to the accompanying antibiotic therapy. The removal of physical discomfort involving one or both testicles could also be an explanation for an instant change of attitude.

We would hope to have all the yearlings cantering in the string by Christmas so as to be able to up the tempo, weather permitting, after the holidays. The old-time trainers would try their yearlings before Christmas to see what they had. The famed 19th century yearling races were probably actually early two-year-old contests as the birthday in those days was 1 May.

It is often possible to predict the better prospects amongst the team even at this early stage simply by observing the way in which they use their hind legs in comparison with their companions. Those horses whose hind legs reach up furthest under their girth even in their slower paces are likely to prove the superior runners.

Mac's Imp (USA), Champion 2-year-old in Ireland, in full cry alongside the Devil's Ditch at Newmarket. Alan Munro up. Compare his action with that of Superpower (p 87). (Photo courtesy of Paul Edwards)

The Christmas and New Year period is normally fairly shambolic in the racing environment due to absenteeism but we should resign ourselves to that fact. We can console ourselves by thinking that any injured horse might well miss much more time than this seasonal upheaval will cost him without suffering any long-term ill effects. After the disruption of the holiday it may take a day or two to get the stable back on an even keel, and we must take extra care to avoid accidents with very fresh horses, particularly as conditions underfoot may be bad.

By about 4 January, weather permitting, the schedule should be back to where we left off.

We can now gradually begin to step up the exercise a little. All increases in pace in a racehorse's workload must be made gradually. It must be made plain to all riders that any unanticipated showings of speed will always be regarded as quite the opposite of a pleasant surprise. Although two-year-olds will not be required to race round a turn for some time, and some indeed may never do so, it is a good idea to include some cantering that does involve turning a well-defined corner as part of the racing education before the serious speed work commences.

Once the holiday period is over we will start to increase the hard food ration. As with everything else, this increase should be gradual. Over two or three weeks the now two-year-olds' intake will gradually increase, as long as they continue in full work, towards the normal allowance for a horse in training. This comprises a fairly dry ration made up of Canadian oats, racehorse cubes and pre-mix fed 3 pounds, 3 pounds, and 6–8 pounds at 6 am, 12 noon and 6 pm, respectively. In fact this will be found to be an optimistic expectation for very many two-year-olds, particularly as they start to work harder. As a general rule, racehorses do not eat as well whilst they are in hard work as they do when their regime is easier.

There is no longer any need for more than a token trot to check that all are sound and the cantering can be increased to three canters of around five furlongs each for all except those that look as if that workload might be too much for them. The second and third canters should be either upsides in twos, or in a larger bunch. We may need to be very insistent to make some lads go close enough to the other horses; however, we really do want them to be banging their irons against their partner's. There is no earthly use in horses merely going parallel to each other. Just because there are rules against rough riding and interference in races does not mean it doesn't regularly take place, and we want our soldiers to be experienced in combat conditions. The old horse should continue to lead so as to control the speed. In the event of any of the juveniles getting a little keen they should be relegated to the rear where they will normally settle down again. We do not want to encourage any overenthusiastic behaviour at this stage.

The two-year-olds should be ready for the first minimal injection of speed by the last week of January. The quietest way to introduce this is by telling the lad on the old horse just to go on a bit once he can see everyone is present and correct. He need not signify his intentions beforehand so as to avoid too much excitability amongst the other riders at the prospect of

having a little feel of their mounts' ability. Of course, the old horse must be easy to rate and the lad on him must know what he is doing. They should go about three furlongs at about 17 or 18 seconds to the furlong, in fact a normal canter for the old horse.

It is not difficult to determine an approximate relationship between stride pattern and speed for some of the older horses that can lead this type of work. We are only attempting to ensure that there is a fairly regular progression in the work times, and it is not realistic to expect the clock-in-the-head racetrack system to be any more accurate than this one. Once we have some idea how fast the old horse is going at a given stride rate anyone numerate can be instructed how fast to go on him. In fact it will be easier to implement this method by using half-furlongs in our instructions because the markers should be so placed; riders charged with the task of setting the pace must continue to monitor their speed throughout as the discs may have been displaced by earlier traffic and not precisely reset, which over only two sections might be misleading. The overall distance will be correct and it is unusual to get three consecutive widely differing sections. It is easier for the average work rider to count off each physical stride than to assess accurately the perception of seconds passing in time.

Most two-year-olds (that is, most horses that are going to be capable of racing competitively at two years) will improve steadily under this regime and by mid-February the normal speed for cantering every day will have advanced to the 17 or 18 second per furlong rate. The third canter can now be dropped and the routine cantering should now revert to one behind the other in order to guard against any horses or lads becoming too keen. Two or three times a week they should work a little more seriously and continue to reduce their times on those occasions. Any signs of excitability, either equine or human, must be carefully monitored. The times or the stride pattern of the old horse should be dropping steadily so that by early March the second daily canter should be at around a 15 second per furlong rate and a three furlong work is completed comfortably in around 42 seconds. This rate can be regarded as a 'half-speed' and they should do it with the last furlong slightly the fastest.

All these times are taken whilst the horse is already moving, not from a standstill, so are not particularly onerous. An early-season two-year-old race, in Britain, might be run in 25 or 26 seconds for the first two furlongs and finish in 1.03 minutes from a standing start, although there can be tremendous variation due to the differing tracks and the state of the surfaces. The standing start costs almost two seconds, and this should always be borne in mind when comparing race times between Britain and America. If two-year-olds win in the same time as the older horses over course and distance on the same day during the first weeks of the season they are potentially quite smart. Unfortunately, some of these early fliers will have been so cranked up by their connections for an early campaign that they will soon fizzle out.

It is not constructive to have two-year-olds working the last furlongs slower than the first, due to having overdone the early pace. Horses definitely do not get the same fitness benefit from this work and they can also become disillusioned very easily at this age if they are finishing tired. This should not imply that all that is required is a flying final furlong, as to get improvement we must see a regular reduction in the overall time; however, to sustain that improvement there must be no falling off in speed at the end. Obviously on raceday most sprints are run at a fast early pace which then slows, but there is no sense in actually teaching horses to slow up at the end. Early speed can easily be introduced at a later date, if necessary, simply by two or three very sharp dashes, which will however be over only

two or three furlongs, allowing the horse to be pulled up before he gets tired.

We are now well into March and as we drop our workday times steadily and in an organised fashion towards the 12 second furlongs which are the standard requirement of a Thoroughbred racehorse we should be anticipating either of two widely differing situations.

The first is that some of the team will not be as comfortable with the increased workload as others, which is only to be expected, and is easily remedied by backing off them a little. We don't need to stop with them altogether, but we may allow them a week or two doing routine canters. We might then quietly have another try, perhaps in company with any others that have lagged behind the main group for various reasons.

The other thing we should be watching very carefully for at this time is the horse that gets a little speed crazy. Even though this one has no problem physically handling the work, his brain is starting to overheat. This too will probably be resolved by our backing off him a little and reducing the speed of his work, but this might not be the right thing to do. This horse might easily be a precocious sprinter, pure and simple; if such is the case, we may well miss the boat with him if we do stop now. This type of horse needs careful consideration, and an experienced lad to ride him and preferably to do him in the box. Lads are naturally more patient with their own horses. The best remedy to give us a chance of covering all eventualities is to move him to first lot with the old horses, and see how he gets on cantering in that string. Very often this will do the trick, as the old ones tend to be going a little faster and also a little further. This in itself may well be enough to prevent him from trying to overdo things, and the more strenuous canters will also benefit his fitness without him needing to work more seriously for a week or two. If he does continue to be headstrong but is physically doing well we should press on and let him do his work behind an old horse, so that he doesn't get in the habit of running away. Obviously the old horse is not to race him, but merely to go fast enough for the youngster to settle, and the two-year-old should be allowed to come through at the end and to finish in front. The sooner this type of keen juvenile gets to the races now, the better. These horses sometimes turn out fine after they have had a run. As long as he is a healthy horse, we should try to run him regularly instead of working him fast at home once he has made his debut.

Obviously it is important to use the best available riders, and we should hope to develop some of our own along with the horses. It is increasingly difficult to find competent lightweights but, for the purpose of argument, we must assume that riders of the two-year-olds following this method are under 9 st, and we must remember that the weights allotted for serious work should reflect the age and the capabilities of the horses involved. Weight for age between two and three over five furlongs early in the year is about 30lb, which gradually reduces to reflect the increasing maturity of the youngsters. The full scale is easily available, and we should instinctively take it into account in all calculations that involve horses of different ages working or racing together.

At this point another golden rule can be recorded, which is that when working a two-year-old with an old horse, the old horse always works for the two-year-old. That is to say he does not try to beat the two-year-old either at the start, where he has the greater experience, or at the finish, where he will probably show more stamina. The rare exceptions are when we are fairly sure that the two-year-old is really smart and are considering how much to bet, but such all-out trials should only be over four furlongs early in the year, as the full five is too severe for the two-year-old. After the work is over, the old horse should be slowed in order to allow the youngster the encouragement of getting to the front even if he was not there at the winning post. Our lads should always be aware of the damage which can be done to a two-year-old's confidence, and they should realise that offences in this area of operations are regarded as very serious. Unfortunately, it is always easier to turn any young horse into a loser than into a winner.

To return to those two-year-olds that are making normal progress, by the end of March we should find that most of those that have kept up so far can work a half-mile in a little above 50 seconds, with the last two furlongs in 24 seconds. We might refer to this rate as 'three-parts speed'. This stage of the training is quite enjoyable to all concerned in as much as it takes the form of what we call 'farmer's races' and there is for the first time some element of competition, although this must be controlled. The pace of the daily second canter will remain a two minute rate of 15 seconds per furlong, although obviously the distance remains around five or six furlongs. This was traditionally referred to in Newmarket as a 'swinging canter'. As a general rule, the more strong cantering work any racehorse receives, the smaller amount of formal fast work he will require. A regime involving 15 seconds per furlong canters most days is definitely beneficial in establishing and maintaining the degree of fitness required to complete an arduous season, but it must be introduced gradually. By now most of the two-year-olds are interchangeable with the old horses in the string, so allowing the light lads to ride more of them than when all the young ones were second lot. The two-year-olds need not canter quite as far as the old ones at this stage, although they will by now be cantering at similar speeds.

Unfortunately, the speed crazy type is not uncommon amongst sprinters and this can cause problems amongst the older horses too. Once they are fit, many of these horses are well suited to doing just one good strong canter and then going home. Doing two canters with the string often fires them up needlessly. If these animals can be regularly raced, so much the better, as the need to go fast at home will then be lessened. In many cases a normal programme has the same reaction on these animals as pouring petrol on a fire. The widespread perception that they need no work is quite illogical and we should continue to train them, but with some tact and diplomacy. The frequent examples of horses that win having reportedly done no work at all are difficult to explain, but those animals would almost certainly do even better were it possible to put them into a regular work schedule. These cases tend to occur in older, lower-grade animals that very rarely change stables into more formally run establishments which might enable the theory to be tested.

At this stage we will have some idea of the real potential of the two-year-olds based on how easily they seem to do their work. Reasonably precocious types will nearly all progress smoothly up to this point but one or two more may now be coming towards the limit of what they can do comfortably, and again we should back off these ones for a short time. As long as they remain in good health we should never stop on them altogether, but they may resume routine cantering without any fast work for a time.

The next couple of weeks will see further increases in speed and these should always be steady rather than dramatic. Some thought should now be given to sending horses of apparently similar capabilities together. We can easily spoil any horse at this stage by working him with one that is far superior, which is merely an endorsement of what we have previously noted about working with an older horse. Two-year-olds must never be worked fast in heavy ground, although they may occasionally be forced to race in it. If the final stages of the gallop being used are severe, such as Across The Flat at Newmarket, two-year-olds should not be required to work as far up

the hill as the old horses, so as to avoid disillusioning them. They will however derive great benefit from cantering uphill, as long as the increased strain is gradually introduced.

Once a two-year-old delivers a sub-50 second half-mile at the beginning of April we can be fairly sure of him winning something, especially should the last two furlongs of the work be appreciably faster, such as in a 26 second and 23 second split. The reverse split is not nearly as good and may well indicate what we call 'cheap' speed. However, even cheap speed is better than no speed, and with care this type of horse should be able to scramble through some sort of a contest, even if only because of the weakness of the early season opposition. He can then be sold, probably to Italy.

When two-year-olds reach this level and are still finishing strongly we can feel optimistic as to their prospects and begin to consider where we should run. If they have followed these recommendations they should have a sound base of fitness and will be ready to compete after only three or four more works. Of course, if we intend to bet heavily on one we may prefer to spend a little more time to ensure his complete fitness, but as a general rule betting should never be considered a major factor in any realistic plan to survive in the racing game.

The remaining works should be at a similar rate, although they might be slightly longer so that they come close to the distance of the race. To be fair to them, all two-year-olds should have at least six works at something approaching racing pace before they run, although those works need not all be over the full five furlongs. Strong canters should continue on nonwork days as long as the animals are thriving on their work.

As previously mentioned, it may be advisable to really send our horse along over two or three furlongs, say a quarter of a mile from a standstill in 23 seconds or so, once or twice, in order to prevent the possibility of being badly outpaced in the early part of their first race. This is combat training, not fitness work, and he should always be pulled up while still full of running. These dashes are essential, however good we may think he is, if we intend betting seriously on him. If, however the result of the first race is felt to be incidental to a likely successful career, we should not bother.

The weather will probably play some part in the completion of this schedule, and it may often be necessary to use all-weather surfaces if they are available. On these occasions we should take care to school the young horses in brushing against the rail and in entering narrow gaps and racing in tight quarters next to it. If the horses are to leave any railed gallop through a gap in the rail after working they must always be made to pass the gap and then turn back to it.

In the event that we do wish to bet, or even just for interest, we may want to work the two-year-old formally with an old horse in order to try him. This can be extremely informative if properly conducted, and in the old days, when it was normal practice, it was said to have two purposes. First, to discover a good horse but second, and equally important, to uncover a bad one! If we do decide to try a two-year-old it is usually a good idea to have a semi-serious dress rehearsal about a week before the real trial. If we really like this horse he should fairly easily go three and a half furlongs with a reasonable three-year-old, say a 70-rated handicapper, in receipt of a stone fom the older one. If he can't, we may have overestimated him. If he can do this easily enough then he should come on enough in a week to repeat the work in receipt of only 7lbs. This does not make him a good horse, but it should be enough to win the majority of early-season maiden races. It is not recommended, or necessary, to go any further than this, or at most four furlongs, when working with an older horse at this time of the year. The result of any trial that takes place on a gallop with marked undulations can prove misleading, as the old horse will normally be seen to greater advantage, and to guard against this happening such ground should only be used to try horses after they have had previous experience of its irregularities. We should bear in mind that the same caution should be exercised in expecting great things from inexperienced horses racing on very sharp tracks, even if their home work has been good. Animals that have already had racecourse experience will normally have a distinct advantage.

Many years ago it was the practice to try the yearlings before Christmas, although they then had much lighter lads to ride them. It was said then that the best horse at Christmas would in fact turn out to be the best at the end of the day. This would seem to imply that early development need not necessarily predict early decay, contrary to popular belief. A recent survey of the participants in the very early two-year-old dashes in America showed them on average to enjoy longer careers than those that were not started so early in the year.

It might prove interesting to refer to the now indiscriminate use of the word 'good' by racing enthusiasts. When applied to a racehorse this adjective ought to imply an animal of at least Listed race class, although to a purist a stakes horse would only be 'nice', and he would demand Group performance from a 'good' horse! Arguably these terms are generally too vague to be allotted any specific value, however when used by professional horsemen they should imply exceptional racing ability.

Other examples of the bastardisation of the vocabulary are the fact that nowadays a horse with 'a leg' is no longer specifically understood to be suffering from a tendon injury, and that one that 'blows up' in a race is no longer specifically understood to have weakened purely through lack of fitness which, by implication, can and will be remedied Obviously, the inappropriate use of much originally specific racing terminology by the media tends to further corrupt correct usage.

We have covered the actual training schedule of the early-season two-year-old in some detail, but as well as getting him fit it is vitally important to teach him something of the technique of racing. This is widely overlooked and almost certainly leads to many horses not fulfilling their full potential, whether or not they apparently race successfully. Funnily enough, those horses that appear completely natural runners at every stage of their training do surprisingly often get beaten on their first start. Everything has come so easily to them that they have no idea what to do in an actual race when they may not automatically be able to dominate the opposition from the start. Even though they may run quite straight, and apparently do nothing wrong, these horses are actually beaten through greenness. Fayruz was well beaten on his first start through this syndrome, causing a certain amount of financial upheaval in the camp, but he bounced straight back and won his next six starts in less than a month. This horse was already inclined to be headstrong, so had not been subjected to the recommended two or three furlong dashes that would have prevented the initial defeat, but which might easily have left him impossible to train.

In any other discipline we would expect to teach the horse his job gradually, and the better he was taught, as long as he had some natural aptitude, the better results we would expect. There seems little reason to believe that just because a racehorse can run around a field instinctively he can teach himself to run fast or slow on demand, whilst carrying an unnatural burden, without some specific training. We should remember before dismissing this speculation out of hand that in the kingdom of the blind, the one-eyed man is king, and that any advantage we can give our horses will increase our prospects of eventual success. As mentioned elsewhere, top harness-racing trainers, who in many cases are also drivers, attach enormous importance to what they term 'racing manners' in their much more arduous and tactical sport. As harness racing is completely time orientated the value of sound practices are presumably plainly demonstrated, which is not always true of Thoroughbred racing.

Even if we accept this precept, we may initially find it extremely difficult to implement properly, but if we do make the effort we may hope also to develop some riders capable of following this system as a matter of course. In the meantime, any efforts we do make will not be completely wasted. Although this concept may to some sound a little far-fetched it is probably not particularly novel. It has merely, like many sound equine practices, been forgotten in the combustion engine euphoria that has swept the civilised world. What we require is a horse that, although running in a relaxed manner so as to conserve as much energy as possible, can be instantly called upon to quicken or to change direction as the unfolding race may require. Obviously this is easier said than done with a big, long-striding horse which must mean that these particular animals will require even more education. Ironically, in most cases they will be the least likely to receive it as they will often be relegated to the back burner by their trainers and never seen again, at least not until they are too set in their ways to be easily taught how to handle themselves to best advantage.

One aspect of this approach that seems to have little relevance in Europe, although it is regarded as vital in America, is the ability to change legs, or leads, on demand. In Europe all horses are allowed to decide for themselves which leg to use in the closing stages of their race, and we may sometimes consider a race to have been lost by changing at a vital stage. In America it is considered essential that all horses change from their near to their off lead when they enter the straight, and failure to do so is regarded as extremely detrimental to their chance of victory.

The farmer's race system mentioned above does give some assistance to the learning process in that the young horses tend to be enthused by the crowd, which naturally makes them competitive, but of course they do not suffer the confusing experience of being punished (as they must interpret it) for going faster. It is essential that young horses see racing as almost a game at this stage of their career, although that should not imply that they do not go straight about their business as required. A top-class work rider will constantly be teaching a two-year-old to pick up speed and then slow down smoothly even when cantering routinely in the string. Although this is now very rarely found it may have been more common when wages were so low that a lad was dependent, in the true sense of that word, on what he could win betting. Fortunately, however, this is not brain surgery, and if we are insistent enough we may persuade our lads to make some effort to work with the natural enthusiasm that most two-year-olds do initially possess in the attempt to shape effective racehorses.

Although whips should by this stage be carried they will very rarely be used on two-year-olds other than on the shoulder as a signal to pay attention or to prevent them from hanging away from or onto other horses. Any use of the whip behind the saddle will only be on our express instruction to a lad. A backhander may occasionally be felt necessary as a wake-up call by a jockey riding work, but he is a professional and he will be asked for his opinion of the horse's ability, so this can be said to be a special circumstance. If the whip is used behind the saddle it must be on the hindquarters, not on the flank.

Two points come to mind here following the above. Firstly, the term 'backhander' is another that has lost its original, precise meaning, which was, very specifically, a slap with the whip in the backhand position. Because all jockeys in the pre-Willie Carson era picked their whip up into the forehand position for their extreme effort the term 'backhander' originally implied little more than a flick, delivered simply as a reminder to pay attention to the rider's instructions. It was quite common for the jockey's instructions, even on fancied horses, to be along the lines of, "You can give him a backhander if you really have to but you are not to knock him about." Nowadays we routinely see animals getting several severe blows even if they are never seen with a chance of winning, and anything up to 20 strokes when the race is a close-run thing. There is no reason to countenance this style of riding as it is obviously needlessly destructive of the horse and simply denotes bad practice; we should aim to have our runners ridden in a manner more in keeping with the old style, if not for humanitarian reasons then as a common sense protection of our investment. Common sense dictates that the problem would be speedily resolved were all those winners that had suffered a breach of the whip rules to be disqualified.

The other point that arises is that the old-time trainers felt any serious trial should involve either all jockeys or all lads in order to avoid the result being confused by any rivalry. Lester Piggott, although definitely one of the truly great jockeys of all time, was notorious for ignoring all prearranged plans when riding work. He had a great tendency to set off before the gallop was even reached and to let his horse run along, whatever the trainer might have preordained. When his mount tired, Lester tended to let it drop right out of the trial, to the fury of the trainer and the delight of the lads who came to beat him. The amazing thing was, however, that Piggott's estimation of the merits of all the horses in the work, not just of his own mount, was extremely accurate. The same powers of observation enabled him to identify countless future winning rides on horses that previously ran in races in which he had ridden.

Starting Stalls Training

Be ye therefore wise as serpents, and gentle as doves.
St. Matthew 10:16

Before any two-year-old can run he must be schooled in the starting stalls. There are several different schools of thought on the best method of doing this, varying from daily practice to virtually no practice at all. The proof of the pudding being in the eating, different trainers will tend to adopt whatever system suits them, and in many cases will practise from the yearling stage. It is never a good idea to allow lads to approach the stalls with their horses in the absence of supervision, as they are likely to encounter difficulties even though these may often not be reported.

The method described here does not advocate regular practice but it has, by and large, been effective over a long career. Most two-year-olds do not take any great exception to the stalls, although funnily enough it is quite impossible to predict which ones will object from their behaviour in other areas. We will not take the young horses to the stalls in most cases until they are near to running and we normally only take three or four at a time in order to avoid rushing if things do go wrong with any of them. It is essential to have a very quiet pony and plenty of helpers when using this method.

The practice gate should have stalls descending in width from wide, through fairly wide, to standard size. All the two-year-olds should be ridden and led through the stall of each width in turn, first behind the stable pony and then alone, until they will enter and leave calmly. When walking through the regulation stall, even with the front gate open, extra care should be taken not to get them caught up on the rear doors due to their not approaching the gate squarely. The pony can now be shut in the first regulation-size stall and left there. His rider should as usual maintain a constant cheerful chat. We now walk the first two-year-old through the adjacent stall and close the door behind him immediately, even though he may not have halted as he does not yet know that this is what is required. It is preferable that he hurry straight on through the stall and the back gate has to be reopened to reload him than he realise that he can get out backwards, which might be the case were he to panic due to being stopped too sharply and the back gate not to be closed. We can easily reload him as long as he has not become alarmed. His recognition of the commands "Stand" and "Back" will prove invaluable at this point, but the rear gate should always be closed promptly in order to prevent a rearward exit. This method is really only a rerun of the breaking process in that we achieve our aim by gradually pressing forward and building on the previous stage. The maxim "More haste, less speed" still very much applies.

Once the pupil will stand quietly and has felt the back door on his quarters we can carefully close the front. We should make quite a fuss of him and someone can give him some grass to pull out of the mesh on the front gate so that he will have to touch the gate with his nose. Although the pony has not been mentioned much, his role is vital and it is his calm demeanour that will give the young ones the confidence to learn this important lesson properly. As long as the first two-year-old is relaxed standing in the gate we repeat the loading procedure with the others until they are all installed.

After a few moments the front gates can be opened by hand and the horses walked out. If one is reluctant to leave he should initially be led rather than chased out. The pony can normally remain shut in, as the less aggravation he gets the longer he will remain happy in this task; in fact, he should also be made a fuss of by everyone so that he regards this as a pleasant duty. After a couple of repeats we can spring the gate normally to accustom them to the noise, but we still just let them all walk out. We then repeat, gradually increasing the pace until they canter about a furlong away from the gate. The two-year-olds should never be allowed to turn back immediately in front of the stalls, even if they are to repeat their lesson. They must always go far enough to impress that they actually leave the gate behind when they come out.

Sometimes the pony may need to be placed a distance in front of the gate to provide a target for a reluctant two-year-old to go to, and this is very effective. Occasionally we will find a two-year-old that just will not come out, usually because of alarm at the noise of the gate springing. Rather than try to chase him out, we should lure him out by means of the pony standing close in front of the stalls, or by having the pony come straight through the next stall, in which case the youngster will often join in. In these cases we may also have to revert to opening the front by hand a few times. When confronted with this type of horse it is necessary to invest extra time to resolve the problem, as bullying often makes things worse.

If this session has gone smoothly, one more visit, involving jumping out smartly two or three times and going a couple of furlongs fairly sharply, will be enough to prepare most two-year-olds to race. Any troublesome horses should, if possible, finish on a positive note, even if they have not advanced as far as we had hoped.

If we do want to bet seriously on any horse on his debut we will be tempted to do a bit more practice with a view to having him very alert. This is not really recommended, as the British system often involves lengthy delays and the starter may well suspend any horse that misbehaves through being too excited. With a view to his future career it is safer to send him to his first race knowing that he will definitely load quietly, and that he will stand in the gate for some time if necessary waiting for poorly behaved opponents, rather than to have him wound up like a watch spring.

Stalls practice should not take place in bad weather as the wind and rain will upset everyone involved, with unhappy results. Many young horses can be so upset by these conditions as to undo several days' progress, and this should always be borne in mind in all aspects of handling very nervous horses until they have become more confident. Horses often seem to get on edge before thunderstorms and, apparently, seem able to detect imminent earthquakes. Presumably animals can detect changes in atmospheric pressure, and this may have given rise to the old perception in rural Suffolk that pigs can see the wind.

The advantage of our method is ensuring that horses never see the stalls except in circumstances that are specifically intended to resolve any difficulty which might arise. This cannot be the case when lads wander in and out of the gate, often unsupervised, as they do in many stables. The proof of the pudding might be said to be the fact that in 30 years we avoided any horse requiring a stalls rehabilitation certificate.

Training The Older Horse

"They shall go from strength to strength." Psalms 84:5

We have completed in some detail the specific training of a yearling up until the time of his first start and we will now turn to more general aspects of racehorse training, particularly with reference to the maximisation of assets and to damage limitation. These twin precepts are the only realistic foundation on which to establish a long-term involvement without having consistently to introduce further large sums of capital. To apply them successfully requires a professional and disciplined approach. For some reason, such a philosophy may prove difficult to explain to many owners and because of this difficulty trainers as a whole have tended to take the line of least resistance, simply preferring to keep their boxes filled.

Truly to implement the various procedures we may need to employ in order to succeed we must, almost certainly, abandon the comparatively recent fashion of delegation. There are various agricultural proverbs dating from the 17th century that might be applied, such as "The best manure is the foot of the farmer walking on the land every day" or "Nothing fattens beasts like the master's eye." The truth is that our financial objectives will only be accomplished with any consistency if the trainer has total hands-on control, as it is unrealistic to expect to find deputies who are genuinely qualified to take decisions for the remuneration commonly offered. This nondelegatory approach will necessitate the number of horses being restricted to 60 at most. Up until 30 years ago 60 was considered a big string, despite the more capable staff then available.

The enormous stables that have become the norm merely reflect the current defeatist attitude that this is purely a numbers game, and one cannot hope to do other than haemorrhage money. As long as it's someone else's money the prevailing system does have certain attractions for a trainer. In the words of philanthropist, owner, trainer and gambler Barney Curley, "Most trainers should carry a Government Health Warning!" As noted above, the modern trainer's attitude may in most cases be a reasoned response to the demands of their customer base, but due to the inevitable loss of attention to detail the numbers-game philosophy of racehorse training has become self-perpetuating. There can be no doubt that most very large strings do not produce results remotely in keeping with the size of the investment made in their raw material. They obviously do tend to include the best runners but require enormous investment and reinvestment to do so. It would be interesting to explore whether some of the biggest strings could produce just as many top performers if a much smaller intake led to less delegation and increased attention to detail. In the present climate no one is likely to have the confidence to attempt such a move.

The revolution in National Hunt racing since Martin Pipe appeared on the scene is almost unbelievable. To define that change in one line we need only note that a two mile novice hurdle might currently be run in up to 20 seconds less than was the case prior to his emergence. This is a phenomenal improvement in a relatively short time. An improvement in overall training methods, leading to greatly improved fitness in very many of the horses in the country, driven by the need to compete with the Nicholshayne horses cannot fail to be a factor. If there was not some truth in that theory, Pipe would still be winning all the races easily without the times necessarily having to improve. Prior to his meteoric rise there may well have been a feeling among jumping trainers that as their horses broke down only too often they should obviously be circumspect in the amount of training they administered. An unfit horse must be more likely to sustain an injury than a fit one and the scene was set for another self-fulfilling prophecy. The style of jump racing that previously allowed a moderate seven furlong horse recruited from the Flat to reserve his stamina sufficiently to win two mile hurdle races is now a thing of the past.

Rather than registering that his success was due to superior training technique, and resolving to examine the shortcomings in their own regimes, Pipe's opponents seem to have wasted several seasons deluding themselves that his results flowed from some magic formula. As the old-time farm horsemen had recognised there was no point in him disabusing his rivals of those suspicions and thus making them try harder themselves! By coincidence, one of the most remarkable training performances of recent years in America was by ex-English jumps trainer Michael Dickinson whose Da Hoss won a second Breeders' Cup after virtually two years off. To train the first five finishers in the Cheltenham Gold Cup, or indeed 12 winners on a single day, as Michael had done previously, are further feats unlikely to be repeated.

The new wave of National Hunt trainers currently coming to the fore may well owe much of their success to the fact that they have been able to observe Martin Pipe whilst they were still young enough to learn from his success, and to some degree formulate their own training strategies accordingly. It is notoriously

difficult to teach an old dog new tricks, and the previous generation of trainers had difficulty in adapting to the new style of jump racing in which most races are strongly run from end to end. As the horses of many other trainers tend to be far fitter nowadays it might pay Pipe to rethink the stable policy of almost invariably making strong running. Fitter current opponents are less easily galloped into the ground than those he previously faced, and indeed their connections may often appreciate someone to do the donkey work for them.

The Thoroughbred is actually a far tougher animal than it is generally given credit for, and with proper preparation will outperform many other breeds in their specialist fields. There was a well-known saying amongst foxhunting men, who required considerable strength and stamina from their mounts in the golden days of the that sport in the late 19th century, that in horses an ounce of blood was worth an inch of bone. That inherent strength and soundness is still genetically present, and probably improved by further selection and refinement, but it still requires training to be seen to best advantage. The common perception that the modern Thoroughbred is less resilient than his forebears is in fact a comfort zone for everyone involved in his racing career, as once it is universally accepted that the modern racehorse is congenitally weak there is obviously less pressure to achieve anything very meaningful with him. Whether the modern reluctance to cull inferior individuals will have serious repercussions on the breed remains to be seen, but the current policy of positively encouraging them by the proliferation of low-grade handicaps does appear very short-sighted. In fact, those in authority seem to have been almost entirely won over to the point of view of the off-course betting lobby that the number of runners is of more importance than the merit of those runners as far as day-to-day racing is concerned.

The current programme of handicaps must

also have a detrimental effect on training standards and practices as it actively discourages revealing the true potential of many horses in Britain. Once a course has been plotted to make any horse appear moderate in order to earn a favourable rating from the handicapper, it seems a small step for his connections to accept that he truly is moderate, and that being defeated is no bad thing in that it effectively confirms, and may even lower, his handicap rating. The true object of training racehorses ought to be to discover any horse's potential, or lack of it, as quickly as is reasonably practical, to win as much prize money as possible, to waste as little money as possible and to sell him for the highest attainable price. The discussion here continues purely on that rather old-fashioned basis.

As long ago as 1804, Samuel Chifney noted in his modestly named work *Genius Genuine* that, "Horse's legs are very soon destroyed at first coming into work; but when they have had time to be well trained, scarce any running or riding will hurt them." There is no doubt that the same is true today, and it must follow that the best protection we can afford our investment is a fairly rigorous training regime. This need not necessarily be the extreme and precise interval training advocated in some quarters. These systems seem far too complex to implement properly in a working racing stable, and in any event, as evidenced by Martin Pipe, they may not be necessary for optimum results. What we will attempt to practise may involve an overall workload similar to that practiced in Newmarket between the wars, although the detail may differ markedly.

As the racehorse has evolved it certainly requires less extreme training to deliver acceptable results, presumably because the cold elements in the pedigree have become more and more remote. The training that both Thoroughbreds and trotters were subjected to in the early years of both sports is unbelievable. In those days successful trainers were obliged

to develop their racing speed, whereas nowadays they have at least some degree of speed genetically present without any training. Old-time Thoroughbreds, which were actually rather less Thoroughbred than the present animal, were subjected to five hours exercise daily and to regular long works in heavy sweaters. Orrin Hickok reportedly drove the trotter St Julien 50 miles at a three-minute rate in a single day, whilst attempting to resolve the problems of his attitude and gait, and in fact kept him away from competition for three years whilst trying to straighten him out. The pair broke the world record for a mile with 2.11 1/4 in 1880, a speed that would be ridiculously slow to the highly bred trotter of today.

There were several connections between the romantic figures of American history and the Turf. Orrin Hickok was the brother of Wild Bill Hickok. Frank James, whilst on the run, had horses in training in Nashville with George Rice. After his acquittal by a rather partisan jury he acted as a starter at trotting meetings and as betting commissioner for leading Thoroughbred trainer S.C. Hildreth. Jesse James, living openly but under an assumed name and with a large reward on his head, was also a racing enthusiast and friend of trotting trainer Col. W.W. Abbott. Railroadman E.R. Harriman who, at least in the film of the same name, organised the hunting down of Butch Cassidy and the Sundance Kid, was, typically of many 19th century captains of commerce, a harness racing enthusiast. Indeed, he founded the Trotting Horse Club of America.

Since those days the training pendulum has swung completely the other way and in most cases training regimes for horses have never been lighter than today. Conversely in the human athlete, the recent increases in speed are accepted as the product of ever more brutal schedules. Some degree of any human athletic improvement must be due to psychological strength, but we cannot explain to a racehorse that once he passes the pain barrier he will be famous, and so the severity of his exercise routine will always be limited by the animal's ability to cope mentally as well as physically with his workload. There seems however, no logical reason to suppose that a progressive and moderately strenuous schedule for our horses will not prove more effective than relying on their inherent ability.

Before embarking on any description of the recommended exercise regime it is vital to note that there will always be horses which, for various reasons, will not achieve optimum results unless adjustments are made to their routine treatment. Much of the art of training lies in recognising these individuals at an early stage so as to avoid compromising whatever chances of success they might have, and also to avoid their disrupting the remainder of the string. In many cases such a discovery may be made by accident by an attentive trainer in close daily contact with his horses. Such unlooked for revelations are not unusual, but we must be aware enough to recognise them. They may present themselves both in regard to daily training and in regard to a horse's style of racing. For example, although it is commonly misinterpreted as bad luck in running when a beaten horse finishes fast after being shut in until the last moment, this may actually be a valuable clue as to his preferred running style.

The standard and numbers of staff employed in a training establishment are governed by both availability and cost. The best plan is to pay a premium above the regular wage in the hope of attracting enough recruits to allow us to be more rigorous in our standards. If we do this and maintain a ratio of about two staff to five horses we should always have volunteers waiting to fill any vacancies. This ratio allows the yard to operate reasonably smoothly even when there are lads away racing. It also attracts those lads that do still take an interest in their horses as they cannot do that in most yards where they may be doing four or five even before they have any spares.

When the weather is warm this system allows the better horses and those currently in a busy racing schedule to be taken out for a pick of grass at evening stable time. If this seems a rather cavalier attitude to cost we should reflect on whether we wish to be merely a livery yard or take training to its logical conclusion, as the latter will be impossible to achieve without adequate manpower. By the same token, no thought should be given to anything but the best quality oats, hay and bedding.

Even if the lads were doing one each, the horses would not be done as they were years ago. However, as long as their charges appear to be clean and tidy no-one, as was formerly the case, is going turn up the animal's coat to inspect for grease or expect a row of knockings from the curry comb on the doorstep. On the other hand, a good horse like St Simon will no longer be driven mad by one lad strapping him whilst another restrains him with a muzzle on. Most stables in the old days contained horses that had become savage largely due to the aggravation of grooming on the basis that, apart from the higher standards of spit-and-polish formerly required, the vigorous pumelling and massaging was felt to be extremely beneficial physically. This was a glaring instance of lack of common sense by our forbears, as any ticklish or body-sore animal was effectively being tortured for up to an hour per day, which can hardly have been conducive to his best performance as a runner. One of the dodges used to be keeping the dust and scurf in a matchbox, and pouring it back onto the body brush to provide instant knockings for inspection on the doorstep the following evening! The hygiene of the stable itself, a safe depth of bedding, and absolute cleanliness of both feed and water mangers must be rigorously enforced. The head collars should be kept clean; to avoid frequent oversights this task can be completed and all brasses can be brightly polished each Friday at midday whilst our lads are waiting for their wages!

It will be hard for girls to break into a chauvinist sport, although the male jockeys are not, by and large, the problem. (Photo courtesy of Jon Nicholson)

Poor timekeeping should not be tolerated, nor should the irritating habit of disappearing before the last horse is fed at evening stables. If we do have the staff structure suggested above it should be easy to insist on our standards being met.

The term 'lad' does not imply a male, but is understood to include girls as well. Actually, as a general rule, girls may look after their charges better than boys, and they are certainly more likely to be able to plait and to turn themselves and their horse out to a high standard. As far as riding is concerned, the girls may tend to have less experience and may require more tuition, but they may also make more effort to follow instructions. Our tolerance level for anyone disregarding instructions should be set at low and everyone must realise that this is not a rehearsal; we are doing it for real.

Unfortunately it does seem that any attempt to make a jockey out of a girl will be doomed to frustration, in Britain at any rate, as the industry as a whole is extremely chauvinistic. Obviously this state of affairs does not tend to encourage those girls who might have a chance to make good horsemen to stay in the game, which further reduces the number of lightweight exercise riders available. However, we might remember that it took a High Court injunction to install the first female trainer in Britain only 30 years ago! A girl will need to perform twice as well as her male counterpart to be regarded as half as good in the racing world, although in very many cases that will not prove to be a particularly difficult assignment. We might also remind ourselves that in 1895 Willie Simms came from America, having ridden 228 winners the previous year, and was able to secure less than 20 mounts. Of course, Simms was black, and adopted the shorter stirrup always credited as Tod Sloan's trademark, which would also have called for a certain amount of lateral thinking on the part of English Turfmen. Within a very few years, however, the riding ranks in England were dominated by Americans boasting less distinguished records. As the physical size of the population increases, female riders may well become more and more accepted through pure necessity.

The most sensible way to organise the morning is for everyone to muck out all their horses straight away, to give them their hay and, lastly, to clean and refill the water mangers. Many horses will not have eaten their breakfast and it should be left for them to eat when they come in from exercise. When the soiled litter has been removed the stable should be set fair with what remains, with the fresh bedding added to the sides. If the daily addition is placed in the middle of the box it will be

impossible to rotate the litter correctly so that there is nothing in the stable more than a few days old. Other methods that deal with each lot or set of horses separately result in the horses that go out late in the morning getting no attention from 6.30 pm until 10 or 11 am the next day, apart from their breakfast at 6 am. There is normally no reason to withhold a horse's hay until after exercise, but if we do particularly want to ascertain any horse's wind fitness we can leave him without his hay until he comes in after work.

Whether any breakfast is taken by the lads before or after first lot doesn't really matter, as long as everyone is ready to go back to work promptly afterwards.

As a matter of course, all racehorses should be rigged as simply as possible in plain jointed snaffle bridles and running martingales with a bib. If the yearlings were broken using the sweet mouth bridle then some thought should be given to making it universal for use on all the horses that have no specific requirements. There is probably sense in each horse having his own bridle in order to reduce the risk of infections. Lads are very inclined to make any adjustments on the near side of the bridle only, which tends to further encourage one-sided mouths, and they are in fact quite likely to make no adjustment at all between horses when they are using the same bridle! The American type of martingale with detachable bib is not as good because it does not run through the neckstrap.

The amount of clothing the horses wear is governed by the weather. However, there is no sense in free-sweating animals wearing heavy clothes; these horses are better off being cool whilst they are out if it means they remain dry and that they come in fit to have their stable rug, or at least a sheet, put on. Any horse that will still sweat on a cold or windy day must never walk home without something covering his loins, nor be left stripped for any length of time when he comes in. It is not good policy to wash horses in cold weather, but if unavoidable this should be done quickly, with tepid water, and out of the draught. The horse should then be scraped and covered with one of the big American coolers as soon as possible and led round until he dries.

It should be stable policy that no horse, ever, comes out of his box without being wiped over and having a quarter mark. The tack should always look as if it has been carefully fitted, with the exercise sheet on straight and not hanging over the tail. There should be a notice in the tack room warning all staff that they are responsible for monitoring the safety of their tack, as they are often very careless in reporting worn or broken equipment. Those lads riding light-framed horses should take care to fit breast girths if necessary and not to set out with their girths already in the top hole at both sides! Frequent reminders will always be necessary on every aspect of tack and equipment, and the fact that a horse has always worn a particular item of tack is no guarantee that that fact will be remembered by his rider.

The string should stay on the premises until the last horse has pulled out so as to all set off together. Any instructions regarding the gallop to be used or the work to be done are better given when all the riders can clearly hear them in order to avoid mistakes. Most lads are very inclined to assume that someone else will be paying attention, and so not to listen themselves. Once the destination is set, the string should walk to the gallops in an orderly fashion, not wandering all over the road and antagonising car drivers, as this only intensifies the traffic problem for all horses. We should place someone on a steady older horse at the front to slow drivers down and to convey our thanks to them when they do so.

Once the string is on the grass they trot briefly to check for any lameness, although horses that are habitually stiff when they first appear may be sent to trot on for 10 or 15 minutes before rejoining the main group. Older horses, in particular, will often move poorly in their slower paces even if there is nothing wrong with them; whether they have enough sense to realise that this action might tend to precede an easy day is debatable, but we should always be alert to the possibility of horses that are actually in relatively good racing condition not bothering to move well until they go faster.

As long as everyone is alert to the possibility of being kicked, it is a good thing for the horses to walk upsides once they are away from the traffic, as this is more interesting and relaxing for them. If care is taken, there is no need to segregate colts and fillies absolutely. This coeducation lessens the chances of a two-year-old colt becoming upset by a filly either in the transport or in the next stall when he runs.

Depending on the distance of the gallops from the stable, the time before the first canter may vary between 10 and 30 minutes. If the first canter is to be a steady one, primarily intended to take the string to the serious work ground, there is no need to delay. The total exercise time might be an hour, or slightly over, as long as the weather is not very bad. If the horses are to be reasonably well done up when they come in, it will take at least 30 or 40 minutes to get the next lot out. Early in the year the two-year-olds do not usually require quite so long, and will tend to make up the second lot, but as time passes both strings will tend to include all ages, so as to best utilise the lighter riders. Any third lot horses are normally 'waifs and strays', or 'lame, sick and sorry', and do not require a long exercise. The walk home should be relaxed and should be long enough that all horses have completely stopped blowing before they go in. There would obviously be great difficulty in adapting these theories to racetrack training in America, but it might prove possible to organise a modified version at a training centre.

The first canter is normally reasonably sedate, probably up to seven furlongs at around 17 or 18 seconds per furlong for the older horses, although occasionally arthritic older animals may require a very steady canter as well as some trotting before doing even this canter. Early in the season the two-year-olds may pull up after five furlongs but as the year progresses the young ones will also go further. Any more excitable horses that may be only doing one strong canter should be sent on ahead to avoid chasing after the others or being chased up themselves. These irritable horses are better suited to getting their work over with as little waiting around as possible, particularly once they are fit.

As mentioned elsewhere it is relatively simple for anyone with a stopwatch to make a reasonable connection between stride patterns and time, even if only for the horses that tend to lead the work. On communal open heath training grounds, the lacksadaisical replacing of the half-furlong marker discs that may have been kicked out by horses when working can complicate matters by making the distances between those markers irregular. It would be simple enough to mow a strip right across the whole width of the ground to be used for the year in order to ensure that at least the furlong markers were always reset in the correct place. One of the drawbacks of Newmarket Heath, although overall it may be the premier facility worldwide, is that there tends to be more interest in grandiose schemes than with such simple matters.

After walking for a few minutes, the second canter is completed at about 15 seconds per furlong by all those in full work. Very backward horses, which we have endeavoured to avoid, or those returning from injury, obviously attain this level gradually, progressing through long trots with short steady canters through longer steady canters to three moderate canters and so on. Throughout this training process each stage must build upon the previous one and this fact needs to be constantly reinforced to all members of staff. Occasionally, a backward horse and his rider may both become so content

with a steady cantering routine that no further progress is made and this should not be allowed to continue. As long as any horse is sound, he must be made to do enough work to derive some fitness benefit from it if we hope to evaluate him.

Any horses that have been rested are returned to full work in this gradual way but if coming from complete rest they will require careful exercise in the arena, initially ridden and led, for some days before going outside the premises. All horses should wear front boots when they are fresh so as to lessen the risk of injury. Although we should beware of the tendency to rely on it regularly, the mild sedative acepromazine can be helpful in returning very fresh horses to exercise without risk of their injuring themselves.

This basic cantering pattern has been designed so as to render too much severe galloping unnecessary, particularly once the horses have started running and if they are in regular competition. It is doubtful whether any exercise at a rate slower than 14 or 15 seconds per furlong can be of much effect in the majority of horses. There may be some confusion over the term 'gallop'; it is used throughout in the English sense to indicate fast work. Canter is used in a more liberal way to describe all routine exercise according to the adjective used with it. The various times referred to throughout are included to give a true idea of what is being described and do not imply total reliance on the watch. As previously noted, traditional descriptions, such as 'swinging canter' and 'three-parts' speed, have largely been lost in the mists of time and can no longer be regarded as trustworthy benchmarks.

The words 'gallop' and 'canter' can also used to indicate the actual strip of ground, but this should be apparent from the context.

Any work done on an uphill gallop will, of course, be of more use in building and maintaining fitness. Care should be taken, however, to ensure that the use of uphill stretches is constructive rather than destructive to young horses. They may quickly become disillusioned and fail to improve with their training if they are initially expected to cope with the degree of uphill work that the older ones take in their stride. For instance, if sending old horses Across The Flat at Newmarket (this is the gallop parallel to the Rowley Mile track), an excellent work is to send them "four and two, increasing up the hill". This indicates that they begin opposite the four furlong pole on the racecourse and continue two furlongs past the winning post towards the top of the town. By commencing at about 15 seconds per furlong and gradually picking it up when they reach the rising ground around halfway, they can derive considerable benefit without ever exceeding a 13 second furlong purely because of the gradient. However, this is far too severe for a two-year-old early in the year, and early two-year-olds should only use a stiff uphill training ground with caution.

It is advisable in many locations that do have grass gallops to press on with the training in the spring before the ground becomes too hard, as although there are many artificial surfaces they all have various drawbacks, and a variety of grass gallops is preferable. If a horse has already achieved a strong level of basic fitness before the ground dries up he can more easily simply maintain it on the artificial surface without overly risking him, particularly if he can compete regularly. Whenever artificial gallops are used the cushion must be regularly monitored for both depth and consistency, unfortunately on communal gallops this tends not always to be the case.

Fast work for older horses should follow the same precepts as for two-year-olds in that there must be a steady process of increasing the workload. Sudden fits and starts are not to be recommended and all riders must be constantly reminded that their mounts are not to be allowed either to stick at a level that they have easily achieved, or to make quantum leaps,

whether they appear keen to do so or not. Many problems arise from horses progressing too quickly for one reason or another. We do not want any surprises, as pleasant revelations in this area have a definite habit of turning sour.

The farmers' race can also be a useful tool in preparing older horses, although some of them will be too free-going to be able to take part without doing too much unless they set off behind the others. As long as it does not become a real race, both lads and horses will greatly enjoy it and it can be a means to get work into those more cunning old horses that are normally careful not to overdo their efforts. For some old horses it is probably as encouraging as giving a track greyhound a live kill. These works will probably be six or seven furlongs in around 1.16 and 1.30, respectively, and as this proves easy for horses working in a bunch most animals can do it two or three times a week quite happily. A gross horse will thrive on this work almost daily.

Early in the season two-year-olds should not normally be sent with old horses on these occasions but as they get stronger they will be up to it, as long as they are getting weight from the older ones. The morale-boosting effect of these performances may be very useful to a juvenile fulfilling a very long and busy season. This type of horse must be kept in a permanent state of readiness for Allowance races without having definite objectives, and he must obviously remain dead fit without becoming sour.

Serious galloping of older horses may be kept to a minimum under this system although two or three fairly serious works, of five furlongs in around even time (a minute), as well as any uphill work and farmers' races, are necessary before the first start. It is rarely necessary for any very serious work to be over the full trip when racing beyond seven furlongs. Although sharp canters over the full trip with an increase towards the end are to be recommended, serious long work is extremely difficult to organise satisfactorily. It is essential

Wind fitness can be gauged by monitoring the line in the flank caused by the movement of the diaphragm.

that all riders (other than those who have specific tasks to fulfil) are instructed to maintain their position in the string when cantering, and not to fall far behind, in order that we may be able to proceed on the basis that all members of any particular bunch have in fact done the prescribed amount of work.

In order to have an idea of how fit any horse might be, we need to observe him closely after his serious work. We do not take much notice of the degree to which he seems to be blowing through his nose as this is very misleading in most cases, although many lads (so presumably their ex-employers) will seem to regard it as their yardstick. A more reliable method is to observe that when the horse is viewed from the side the line caused by the movement of his diaphragm will be clearly visible from the girth back to his flank. If he is blowing fairly hard, having derived some benefit from his effort, then this line may initially appear to be two inches deep as he breathes (see above). We should judge that the

subject has finished blowing when the line disappears, which, if the programme is working properly, should normally be in around 15 minutes after he pulls up. This presupposes that the work increases in accordance with the level of fitness so that by the time of the first start he will blow this much after a fairly strenuous effort, such as five furlongs in a little over a minute, although earlier in the programme he will have blown similarly hard after either a shorter distance in the same time or the same distance in a longer time. To have a horse blowing for a much longer period at an early point in the training is obviously easy to achieve, but is to be avoided. Recovering from such distress is likely to result in an overall slowing of his steady progress. A fit horse running over a trip of less than a mile will probably blow for between 20 and 25 minutes if he has a hard race. If he should unexpectedly blow for considerably longer then something may be wrong with him. Once we are comfortable using this means of evaluating fitness, any horse that does blow much more than we anticipated, should be regarded as being possibly off-colour and should be carefully observed for a day or two. As with the stride pattern method of speed estimation, this method may seem a little rustic; if so, it will be relatively easy to calculate some relationship between it and a more sophisticated one involving respiratory rates and heartbeats.

The practice of weighing horses daily has become fashionable over the past few years, but it is unlikely this could reveal anything we should not at first glance see for ourselves as regards any horse's condition and wellbeing. Quite apart from the obvious drawback that it is impossible to assess accurately whether or not any animal has emptied himself (or taken on water at a weight of ten pounds per gallon) to the same degree as on previous days, the fact that there is absolutely no way of proving whether just because a horse won at a certain number of kg that is his optimum weight, must cast further doubt on the procedure.

Some animals are prone to becoming setfast after their exercise. This is an acute attack of muscular cramp which can be so severe as to make getting the horse home difficult. It was originally assumed always to be associated with unaccustomed strenuous exercise or with exercise following an easy period, being referred to as 'Monday morning disease'. There is also thought to be a connection with diet. Those horses that are susceptible should have some exercise on Sunday, should possibly have their protein intake reduced and should be jogged part of the way home after exercise in order to allow their muscles to warm down gradually. This syndrome seemed to occur quite frequently in those of our animals that subsequently tested positive for Lyme disease, and to abate following antibiotic treatment.

Any horse that carries his head down after his work and has a rather glazed look in his eye should be scoped, particularly if he coughs, as he may well have bled without doing so visibly.

Those animals that do bleed in their work, or in their races, can be treated with minute doses of a homoeopathic preparation of rattlesnake venom (Crotalus Horridus 200) which the vet will obtain. This seems at least as effective as any other suggested cures, and horses can run whilst being treated with no risk of failing the routine test. The extent to which racehorses are or are not affected by bleeding is far from clear, but those that do bleed visibly are almost sure to be compromised by doing so. A very high proportion of all runners have been demonstrated on scoping to bleed to some degree, so presumably many horses do cope with the minor episodes. It is, however, fair to say that if any horse bleeds visibly more than once in a short period there may be a potentially serious problem, and he should be given a break.

Gross animals are often very thick in their wind when first put into strong work without having anything wrong with their respiratory system. If endoscopic examination reveals no abnormality their work should be increased in order to resolve the problem. Their hay should be reduced and they should be bedded on something inedible. Susarma was cheaply purchased as a five-year-old, being announced as making a noise, and having run very poorly all of that year. He certainly did make a noise and was a gross Quarter Horse type, but as the result of his scope was normal he went into vigorous training, to say the least. Susarma was a good-natured horse and a good ride and he went out two or three lots every day for some time, both doing his normal exercise and then leading the two-year-olds. Eventually, after some weeks of this and two races - in which he blew up - he did get fit and became one of the best sprinters, although he always made a noise. As they get older, males in particular may need more work as they tend to become more gross; unfortunately, many of them also tend to become lazier and more resentful of being obliged to do their exercise, so these horses should be handled with extra tact.

If, at the end of his work or as he pulls up, a horse is heard to gurgle - a noise sounding rather like water running down the waste pipe of a bath - we can usually expect the problem to resolve itself gradually in many cases as fitness develops. However if this is not the case, and if the gurgling persists even after experimentation with a tongue-tie, some problem involving the soft palate is probable and veterinary advice must be sought.

Many yearlings may make a noise when cantering at first, but the majority of these will be proved on scoping to be suffering from a throat infection. If cantering is suspended for

the duration of the antibiotic treatment they normally recover completely.

Very often the older a horse gets the less inclined he may be to put much effort into his training. We have to use our imagination when faced with this type of horse and try to get the work into him without him realising that he is doing it. Bullying these horses rarely produces good results, but the rider should be alert to the possibility of allowing such a horse to do a bit more than was scheduled should he ever seem keen to do so. This is one of the very few occasions when improvisation by exercise riders should be encouraged. Group One winner Superpower was an appalling worker and he

Susarma (USA) was an extremely coarse winded horse requiring a lot of work. Tony Ives up. Here Tommy Kelly holds him after winning at York. (Photo courtesy of Kenneth Bright)

Superpower with Walter Swinburn up. Compare his action to that of Mac's Imp (USA) - hindlegs reaching far under the body. (Photo courtesy of Liam Healy)

regularly galloped with a two mile maiden claiming horse in an attempt to enthuse him. He was an extremely surly individual and wore blinkers every day at exercise, although he normally ran without them.

An older horse that has become disillusioned may often respond to being used, if he is suitable, as the trainer's hack. This means he can canter about less formally, and can be given short sprints here and there on the unused and unmarked ground, to the delight of himself and his rider and the fury of the ground staff! If horses like this are sent with the youngsters that are just beginning to work they will be heartened by the fact that they are being restrained at the end so as not to overdo the

juveniles. It can sometimes prove extremely difficult to get an old horse back to being competitive after a complete break such as being turned out, and rather than risk this happening it is safer to give him a change of routine if he seems a little stale. Generally speaking we should not be too strict with the older campaigners as long as they are not getting too much above themselves. All horses will tend to race more productively if they are kept as happy as possible.

It is quite common for racehorses to become more excitable as their workload increases, and we should always be alert to this. On the other hand if any animal readily accepts a fairly severe training regime and thrives on it, mentally as well as physically, the omens are very favourable. This does not imply that we should try to determine just how much a horse will stand, but an individual that has remained calm throughout a successful preparation can normally be relied upon to run his race.

Horses that jib or otherwise behave disruptively at exercise should not be allowed to become a bad influence on the whole string. Before banishing them to a solitary routine with the pony, however, it is worth trying them in blinkers. The traditional Newmarket use of blinkers as part of an extreme punishment session is not called for. It is remarkable how many horses will settle down to their work simply by having blinkers fitted, although this fact seems little understood in the British racing tradition. Alternatively, very badly behaved horses sometimes respond well to an absolute routine and will go to the same place each and every day without too much fuss. In this case they should be allowed to do so rather than have daily confrontation. We should be careful not to diminish the attraction of this one exercise ground by going too fast, as we would prefer to get this type to the races half-fit than not to get there at all.

Generally speaking we will tend to do the last serious work about five days before a race, which leaves time for a blow-out two days before or on the eve of the race if necessary. This might be two furlongs at three-parts speed, or in about 25 seconds, and will sharpen horses up whilst being too short to take anything out of them. A very gross or stuffy horse will benefit from doing some work on the morning of his race, but with the problem of travelling that is often impractical. If a raceday work is used it is essential that the rider does not do too much, or go too far.

As a general rule no serious work should ever take place in the trainer's absence, and any work that must be done should be set so as to preclude the danger of the riders racing or trying the horses involved. Any discovered breach of this rule is a hanging offence. Richard Darvill in his *Treatise On Training The English Racehorse*, published in 1828, repeatedly remarks that "[stable] boys are very inclined to be tricky", citing his own youthful transgressions whenever the trainer's back was turned as reinforcement of his warning not to leave young staff in particular unsupervised with horses in training.

Any horse that showed top-class form in the previous year should be fit before he is allowed to run, because his reputation and his capital value are subject to review. This type of horse should be tried with horses that have recently proved to be in good form and at weights that reflect to some degree his ability. If the trial is not reasonably satisfactory the horse should not run. Although we may be tempted to seek excuses for him, it is virtually certain that a poor work predicts a poor race. At this point a sound relationship between owner and trainer can avoid the considerable capital loss that might be incurred should the horse disgrace himself. This is a potentially disastrous situation and cannot be regarded as lightly as running an ordinary horse before he shows that he has retained his form. In the latter case a moderate display or two might serve to get him rehandicapped, which might ultimately result in a successful campaign. Unfortunately many owners of a classy horse will insist on running in these circumstances, often having been influenced by the opinions of people who have nothing to lose if the wheel does come off, and who can advocate a bold strategy. We should remember that it is easy enough to roll a barrel down a hill; the hard part is pushing it back to the top. If any horse running poorly when that event should have been anticipated cannot be successfully rehabilitated then his owner may have learnt a costly lesson.

Francis P. Dunne summed up the difficulty of this particular situation when he observed, "Nothing brings out the prick in a man sooner than his first good horse."

A twilight horse. Mac's Fighter won The Wokingham Handicap under a record 9 stone 12 pounds, but was never given a chance by the handicapper subsequently. Here, he and Emma appear through the winter twilight at Lingfield. (Photo courtesy of Jon Nicholson)

One of the most frustrating aspects of the British system is the proliferation of handicaps, in which those who are unwilling or unable to produce the true potential of their animals receive weight from those who do try to run their horses to the best of their ability. Actually it may sometimes appear that the Official Handicapper may be unduly influenced by the trainer's name, while at best he certainly fails to penalise some who shamelessly work the system, including some whose position in racings hierarchy ought to ensure different tactics! Although we may find this situation annoying when our horse is defeated by what will likely prove an impossible weight concession, we will largely avoid it if, as anticipated, the majority of our horses are sold before they need to enter the handicap ranks.

In his excellent little book of 1892, *How To Train The Racehorse*, Lt. Col. Warburton, R. E., says, "We can easily understand and appreciate the pride or vanity which impels a rich man to give a large sum of money for a good horse in the hope of seeing him successful in weight for age races, and many of us will approve of it but few will think it a feather in any man's cap if he wins a race with an indifferent animal through the mistake of the Handicapper or his own cleverness." Cleverness is of course not in this sense to be regarded as a virtue, rather the reverse! The Colonel's philosophy should be very much the basis for our own organisation, and we should ignore any perceived success achieved by the handicap brigade as irrelevant to racehorse training in the true sense.

Fortunately, the two-year-old programme is based on allowance races, but these are few and far between for older horses, to the extent that fairly useful allowance horses, falling somewhere between handicap and Group class, are referred to as 'twilight' horses. Reasonably talented performers hover between two worlds in Britain because the system is primarily geared to providing a large pool of inferior runners for the off-course betting market. This type of horse does, however, find a ready market, both in America and in Hong Kong, as long as we can keep him fairly clean and sound. Because of the premium export value of higher-rated animals, as well as for sporting reasons, it is advisable that all our horses do their best. The only exceptions to this might be, as above, running an ordinary horse which we suspect may be out of form, as long as we are certain that it cannot much harm either his prospects or his value. If by any chance he does run surprisingly well after showing us little in his work then we might debate whether to allow him to continue to train himself, rather than think how much we can improve him at home by altering his own preferred programme which has been proved successful.

There might be a little confusion regarding the different interpretations of the term 'handicap horse' here and in America, as their interpretation implies a horse of four or older that competes at the highest level, whereas in Britain, unless prefixed by some qualification such as 'very useful', it is an almost derogatory term.

There is excellent prize money available in an increasing number of British handicaps but these races are difficult to win with exposed horses, which are handicapped to the hilt, and we should beware of running a twilight horse into the ground on too many wild goose chases. The size of the pot makes very little difference if you are too high in the weights to get any of it, and we must be careful to sell these animals whilst they are still sound and competitive. Quite apart from the physical dangers and the expense of running regularly and without realistic hope in these cavalry charges, many horses do eventually just get sick of hopeless tasks and lose all interest. Once again the owner must be prepared to remember the overall objective, which is to maximise sales and move on, before we reach this point of no return. The British handicap ratings are usually well understood by regular American buyers and they are quite prepared to take these overburdened horses as long as we do not wait too long after the last positive effort.

As we do not wish to see advertising stickers making our horses or jockey look like a contestant in a stock-car race it is doubly important to follow a sound trading strategy in order to demonstrate to the Customs and Excise Department that our owning racehorses should be allowed, as a business, to reclaim the VAT of 17.5% on all the expenses involved. The reason that most owners in Britain opt for the ludicrous pretence that their horses are generating advertising revenue is because they are incapable of running the horses as any semblence of a bona fide business. The Inland Revenue does not necessarily demand that a business actually shows a profit, only that it is run in a way that clearly indicates the intention and the possibility of doing so.

Racing colours are the livery of an owner and they look much more classy in their pristine state, rather than covered in logos and resembling something better suited to a speedway circuit. The question of colours is obviously very subjective; but a more traditional and plain design is far more sophisticated and seems preferable to many of the fussy designs in current use. It would be well worth our buying and reregistering as plain a set of colours as possible if we intend to be serious players; like personal car numbers they will always hold their value. Plain gold and plain cerise were amongst those recently sold, and either would have made an excellent statement of intent to succeed for an aspirant owner. Plain colours originally tended to be those of the aristocracy, and to imply a certain amount of style, which would have been understood to decrease in direct proportion to the flashiness of the colours' design. In the words of Oscar Wilde, "All vulgarity is crime."

Naming of yearlings is another field in which the general standard has dropped dramatically, although many owners do still take the time and trouble to find a name that bears some relevance to the names of the sire and dam. There is some truth in the saying that a good horse can't have a bad name, but it may be better to give our string decent names to start with, rather than rely on their turf record investing ridiculous ones with respectability! Overnaming is also to be avoided, as there will always be very pretentious names such as Emperor's Diamond attached to animals that will finish (or even commence) their careers at the lowest level. The Royal string is invariably cleverly named and demonstrates that attractive names sound equally at home in any circumstances. Recent examples include Whitechapel (Arctic Tern x Christchurch), Feel Free (Generous x As You Desire Me), Hebrides (Gone West x Sleeping Beauty) and Nightingale (Night Shift x Grey Angel).

Horses and their lads must always be well turned out at the races, although that does not necessarily imply horses need both mane and tail plaited and their quarters covered with designs applied from a plastic pattern sheet. Quarter marks should be limited to those applied with a brush; the intricate ones used to be done with a comb or a matchbox and those now applied with a plastic template can hardly be regarded as evidence of much skill in the groom. Plaiting tails was traditionally an amateur practice never associated with flat racing, although careful plaiting and knotting of the lower part of the tail can be sensible in very sloppy ground. Racehorses in Europe tend to have their tails cut fairly short, but in America tails tend to be left in the natural state. The theory behind the latter style is that a following horse is less likely to run up onto the heels when a long tail streams behind. A very idle horse, that requires a lot of hand-riding, should have his mane either pulled short or plaited so that it does not make his rider's task even more difficult. Too long a mane might easily cost this type of horse a close-run race should the jockey get momentarily entangled at a crucial point in the proceedings.

There is no reason to suppose that horses from a well-run yard should look any smarter at the races than when we look round at evening stables, although whether that is invariably the case with some stables that regularly receive Best Turned Out awards is very questionable judging by the standards delivered by their lads when they change stable. We should look at every horse stripped, with his lad standing him up for inspection, every night when we are at home, except Saturday and Sunday. The horse should at least appear clean, including his face, his mane should be damped down, his tail free from tangles, and he should have both a regular quarter mark and another one curving down from loins to flank. On Saturday the rugs can be refastened as soon as the horses are done because half the lads are off, but we still see every horse's legs. On Sunday the horses are not dressed over at evening stables, although they will have been wiped over quickly in the morning, and we need only inspect the legs of any that went out. Monday and Tuesday runners will require some exercise on Sunday, and any runners from the previous day must at least be led out.

Most stables employ a travelling head lad to ensure that the lad with the horse attends to his charge correctly at the races. However, it is probably good policy firstly to allow only lads that are reliable to go away, and secondly to share any travelling head lad duties between two or three individuals, so as to encourage some competition. Travelling head lad is a position that invites contact with regular racegoers, the Faces, whom we will not wish to be kept informed about our horses. Any outside betting moves on a previously unraced horse of ours should be regarded as cause for concern in this department. Owning and training racehorses is an expensive business and we are not doing it for any outsider's benefit. If we could keep a pool of

different lads, all reliable enough to take their horses on their own without a regular Travelling Head Lad, then this problem might be largely avoided. Even if the lads have telephone punters their relationship with those people is unlikely to become as close or as much of a problem to us as when there is regular physical contact at the races between outside influences and a single individual. Because bettors are generally extremely chauvinistic there are most unlikely to be any problems with punters involving female members of the team, and in fact most girls will also put their horse away better after his race than will most males.

The care of the horse after his race is easy enough, but is often not carried out correctly due to lack of interest, particularly in beaten animals, once the race is over. The horse will need to be cooled out, carefully watered, then loosed and given a little time to relax before being loaded. He must not be allowed to get cold. Those horses required for routine tests after their race deserve the same consideration and the test should not, as is frequently seen, be an excuse for the lad to abandon his charge and to go for refreshment. The testing team are only too willing to allow that to happen as they have no interest in the welfare of the horse. Our lads should understand that they are never to leave the horse completely, and that he is not to be let loose in the sample box until his breathing has regularised, despite any initial bluster from the testers. We will require an accurate report on how long all our runners blew for, and whether anything untoward was observed, including in the testing procedure. Apart from treating any minor cuts not obvious immediately after the race, that is all there is to it. The evening feed will be left by the head lad, although many stables feed mash after racing, our runners be will fed as usual but at slightly reduced level. If possible we should see every horse after he returns from racing.

Care Of The Racehorse

"A righteous man regardeth the life of his beast;
but the tender mercies of the wicked are cruel." Proverbs 12:10

The head lad in the yard will be expected to ensure supplies of everything are always on time, of top quality and in full measure. He should have the authority to hire and fire but should use it sensibly. All medical treatments must be accurately recorded for future reference, with worming and dentistry programmes and all vaccinations kept up to date. He need not bother taking temperatures routinely, but any horse that does not eat up should be checked, as well as any known invalids and any that may appear a little dull or off-colour. The thermometer should be attached to a clothes peg, which can be clipped to the edge of the rug. The head lad will be expected to notice anything amiss when he feeds first thing and again when he checks the mangers before evening stables. He must make absolutely certain that any medication cannot possibly reach any horse other than the one being treated, and that treatment stops the required time before any race so as to avoid positive tests. He will be responsible for treatment of wounds and removing loose shoes but for best results the trainer himself should be responsible for day-to-day monitoring of the horses' legs for work-related damage. However, the head lad should be familiar with the current status of any ongoing problem legs, as he may be required to stand in when the trainer is away. Assistant trainers, in Britain at least, tend to be pupils under some degree of instruction; by the time they are even vaguely capable of making an informed decision they are normally training in their own right.

The trainer must, for best results, examine each horse's forelegs every day when he is at home. When his runners are in early races he is better employed returning home to see the remainder of the string rather than socialising, although most owners fail to grasp this relatively simple concept. The changes that take place in the legs of a racehorse in training are often subtle and easily overlooked, but on the other hand many horses never do have cold and fine legs whilst they are in hard work, hence this is a vital area of operations and not one in which to delegate. Horses rarely break down with a soft tissue injury without warning signs having shown previously. If the trainer cannot be present at evening stable time he should be certain to feel, at least, the legs of any problem horses before morning exercise next day.

This is in no way supposed to be a veterinary paper and any observations on soundness should be interpreted with common sense. The vet is the technical expert and should always be consulted in case of doubt. A long-term relationship with one individual is to be recommended, although he may be part of a group practice and so have the opportunity to compare notes with his colleagues in unusual cases. It is important that the veterinary advisor be aware of the realistic expectations and principles on which the stable is to run and that his professional advice should be formulated on that basis, bearing in mind that very often we will be looking at financial as well as physical damage limitation and at making firm decisions in a war situation. As a rule, expensive and long-term procedures, particularly those with questionable outcomes, should not be applied to marginally talented horses.

It is not uncommon for a horse to be terribly lame with a comparatively minor infection from a wound. This possibility should always be considered and addressed if there appears to be any evidence at all of broken skin near the site of the problem, as even a chafe from the boots can sometimes result in an alarming scenario exactly reminiscent of a major injury. Dermobion, or something similar, should be liberally applied to these cases whilst awaiting x-ray, and in many cases a miraculous improvement will take place.

The most devastating nonfatal injury for a racehorse is a tendon strain. Once the horse himself is conscious of any tendon injury the prognosis is always bad. In fact, as a generalisation, all time spent rehabilitating genuine established tendon injuries is time wasted. Most of the successful rehabilitations may not have been bona fide tendon strains, despite giving the appearance of being so. Mathew Hodson's *Reader*, published around 1700, recommends that we "take a live cat, either wild or tame, and cut off her head and tail, then cleave her down the chine, and clap her hot, the Bowels and all, upon the strain, and remove it not for forty-eight hours, and the effect is great". Although less high-tech than some of the more recent brainwaves, this is not recommended! Avoidance, rather than cure, of tendon injuries should be foremost in our minds, and visual monitoring of tendons is as important as feeling them.

Fortunately, with proper shoeing and training, this disaster should be an uncommon state of affairs. A major tendon strain out of the blue is most unlikely in any flat racehorse following a programme of progressive exercise loading. Sometimes a slight irregularity will occur which can be seen but not felt, and tendons should instinctively be inspected as well as felt, both from the side and from above. If we stop immediately at this stage, whatever

the horse's racing programme may be, the prognosis for recovery is excellent. Experience will show that minor degrees of heat and fleshiness need not be the cause of stopping work in many horses, but any visible deviation from the perpendicular in any one tendon should be treated with grave suspicion from the outset. Initially any slight heat should be removed by cold hosing and then the leg should be either lightly blistered with iodine or painted with DMSO to increase the blood supply. The blister should be a working blister, not a strong one, and it is usually sufficient to paint the leg with iodine without rubbing it in. If we don't think we did enough we can very gingerly repeat in a day or so. The second application should be cautious for fear of overreaction, and in fact we should be extremely cautious even with the first application on anything other than black legs; on a white leg even a diluted solution may seem severe. All we need to do is to excite the blood supply to the extent that the tendon itself may appear up to double in size, not the whole leg. In a few days it will be back to normal and usually all sign of damage will also be gone. Never bandage over an irritant. The return to serious work should be cautious.

A bandage bow or disfigurement on a tendon caused by ill-fitted boots or bandages should immediately be dispersed by vigorous hand rubbing before it can become a long-term disfigurement.

This basic minor irritant treatment should also be applied to slight fetlock joint wear and tear as long as x-rays show no actual damage. DMSO is also quite effective and will increase the blood supply without giving the filling; however, care must be taken not to use it too close to a race. Windgalls, or soft swellings on the upper aspects of the fetlock, are very common and, if minor, cause little inconvenience. However, deterioration in the situation normally predicts at best some arthritic change in the joint. Those horses with windgalls should be treated daily with either a proprietary cooling lotion, or with a mild irritant, according to which suits them best. Such treatments should always take place after the trainer's inspection.

Many older horses may have joints that look fairly rough and still race quite normally. They should, however, be carefully observed and the exercise rider must always be careful both to choose the very best available ground and always to keep his mount well balanced with no careless stops at the end of his work. These joints can be treated as for windgalls, or they can be regularly hosed. In more severe cases a course of Adequan injections is advisable, or an oral supplement of chondroitin sulphate can be fed to provide the same therapy. Old horses with these chronic minor problems may stand in bandages, as discussed below.

Although these measures are rather simple and old-fashioned they have proved effective in maintaining soundness in hard-raced horses over a long period. There have, however, been one or two fairly recent developments that make our life easier, including arthroscopic knee surgery and scans of bony and soft tissue, and these of course remain in the vet's domain.

As a general rule, standing bandages are not to be used except on horses whose legs we accept as already being a serious worry, because they definitely prevent proper monitoring and also because the bandage marks will be seen, in Britain at least, as advertising damaged goods. If a horse is obliged to stand in bandages, perhaps because his fetlocks are so fleshy as to cause concern, great care must be taken that they are always correctly fitted. In fact it may be safer if only certain members of the team are ever allowed to put a bandage on, so as to ensure that this is done properly. Quilted pads are best under a standing bandage. When it is correctly fitted the horse should give the impression of having his leg encased in a regular tubular shape from the bottom of the fetlock to the top of the tendon. Each lap should be the same size and the

tension just enough that everything will still look very similar next morning, neither like a tourniquet nor hanging off like a pair of football socks. Actually if it looks right it probably is right, and if an aerosol marker is lightly sprayed from top to bottom it will be easy to follow the pattern subsequently. If it looks wrong it should be done again, before using the spray. The thickness of the quilt should protect against bandage bow, but great care is essential. Any small irregularities or wrinkles visible on the leg when the bandage is removed should be vigorously rubbed by hand to disperse them. The lad doing any horse standing in bandages must take them off as soon as evening stables begins so as to allow us to examine the legs after an hour and a half without the bandage. The bandage disguises a lot from both eye and touch, which is why we are reluctant to use them. Bandages must never be fitted over any irritant, as the reaction will be too severe.

Anti-inflammatory drugs also disguise what is happening in the legs of a horse in training, and should only be used on a horse in work under exceptional circumstances and in consultation with the vet.

In some cases good results can be had by standing very fleshy-legged animals with their forelegs coated to the knee in an amoricaine clay. There are several proprietary brands and this method does away with any risk of bandage bows, but it will still disfigure the hair on the legs. There are also many jointy horses that are greatly helped simply by hosing their legs, which has no contraindications. There was a box that had a stream running through it when the Old Man trained at Exning, near Newmarket, in the Harraton Court yard where Percy Peck trained Cicero to win the 1905 Derby, although by my father's time it had fallen into disuse. In fact, anyone with a stream on their premises could easily construct an open-air stall for this purpose. Exning was the original settlement in the area that subsequently became the headquarters of British racing, before the 'new market' became a town in the Middle Ages. Lord Rosebery had three Derby winners trained there, the others being Ladas in 1894, and Sir Visto in 1895; both came under the charge of Mat Dawson at Melton House, where the bungalows now stand next to St Martin's Church. Golden Miller, winner of five Cheltenham Gold Cups and the Grand National was trained at Beechwood House, which stood opposite the White Horse. Grand Parade, winner of the Derby in 1919, is buried at Rose Hall at the other end of the village. George Digby trained Souepi to win the Stayers' Triple Crown from Harraton in the 1950s, and may have been one of the last trainers to have his string out twice a day.

Exercise bandages are, in most cases, to be used only when we really are already in tiger country. They are difficult to fit correctly and positively dangerous if fitted wrongly. There must definitely be only one or two trusted lads allowed to fit them and these should be firmly impressed with the serious nature of the task. Any exercise bandage on a foreleg not extending right to the top of the tendon is risking catastrophe, just as a hose pipe will probably fail adjacent to any binding. This risk does not seem to be the same on a hind leg and here rundown bandages need not go right up the leg. In order to strengthen the horse's suspension it will help to incorporate a splint between the down run and the return of an exercise bandage. This splint is made from several pieces of Vetwrap pressed together and the length can be easily trimmed as required. We first bandage down, make a figure of eight, fit the splint below the fetlock, repeat the figure of eight and continue back up with the splint neatly incorporated into the bandage. Again, all the laps should appear regular in size. The tension of an exercise bandage is critical, and whilst it should be tighter than a standing bandage, care must be taken that it is not too tight, and that the tension throughout is absolutely even. When correctly fitted, exercise bandages should look as if they have been painted on. Although they do have a Velcro fastening this should be reinforced with tape which is applied without added tension. If in doubt, expert instruction in bandaging for work should be sought before embarking on this practice. If any horse has broken skin, such as a chafe or a rundown, in the area to be covered by a bandage it is a good idea to first pull on a section taken from a pair of tights under the bandage to avoid further irritation.

Knees should probably not be x-rayed unless there is some reason to suspect a problem. Our programme is largely dependent on two-year-old runners and very many of their knees, on x-ray, will be seen to be immature. This may often result in horses being put aside which could be competing successfully, and it may also result in even more time being wasted on those that will eventually fail anyway. As long as our charges are sound we must, as throughout this method, believe what we can see with our own two eyes, and get on with it. At the same time we should be certain to use those eyes to spot any changes immediately they occur. Any localised lump on a knee must be x-rayed, although more general soft filling may, as long as the horse is moving well, be due to a bump in the stable, possibly on the manger by a greedy feeder, if that should be the case his feeding arrangements must be changed. The fleshiness should be closely monitored and treated as other minor soft tissue problems. Whenever any horse in training begins to toe out markedly at the walk he is probably trying to save his knees, and the vet should be consulted. If knee lameness is indicated by nerve block, but the normal x-ray views appear clean, a skyline picture will often reveal changes. Knee problems are far less serious now that chips can be removed without invasion of the joint, and a speedy recovery is greatly assisted by treatments such as Adequan. Of course, the resale value of the

Cartoon from 1953 featuring Paddy O'Gorman's first winner as a trainer, Cesarewitch hope Galloway Hills. 'Tishy' was a notoriously unreliable performer and the bête-noire of cartoonist Tom Webster. (Courtesy of Daily Mail)

horse may be sorely affected.

Two other common injuries to the foreleg are suspensory ligament sprain and damage to the sesamoids, either by fracture due to a blow or by having a piece of bone torn off where the ligament attaches. These can both occur out of the blue and the outcome is hard to predict, particularly when both aspects are involved.

Split pasterns are fairly common, and these frequently occur without warning, although certain training grounds may be a contributory factor. However the prognosis is normally very good, and although some cases may require surgery to stabilise them, many will heal with box rest alone.

Pulling up too sharply or too sloppily after work may well be implicated in many injuries; riders must be constantly reminded to pull up carefully, and to trot their mounts out properly after all work. Overall it can prove difficult to persuade exercise riders to achieve the correct balance between having horses relaxed in their work and keeping enough hold of their heads in an attempt to prevent needless injuries. There is always the danger of horses either hurting themselves because they are absolutely uncollected or becoming far too keen due to being grabbed hold of too severely. The current fashion for one-handed salutes by winning jockeys is very unprofessional as the dangers to tired horses are obvious. It should not be countenanced by any trainer with even a basic understanding of racehorses' legs.

Leg Care and Soundness

"A righteous man regardeth the life of his beast: but the tender mercies of the wicked are cruel." Proverbs 12:10

Sore shins, the most widespread problem with young horses' legs is, happily, time wasting rather than serious in the majority of cases. This condition involves stress-induced changes in the cannon bone, usually in the foreleg, and these then cause discomfort in the tendon running over it. If we hope to run the stable as planned we can assume that perhaps two-thirds of the team will be effected to some extent. There appears no way to avoid this syndrome short of a very light training regime. However, as previously discussed, the success of the enterprise depends absolutely on rapid turnover of horses, and as there is every likelihood of horses unaffected at two years suffering at three, we will attempt to accept this problem and to address it in the most practical manner.

As soon as the two-year-olds get to a two minute rate of speed we should always have the prospect of sore shins in mind. There is no way of predicting exactly when, or indeed whether, any particular horse will be effected. Particular attention must always be paid to the shins of all two-year-olds at evening inspection, but the manner of this inspection is important. The shins must be felt very lightly, with minimal pressure, and the contact should start at the knee. Both shins should be instinctively visually inspected for any forward deviation in the profile. Immediately any animal gives reason to suspect any awareness of his shins a basic plan must be implemented. The lad must be instructed that on no account should he touch this horse's shins, as in many cases a completely cured horse will continue virtually to fall down due to the association of pain from previous handling of a sore shin. If his legs get dirty at exercise they should be hosed and not brushed until the episode is over. The shins should be treated with a cooling lotion, but this must be liberally applied without putting any pressure on the leg at all. The horse should be immediately restricted to walking exercise for a day or two. After a couple of days he can resume gentle trotting and assuming he moves well, which he should, as long as we did spot the first sign, he should have lengthy trotting exercise for ten days. Most cases can then be gently returned to the normal routine, and may be back in strong work in less than a month. It is pivotal to the early return to work that the shin is spotted before the horse is lame, and that considerable trotting exercise takes place, both to accelerate the healing process and to maintain enough fitness for an easy return to work. Obviously, as in all soundness matters the horse's upcoming races must be regarded as secondary to the treatment. Horses with sore shins do not wear boots at exercise, and the farrier can be advised to handle their legs gently. Occasionally stress fractures occur in a shin. These horses will normally be very sore and should be x-rayed to determine the extent of any damage. Although a rapid return to work is impossible for these animals, the long-term prognosis is good in most cases. Although possibly dismissed by some as crude, this method has proved sound practice over an extended period; it does require considerable vigilance in order to prevent exacerbating the first damage to the shin.

Once again, the absolute necessity of all horses being carefully pulled up after their work, and of downhill stops being avoided when at all possible, should be stressed on a daily basis if we wish to minimise these injuries. Many horses are prone to taking a bad step when tired, and one bad step can be enough to do catastrophic damage. The stable jockey must also be aware of the importance of pulling up correctly after a race, and particularly when cantering back to the paddock area.

It is extremely common for horses in hard training to lose the fluency of their action to a greater or lesser extent, particularly as mentioned elsewhere, in their slower paces. Traditionally these animals are referred to as 'jarred up', and some degree of shoulder or knee soreness is usually suspected. Dramatic improvement has been demonstrated in some apparently typical cases by the use of Isoxsuprine, which would appear to indicate that some of these horses were more likely to have been suffering foot problems rather than simply from being jarred up in the accepted sense. This is worthy of further investigation. Under the bizarre English Jockey Club Rules

there is no indication of a safe withdrawal period for this extremely volatile medication, and it should therefore be used with great circumspection on horses that are likely to run.

Fortunately in Flat racers the hind leg causes comparatively few day-to-day problems and these are often, like curbs, thoroughpins and spavins, easy to identify and not difficult to treat.

There seem to be a surprising number of pelvic fractures, and whether or not these are due to damage initiated by horses slipping when getting up in the stable is not clear. However, all horses must always have plenty of bedding, not just in the box, but in the middle of the box. The bed should not be, as is often the case, all banked around the sides so as to facilitate mucking out.

Stifle lameness is not uncommon and usually seems to involve a bone cyst, or OCD lesion, which may have to be removed, although many settle down with rest. These are a relatively new phenomenon, whether due to dietary changes in yearlings or improved x-ray facilities is not clear.

Stress fractures to the tibia occasionally occur but normally heal themselves with box rest.

Undiagnosed hind lameness or discomfort, with no obvious visible reason, has caused, in Britain at least, a proliferation of back specialists. Despite the earnest opinions of these opportunists, the vast majority of these problems are secondary and result from problems elsewhere. Listed winner Bestplan was repeatedly treated by a specialist for awkward hind action, but eventually showed a small knee chip that he was attempting to protect. Front limb involvement should always be investigated in these cases and the bona fide back injury may actually be quite rare.

In all cases of lameness that show no more obvious cause, some degree of foot involvement should be suspected. It should be remembered, however, that a sore foot does not guarantee that there is no other problem; a problem in the foot, such as a corn, might occasionally result from the animal trying to protect something higher up the limb.

Injuries caused by interference are usually not serious, although they are a nuisance, and thought must be given to their prevention by alteration to the shoeing. Every effort should be made to eliminate even minor blemishes as they are always liable to infection and because they obviously take a horse's mind off running. Interfering injuries can sometimes be extremely difficult to remedy, as similar wounds can often result from different causes. With this in mind any changes should not initially be too drastic, so as not to make matters irreparably worse in cases of misdiagnosis.

Shoeing and Interference

"Stablish their feet." 2 Esdras 2:23

One of the most vital members of any serious racing stable is the farrier and it is essential to recruit one who is prepared to implement sound practices day in and day out. Unfortunately demand for farriers outstrips supply and best practice is far from universal practice. To complicate matters further, certain policies, which are definitely detrimental to correct foot care, are widely demanded by the customer base, and to a certain extent farriers, like trainers, merely respond to what the marketplace requires. Two obvious examples are the routine corrective trimming of foals and short heel shoeing to prevent shoe-pulling at exercise. It is common to hear someone praising his farrier for making an animal appear correct or because he never loses a shoe, irrespective of the outcome for the horse, so we can have some sympathy for the farrier's situation.

As observed in the section dealing with soundness, there is no pretext that this is a technical document, and it is simply intended to give practical guidelines for a successful racing stable to follow. However, these recommendations are based on long experience and observation and will not be found to risk any contraindications, unlike many common current practices.

Although many stables do employ their own farrier, the practice does have its drawbacks as it is not unlikely that their man will suffer illness or injury, leaving them high and dry. It is better to try to select a suitable farrier from amongst those working for a firm, as this should guarantee cover in such an emergency. It is well worth making some additional arrangement to get the one we want. If the firm does employ a qualified girl it may be well worth giving her a try, as this job no longer requires such hard labour, due to the advent of machine-made shoes. A girl may prove to have a better attitude and more patience, both with the horses and the requirements of the job. She may also possess a surer touch when shoeing sensitive-footed animals, and she should have more time for our animals as other trainers normally prefer a man. We must insist on punctuality and reliability as very often a first lot horse will require attention before exercise.

We want the basic principles to be observed in shoeing these horses. The feet are to be kept as balanced as possible, remembering that they may have been previously corrected. The toes are to be kept short and the hoof angles are to be kept fairly high, probably around 50° in front and in most cases at least 54° or so behind. There is no need actually to measure Flat racers' angles in most cases, and as with the training times, these figures are mainly intended to convey the principle involved. It is impossible to maintain these angles once the heels have become too low, or as in many horses, nonexistent. If we think of the foot in terms of a mass of tubes, and then think of a Coca-Cola can, it is obvious that the more upright the tubes remain, the stronger it is. Once more, this is not rocket science, it is simple common sense. The increase in strain on the lower leg if the load is allowed to descend even half an inch further back from the fulcrum than is necessary must also be considerable. Certainly if we hope to push our horses to anywhere near the limit of their speed we must not increase the basic mechanical problems. Any radical changes which may be necessary in animals coming from elsewhere must be implemented gradually over two or three shoeings, although these shoeings need only be a few days apart.

Toe grabs are forbidden in Europe and are therefore not a subject for much heart-searching here but, viewing the question mechanically, it would appear to indicate that their use must greatly increase the destructive forces at work in any racehorse's foreleg. Lack of traction in the absence of grabs does not seem to present a problem on some fairly hair-raising tracks in England, although the surface can often be like a skating rink. Quite apart from the 24-hour-a-day strain imposed on the tendons by a toe grab, the extra shock to all hard and soft tissue when the foot is prevented from sliding slightly forward as it hits the ground must be very considerable. The fenders or bumpers on most modern cars are designed to reduce the shock of impact by one or two inches of movement and the same theory must apply to the foot when it hits the ground. If extra traction is felt to be essential some experimentation with a couple of grooves cut at 90° to the swedge or fullering might be worthwhile as a less destructive form of grip.

As a rule all our horses will wear plates with solid, not pencilled, heels. However, this might mean refitting hind plates for the front if only the pencilled-heel front plates are normally available. We might occasionally fit pencilled heels to a horse that persistently gets a front plate off at exercise to see if it helps, or we might try them on one that is interfering. The reason we reject them for general use is that the foot will tend to grow towards where the weight hits the ground, and as this design of heel must tend to move that point forward, it tends to encourage lowering of the foot angle. At best it

must make it more difficult to maintain the angle we require.

It is amazing how quickly the heels do collapse in some horses and, as mentioned elsewhere, many yearlings are now in this condition before we ever see them. There may be two reasons for this: firstly, the systematic destruction of yearlings' heels due to attempted correction of crooked or too upright stance, and secondly, the shoeing of yearlings very short in order to avoid losing shoes whilst lunging. Because of the latter problem, we break all yearlings barefoot, but it is often necessary to address damage that has already been done.

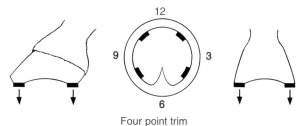

Four point trim

A fairly recent discovery, or more likely, rediscovery, is the four-point trim which attempts to reproduce the type of foot encountered in wild horses in desert areas, a much stronger and more upright foot. This is the high and hollow foot recommended by Xenophon three centuries BC, and by Simon of Athens even earlier. Basically the foot is trimmed to give bearing at what might be considered the four corners only, that is at 10 o'clock, 2 o'clock, 4 o'clock and 8 o'clock, if we regard the underside of the foot as a clockface. As the foot growth will tend to follow the weight, the wall should gradually become more upright. The rolling, or rounding off, of the toe (between 11 and 1 o'clock), and similar trimming of the sides (around 3 o'clock and 9 o'clock) also serves to reduce the flare that many British vendors find so desirable. The entire wall should be rounded off as for a horse that is to be turned out to grass. Quite good results have been obtained with the small number of cases tried so far. This experiment is worth pursuing and has no discernable drawbacks, although it is recommended as a barefoot system to improve the shape of the foot, and is unlikely to suit shod animals.

In all barefoot systems the edges of the hoof must be rounded off to prevent splitting of the wall, and pains should be taken to keep barefoot horses on the grass whenever possible. It may prove advisable to pursue the four point system for several weeks before reshoeing. By the time the yearlings are reshod they will often have reduced the size of their feet considerably by natural wear and tear from the size which they were on first coming into the yard, which should tend to make angles higher and the structure stronger. They should be shod with plates or with light steel shoes, and reshod in about 25 days. Once yearlings are correctly shod in front, the turning and figure of eight exercise should be kept to a minimum, particularly on soft ground, as they may easily step on a full-fitted shoe. In most cases there is no need for hind shoes at this stage.

For older horses with very flat feet or those with no heels, we may need to use wedge-heeled plates to achieve a more acceptable angle. The Elite Competition Shoe has about 2° of lift and it also has a lot more substance to it than regular aluminium plates. Unfortunately in some cases there might be a tendency for the wedged shoe to further crush the horse's heel and the situation should be monitored at each shoeing. A horse with very underrun heels may be helped by a bar shoe in order to attempt to bring the foot more under the column of the limb and to encourage the foot to assume a more upright growth. A front plate can easily be altered so as to be fitted to the foot backwards to do the same thing. The open toe is an added advantage when using a reversed plate for this purpose, but the original heels must be very well pencilled so as complete the rolled toe effect. After two or three shoeings most horses should be much improved, will have naturally

shortened their toe, and might be able to accept a more normal shoeing. Care should be taken to restore, if possible, the angle of the sole between the wall and the bar, which has often become a blur in these animals, at each removal. Wedge heels can also be helpful in the case of a horse which tends to run down either in front or behind.

Horses that have front feet of widely differing size are not uncommon. One foot tends to be big and flat and the other smaller and steeper - a box foot. This situation is not normally evident in very young animals and develops due to uneven loading of the two limbs being absorbed by the feet. The fact that the condition seems to become increasingly noticeable as the animal gets older implies that either the increased strain of exercise is to blame or that it may actually be an ongoing problem resulting from one or more faulty shoeings. It may result from the horse bearing his weight unevenly due to pain somewhere in the limb with the upright foot. If, as is normal procedure by many farriers, the higher heels on the tall foot are then reduced with a view to making it less boxy then that foot will be even less able to bear its fair share of weight. The bigger foot will be further crushed by assuming an ever bigger proportion of what should be an equal burden. Once this cycle is confirmed it can prove difficult to resolve. Thought should be given to reloading the tall foot with its full half of the bodyweight in order to reduce the crushing of the flat one, if necessary by the use of a pad or marginally thicker plate. If the problem of uneven stress on the forelimbs is not resolved there are likely to be more serious repercussions than odd feet.

It is essential that all our horses be shod as full as possible at the heels in an attempt to guard against collapsed heels and the corns that often result, although unfortunately this will always increase the risk of getting shoes off with badly behaved horses or when doing repeated turning.

Although there are schools of thought that advocate leaving the sole and the frog untouched, that theory is not suited to racehorses in training. If the sole is allowed to thicken there is every likelihood of the toe lengthening and the angle of the foot may then fall considerably. If the frog is not kept tidy there is danger of some degree of thrush flourishing beneath the surface.

It is most important that all horses are shod so as to wear their plates evenly as this will indicate that the foot is landing evenly, which in turn indicates that the leg encounters stress evenly. Any horse wearing one side more quickly should have the other side of the foot taken down slightly. For example a pigeon-toed animal will be seen to wear the outside of his plate more. Although this may not start for some days after he has been shod, once it does start it progresses more rapidly. The horse probably grows foot more quickly on the inside, which after a time makes the inside edge land first, and he then rolls all his weight onto the outside edge. The same thing happens to a human shoe; the heels may remain perfect for some time, but as soon as there is any lowering of the outside, perhaps initially caused by turning, that side quickly wears right away due to the extra loading.

We should always stress the importance of not inflicting any unnecessary damage on the foot. Clenches should be big enough to be secure but small enough that any pulled shoes cause minimal breaking of the wall. The use of the clenching tool or alligator should be careful so as to tear the wall as little as possible. The practice of cutting a deep groove across the wall to bed the clenches in should be discouraged, as again the wall is being destroyed. If for any health-related reason the horse stops growing foot at the normal rate it is essential that what he does have is protected. To further avoid breaking up of the wall the nails should not be pitched too low, but any nail inadvertently straying too high should be immediately removed, and not, as is too frequently seen, left without it even having re-emerged at the wall.

The importance of the horse's foot as a barometer of his general health and wellbeing tends to be overlooked on a day-to-day basis, although the basic idea is universally accepted. A horse that seems to have very poor quality horn may well be suffering from some systemic disease and this possibility should be discussed with the vet, particularly should the situation develop in an animal which causes any other strange problems in his daily routine or which inexplicably loses his form. The recent reliance on dietary supplements, which supposedly improve the quality of horn, should not be the only action taken in these cases, and if several horses in the yard are affected there is likely to be more than a dietary problem. Minor laminitic episodes due to the same cause may be quite common but misdiagnosed, and this should be thoroughly investigated if any horse demonstrates reddening around the white line or in the wall of a white foot. The farrier must report all such cases on the understanding that they in no way reflect on him. Steaks or blotches of white on a black foot with no white hair at the coronet seem likely to be definite signs that all has not been well with the animal's general health. An unusual number of horses that interfere, even to a minor degree, in a stable with sensible shoeing policies may be another indication of possible disorder to the central nervous systems of the inmates. Veterinary advice should be sought and systemic antibiotic treatment initiated immediately. These marks tend to be common in the graduates of certain stud-farms and they are not omens of likely good fortune, in fact quite the reverse. Colonel Warburton seemed well aware of this indicator a century ago, as he wrote, "The foot should be of good size, at the same angle as the pastern, and the horn smooth and without rings and steaks, which are sure indications of disease."

There were a very high percentage of these white marks on black feet and red marks on white feet in the horses sold at Keeneland in September 1997. This might well have indicated some widespread sickness in the area in previous months, and it would be interesting to determine whether those horses as a whole achieved what might reasonably have been expected of them, or if they demonstrated any higher percentage of physical and temperamental weaknesses than any other group.

If any horse has feet so weak, due to poor quality and separating horn, that he is obliged to wear glue shoes we should, unless he has an imminent and attractive engagement, stop with him and attempt to resolve the situation. A very effective method of doing this is to remove the shoes and poultice the whole foot right up over the hairline for five days, replacing the poultice daily. The horse should then be left for three days before repeating the whole procedure two or three times, which may involve a month of box rest. In many cases the result will be enough foot to complete the season with careful shoeing. In case some systemic disease might be implicated we should seriously consider antibiotic treatment orally for the whole of this period. So as to avoid the possibility of removing the whole hoof with the poultice, it is essential to observe the periodic drying out stage with the poultice removed. This procedure was discovered by accident whilst trying to resolve a lame animal with a suspected splinter in his foot; although no splinter ever did emerge, the animal grew a great deal of new foot, and the method has proved very useful in re-establishing a healthy foot on several occasions since.

A milder stimulation such as iodine or Cornucrescine can be regularly applied to the hairline in less serious cases, and the animal can be kept in work. Great care should always be taken on white-legged horses, so as not to start any irritation that might turn into a sore heel. In white-legged animals DMSO might be preferable, but cannot be used close to race day. It is not normally recommended to use hoof dressings as they prevent the foot from breathing. The moisture from the grass combined with the washing of legs and feet will normally keep the feet in good condition. The nail holes of a horse with weak feet can easily be reinforced after shoeing by using super glue around them to prevent the wall from breaking; the glue should only be applied in a stripe half an inch wide connecting the nail holes on the same side. Weak-walled horses may be better gently clenched up with the hammer rather than the alligator so as to avoid tearing the wall.

The shoeing of the hind feet causes few problems in itself, and most of the string should wear plain plates, or sometimes light steel, with a toe clip in order to avoid the shoe shifting back. This programme assumes no roadwork, on the basis that cars and horses do not mix well, and most of the horses can be kept in plates all year in front and in plates or light steel behind. The advantages of this system are that any horse can run in what he already has on, should an opportunity suddenly present itself, and that the horses never go too long without being reshod, which may easily happen to a good wearer with regular shoes on.

Some alterations may have to be made in shoeing those horses that incur injuries through interference, and discovering the answer to some cases may prove difficult. However, no horse will give his best performance whilst he is hitting himself, and time devoted to this problem is normally time well spent.

The most common interfering problem is simple brushing of the inside lower hind leg with the opposite hind leg. The balance of the foot should be checked. If the foot is balanced, a three-quarter shoe is fitted with the short

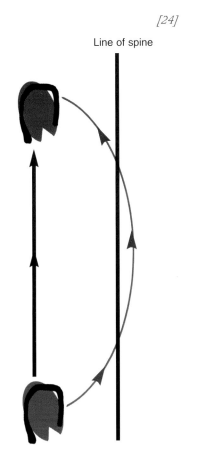

[24]

Line of spine

Original ground placement and foot flight.

Ground contact and flight with medial extension shoe.

original shoe prints of a horse with this conformation will be similar to those of Charlie Chaplin, with the centre of the toe at an angle of perhaps 30° to the animal's spine. We should aim to place the ground surface of the shoe, if not the foot itself, in as close alignment with the direction of the spine as possible. The toe of the shoe should be squared and will form a moderate extension towards the inside, but will not extend to the outer toe of the foot itself. Although there may appear to be an increased danger of damage from this medial extension shoe, the change in foot flight due to the alteration in the breakover point should now prevent any interference. The outside branch is left a little long and fitted slightly inside the wall at the toe but slightly wide and long at the heel. The extension makes the inside branch slightly wide at the toe, but this branch is fitted very close at the quarter and at the heel. The resulting standing shoe print should now more nearly agree with the direction of the animal's spine [24]. A bandage covering the site of the interference should reveal no brush marks after exercise following this shoeing, and if so it can be dispensed with.

A cautious attempt at this solution might be tried in front with a badly toeing-out horse that interferes excessively with the opposing sesamoid area. These horses should normally wear boots. One advantage in attempting this plan is that, even should it prove ineffective, no radical change has been made to the foot.

Interference caused to the hind limb by the front feet is often much more of a problem and can seriously disrupt a horse's career. Most of these injuries are in some way scalping types of wound, usually in horses whose front feet tend to turn in, and they can occur from the hairline right up the pastern and even in some cases the fetlock. In many cases protection is ineffective due to the angle of the blow. To reduce the solution of the problem to its simplest, we need to encourage the front foot to break over as

branch to the inside. In fact this is very common shoeing in Newmarket anyway. If this does not resolve the problem, in many cases reversing the shoeing, so that the short branch is to the outside, will. Many young horses brush out of weakness or when they are tired, and improve as they get stronger.

The more confirmed hind brushing cases tend to turn their feet out markedly and tend to be cow-hocked. We should visualise where the shoe print would be with normal conformation and shoe these horse in an attempt to achieve something approaching that normal placement of the foot. The quickly as possible whilst minutely retarding the flight of the hind foot, in order to reduce the chances of their paths coinciding. The front feet should be well balanced and as short as is practicable and the toes should be squared or rolled. The hind feet can be left a little long with the angle slightly lowered, and the hind shoes can be a little heavier than normal. An outside trailer, perhaps with a calk, can be added if necessary, although cutting two or three grooves across the shoe behind the last nail may tend to grab hold of the ground just long enough to make a difference. Apparently Curtis and Sons, the Newmarket farriers, refer to this particular shoe as the 'Billygripper'! [25] Trailers are not recommended for horses that regularly use transport as they may catch under the partition, although a long travelling boot should prevent this. There is also the danger of the trailer becoming caught in the head collar when the horse is scratching his head in the stable with disastrous consequences, and the head collar should always be removed when the horse is loose in his box or turned out.

The Billygripper hind shoes are effective in curing those animals that can be heard to clatter their front and hind feet together, known as forging, when they are cantering. Even if they are not damaging themselves, these horses do tend to be paying attention to the noise rather than to what they should be doing.

Horses that hit high up, inside the hock, are

[25]

fortunately uncommon. This is very difficult to resolve, partly because it is not clear exactly how the damage is inflicted, and obviously because protection is very difficult in this area. With a bad case even the option of stick-on patches can be unsatisfactory, and when riding the horse at speed it will be obvious that he is severely compromised. If the outside edge of his front shoes is felt to be causing the damage then it should be well rounded off right back to a pencilled heel and we should attempt to slow the hind feet down by the means described above. The rider must be strictly instructed to keep him balanced at all times, as these horses will often move well until they do touch themselves, after which they will naturally try desperately to save themselves by constantly changing leads. If the horse is inclined to turn his feet out behind he should be shod as recommended above. Pleasure Beach, our worst case was, apparently, subsequently cured by a trotting farrier in Macau who left him barefoot behind. This would imply that it was, for that horse at least, purely a hindlimb problem, and this theory is worth consideration. The medial extension shoe might well have resolved this case had it been tried.

Possibly one reason for the widely differing theories on curing any interference in gallopers is that gait peculiarities cannot be nearly so well observed from directly behind as they can in a harness racer. The fact that the directly opposite solution to one originally recommended is sometimes successful in resolving interference problems may be due to the difference, commonly accepted in harness racers, between line-gaited and passing-gaited horses. It is often apparent, when directly following another galloping horse, that the flight of his feet is extremely odd, to the extent that he may give the impression of trying to flick his front foot off his leg altogether.

It is worth considering whether many interference problems, particularly any which prove difficult to resolve, might involve some slight co-ordination problem which in turn may be symptomatic of a systemic disease such as EPM or Lyme disease. Certainly, should a high percentage of horses from any particular source seem to suffer interfering tendencies, or even to tend to be particularly clumsy or stumbling types, that source should be regarded with extreme suspicion. This question may arise in many more aspects of training than is generally supposed, and it should always be considered as a factor in any difficult to resolve situation concerning the training programme. It is impossible to achieve maximum results working with damaged material, and both we and our vet should remember that not knowing what is amiss is by no means the same as nothing being amiss. EPM is certainly far from being the only systemic disease compromising the equine population, although disastrous racing results have normally been attributed to 'The Virus'. In his lecture *Horsemastership*, published in 1911, Derby-winning trainer Col. F. MacCabe refers to tick-borne Relapsing Fever and its serious effects on both humans and animals. This disease is very similar to Lyme disease.

This line of thought reinforces previous warnings concerning both homebreeding programmes and vendors who have proved unlucky for us. Obviously there is no reason to suppose that any stud is immune to athlete-compromising disease. However, in a high stakes business, we must shun any sources that provide even circumstantial evidence of increased risk, based on our previous experience of their stock. This type of unscientific observation may nowadays be dismissed as unsatisfactory, however bitter experience teaches that we ignore it at our peril! It is widely accepted, for instance, that many farms have had land on which particular stock would never thrive, fields that were eventually proved to harbour poisons of vegetable or mineral nature. There is no reason to suppose that unsuccessful or disappointing horse-rearing establishments should be immune to

similar problems, possibly originally of some parasitic nature. Occasional success stories do not necessarily give any farm a clean bill of health if they regularly produce disappointing stock. The norm of any farm's achievements should be the basis for judging the likely future performance of its graduates. In *The Twentieth Century Book of the Horse*, published in 1905, Sidney Galvayne states (pages 227–8): "Stringhalt is a nervous disease... It is very common in some parts of Australia and South Africa... In Australia I have frequently heard some such remark as the following, 'I shall not put my horse in this or that paddock, or it will be sure to get stringhalt'." Careful observation might make us too suspect that unusual patterns are to be observed in the former inmates of various properties.

Feeding

"Give me neither poverty nor riches, feed me with food convenient for me." Proverbs 30:8

The nutritional requirements of the racehorse are the subject of an enormous amount of literature; how much of it is great literature is open to question. Unfortunately, very little relevant work exists on the nutrition of the racehorse under combat conditions, certainly nothing that vaguely justifies many of the claims and counterclaims made by the feed industry. A stable winning important stakes with horses fed on 'Product X' is almost certainly performing moderately overall, considering the capital cost of its equine raw material. If there truly were an elixir of life all advertising would become obsolete due to the vastly superior results obtained by its users. This has not yet happened. The truth is that the horse is a remarkable adaptable animal, up to a point, and in nature he successfully inhabits many different climatic regions with correspondingly differing vegetation. This presumably accounts for the fact that racehorses appear to thrive on a wide variety of nutritional programmes; there certainly does not seem to be any great evidence to show that normal common sense cannot get good results. The considerable expense of some of the more exotic additives should rule them out immediately, particularly when their manufacturers seem very coy on the subject of cost-effectiveness. In the real world, more expensive fuel is only adopted following research that demonstrates superior power or stamina!

We should confine our feeding programme to a fairly basic and traditional one and we should not propose to make any dramatic changes until some serious work is produced involving the study of horses in training and currently racing.

The only thing published that does spring to mind is the 1950s survey of, if memory serves, the Windfields Farm racing division which appeared to indicate that those horses raced more productively when fed 2,000 iu vitamin E daily. As we have had some success in getting horses through long and arduous campaigns on this regime we accept its value. Almost all of the other material is smoke and mirrors, possibly on a par with shampoo advertising on television.

The one thing horses do appreciate is routine, and the feeding schedule should be as regular as possible. Feed times should also be spaced, although whether to the degree sometimes advocated is questionable based on the results achieved by some of the more extreme 'little and often' enthusiasts.

Another indisputable fact is that whatever feed is selected there must be no compromise on quality control. All suppliers must deliver consistently high-grade forage. If we do hope to obtain this service we must in return be meticulous in settling their accounts on time. We aim to form an association with the feed man which should guarantee that if top-class material is ever in short supply, then we are at the front of the queue. In fact this philosophy has traditionally found little favour in Newmarket, Mr Wilde's observation that "It is only by not paying one's bills that one can hope to live in the memory of the commercial classes" being widely accepted amongst the local racing fraternity.

Racehorses in hard work may not require, indeed they normally will not eat, the amounts that are often quoted by many sources, including head lads, feeders and trainers. The traditional measure used to be a stone of short food and a stone of long – 14lbs of grain and 14lbs of hay – daily. For many young racehorses these targets are still too high yet we often hear of animals apparently avidly consuming 20 and more pounds of grain per day. The occasional glutton that might devour these amounts would certainly have his enthusiasm at the manger dramatically reduced were he put into an appropriate training regime. Any trainer who has been told that all his horses are eating 20lbs of oats per day, and whose corn bills seem to support that figure, is almost certainly being robbed. Feeders as a whole give rather optimistic reports of their charges' consumption, and it is important to define accurately what measures are being quoted.

As we are using a traditional approach we will aim to achieve the traditional consumption for the older horses although from experience we may be disappointed by the intake of most of the two-year-olds once their workload increases. The older males will often eat quite large amounts, at least until they have a hard race or two, when they realise that this life is no longer quite so easy and that they aren't really very hungry! The basic ration we use is very lightly bruised Scots or Canadian clipped oats plus about 10% racehorse cubes and 10% proprietary sweet feed. Oats should weigh as heavy as possible in order to reduce the bulk to be consumed. Oats, like hay, should always appear clean and bright in colour, and should smell sweet. The 'naked oats' now widely available weigh very heavy, due to their having no husk, but are inclined to make the droppings very soft. Several manufacturer's produce a balancer supplement with a protein

Manor Farm Boy wins the Gosforth Park Cup under a welter burden as a 4-year-old; he won seven races at two and was a smart winner at three. We got him by swapping for another horse after he was unsold (for £1,000) as a yearling. Tony Ives up. (Photo courtesy of Kenneth Bright)

content of almost 20% as opposed to that of regular oats at around 10% or 12%, and this can be usefully employed for delicate animals. Australian oats tend to be rather sharp and hard, so can aggravate any minor cuts a horses might have inside his cheeks. A small amount of corn oil is added to the night feed, as well as a simple vitamin supplement which should deliver 2000 iu of vitamin E daily. Salt is supplied in a block but is also added to the ration in an attempt to ensure adequate water intake. Electrolytes are added to the ration during hot weather, and are given regularly to free-sweating horses. This feed is used every day, with no mash or cooked feed days. Should the droppings of any horse appear to be very dry and firm the proportion of cubes may be increased for a day or two. The sweet feed is included to give the vitamin powder something to stick to, as many horses tend to sort out any additives and leave them in the manger.

The main thing to remember about feeding racehorses is to feed them so that they normally manage to eat up their allowance. If any horse does leave unaccustomedly he may well be off-colour and his temperature and general appearance should be checked, although if he goes straight to his breakfast he is probably fine. The art of the feeder, of course, is in judging just what a horse will eat and keeping his total daily feed a double handful, or about one pound, below that limit. Attempts to overfeed may result in horses leaving so frequently that no one knows whether they are well or not.

The ration is fed in the following proportions: 5 am: oats, 3lbs; 12 noon: oats, 3lbs; 6.30 pm: oats, 5lbs; racehorse cubes, 1.5lbs; sweet feed (as carrier for supplement powder) 1.5 lbs; oi1, 1/3 cup; supplement and salt. This is for a horse that eats fairly well, and adjustments can be made as necessary over the three feeds, in fact many animals that are poor daytime feeders do eat quite well at night. Many horses ignore their breakfast until after they have been exercised, but will go straight to it when they come in; in most cases the midday feed will have to be reduced for those animals that have not by then finished their breakfast.

Once the horses are in strong work and their hard food ration has increased the hay allowance is reduced and the hay itself is changed from timothy to a strong alfalfa or clover and timothy mix, which must be of top quality. The protein content of the alfalfa is considerably higher than that of the timothy. The hay should obviously smell fresh and sweet, the leaf and flower should be intact, and the colour should always be bright rather than dull. As the work intensifies, the hay intake seems to drop naturally as evidenced by what is left in the shavings bedding, and the

ration is reduced as indicated. Although it is not so readily apparent amongst horses bedded on straw, animals in hard training may tend to eat surprisingly little hay, and obviously hay that is dragged through their bed does not count as intake. The two-year-olds not yet in full work can easily tend towards fat if allowed too much alfalfa, and this situation must be closely monitored. All horses appreciate greenmeat during the spring and summer. If a daily supplier of fresh cut lucerne or alfalfa can be found, the hay ration can be reduced, if necessary, for as long as this benefit lasts.

Water

"Thirsty and you gave me drink." St. Matthew 25:35

The amount of water consumed is thought to be important and fresh clean water should be always available. However, despite being fed salt, Manor Farm Boy rarely drank three or four gallons of water in 24 hours, yet was near the top of his generation through long campaigns at two, three and four years. This may be another area deserving of more research. There might be some sense in those horses that tend not to drink whilst away from home always having their water lightly flavoured with something innocuous, in order that they be less aware of changes in the taste of the water at the racecourse. Care should obviously be taken that any such additive does not fall foul of any medication rules!

Racing Strategy

"In the day of prosperity be joyful, but in the day of adversity consider." Ecclesiastes 7:14

Although prize money in Britain is very low on a day-to-day basis, we should endeavour to keep our team in competition as much as possible. Galloping for brass, as they say, is much better than galloping for nowt. This may prove easier to achieve with two-year-olds than with older horses simply because they can compete in condition or allowance races rather than be at the mercy of the handicapper. Those horses that do run up a number of handicap wins have almost all commenced from a mark far below representing their actual ability. Despite what we may read, very few of these animals have been improved by clever training; they are simply revealing that they are not as bad as the handicapper had originally assumed, based on what had been previously exposed. The majority of well-handicapped horses have achieved that happy state through incompetence or villainy in that they have either raced when patently unwell or unfit, or they have been 'having a run round', as they say. Regrettably these very questionable practices find favour even at the supposed higher levels of the sport in Britain, but as they are neither sporting nor skilful, and in most cases fail to maximise the resale price of the horse, they are of little interest to us.

Although a favourable handicap rating may be regarded as essential in many quarters, the reverse is true if we hope to sell our horses for premium prices. In fact, there are one or two trainers who do set out to manufacture an artificially high rating by running horses over their heads, and they have often proved successful in doing so. Of course, the secret to making this plan really work is not to start believing any inflated rating ourselves, as the fall in that rating and in value can be as meteoric as the rise. This policy is similar to making money on any rising market, in that it is essential to hop off the merry-go-round before it stops. A more moderate course is advisable in which we should attempt to pick up as much prize money as possible whilst keeping a strict eye on both the saleability and soundness of the stock. Particularly in small fields it is very easy for a horse to get sucked along into a placing well beyond his normal capabilities. We must be aware if this does happen and our horse should be sold on as quickly as possible on the strength of it.

A maiden race will in most cases be the first objective for all our horses as they will tend to run against similarly inexperienced opposition. However, it is often possible to find a conditions race that may be less competitive due to most trainers shying away from previous winners. Rather like children playing conkers, if we do beat a previous winner, or even run him close, we assume an added reputation, which may or may not be justified, and the scene may thereby be set for further success. There did use to be a certain advantage in always winning a maiden first, in that the American market much preferred those horses which were "nonwinners other than maiden or claiming". They now seem increasingly to write those races for "nonwinners of two races" that now gives us a little more scope when reselling. With the American market in mind we should always consider targeting the maiden races on the all-weather surfaces, as a dirt winner will always be more desirable than a horse with the equivalent form on turf. It is also important to bear in mind that the American programme, because of the course layout, does not cater to any great extent for pure five furlong runners.

Horses that are expected to stand up to an arduous campaign must be fit, but it seems that they do last longer if they come to their first start just needing it. For some reason the harder training necessary to absolutely guarantee success on the debut almost equally guarantees earlier decline in performance. Obviously many horses do win first time and then go on all year, but they tend to have initially defeated opponents which subsequently prove be considerably inferior. We should aim to produce all debutants to do their best without being hurt, and should anticipate that the race will bring them on 7lbs in condition, apart from the benefit they derive from the experience of racing. The 7lbs improvement means that if the two-year-old had previously galloped with an older teammate receiving 14lbs we should expect him to repeat the performance receiving only 7lbs. This improvement is equivalent to roughly two or three lengths. Obviously a punishing race when not dead fit will tend to take a lot out of any horse. Our jockey should be well aware of the situation as regards his mount's fitness and also that we regard this as merely the start of a horse's career. This is particularly true in soft ground in the spring as even five furlongs is at that stage a stiff task for any two-year-old. If any horse runs particularly green it is reasonable to anticipate more improvement than that based on improved fitness; this applies equally to the opposition and we should objectively watch how they perform when viewing the replay, so as to correctly anticipate the result of any rematch.

Once a two-year-old has won his maiden he should, unless he is highly regarded enough to be aimed at specific targets, be maintained in a state of constant readiness. Any open or condition races for which he is eligible should be entered and no suitable opportunity should be missed. Obviously, to define what may be a suitable opportunity requires an accurate assessment of our own horse's capabilities. This means his current capabilities as demonstrated in his exercise. It should not be necessary repeatedly to try a horse that has established recent form, but we will use him to assess his team-mates before their debuts. The performance of these horses will give a reasonable estimate of the form and prospects of the original winner, and enable us to decide whether to retain him or sell him. There is normally a buoyant Italian market early in the season for winning two-year-olds and unless our observations lead us to believe his value can be increased, or at least not diminished by racing him on, we will sell him. In the event that we are concerned as to the true value of his form, but are unable to get him sold, there is no need to run him until an easy race does appear. One invariably does appear as long as we are prepared to wait. Oddly enough any minor race which seemed rather uncompetitive last year may well be the same this year, and this fact is worth bearing in mind. This also applies to unusually hot races; some maiden races, where the previous winners have subsequently excelled, can be very tough and should be avoided.

If the stable does have several horses of similar ability at any one time, this may occasionally pose problems as to which horse should fulfil which engagement. In practice we will normally find that due to a wide range of hopefully minor setbacks we cannot have too many useful animals for the opportunities available. Running two horses in one race for different owners can often lead to unpleasantness; even if nothing is said at the time, the ill-feeling, particularly after an important race, may remain for years. If possible it should be avoided.

The heavy ground in Britain early in the year can be devastating for two-year-olds and

Sayf El Arab (USA) scampers clear in the King's Stand Stakes under Taffy Thomas - beating favoured stable companion On Stage into third place. He always wore a neckstrap after having been withdrawn from his intended debut after getting loose.
(Photo courtesy of Leslie Sampson)

this fact must always be borne in mind when deciding on whether to run or not. A seemingly weak race should not normally be passed up with a run of the mill animal as a bird in the hand is certainly, in this business, worth at least two in the bush. We should not expect any two-year-old to recover as well from a hard race in heavy ground as from one in normal conditions. This fact seems often to be ignored, and we may sometimes anticipate a lesser effort from an opponent that has recently run on heavy ground. If we do want always to keep the percentages in our favour we will not run our own youngsters back too quickly in these conditions. Firm ground on the other hand is ideal for running sound horses regularly, particularly as the opposition is often reluctant to take part. Hard ground on the old scale is very rarely encountered nowadays, but fit animals with well-trained legs rarely take any harm on fast ground, and the small fields are an added attraction for us.

Better-class horses tend to have their careers more formally mapped out in advance with a view to being brought to peak fitness for a particular objective. By definition it would appear that all trainers fail to judge this difficult process correctly most of the time, since all but one horse in any particular race fails in his objective. It makes sense for our operation not to embrace this policy too warmly except when we are quite sure we do have a genuine Saturday horse since, as noted, a bird in the hand is worth two in the bush. In fact, too rigid an adherence to the advance programme book might be similar to using the list system for purchasing yearlings, in that any attractively framed race has appeared in everyone else's book too!

It is worth bearing in mind that we should never be afraid of one horse when assessing the entries and deciding where to run. This is particularly true with two-year-olds that are ultimately to be sold, because raising their handicap ratings can be an asset rather than a disadvantage. Very often a useful horse might be entered at a minor track because his connections are not altogether happy with his progress, and are hoping for a virtual walkover. If our less highly regarded horse is second he can lose nothing, but should he win his record and his value are both enhanced.

With most of our the older horses, but also with the two-year-olds as the season progresses, the different distances of races eventually becomes a consideration. There are two distinct schools of thought on this matter, as some trainers never do experiment at all, whilst others never stop chopping and changing. We should aim at a balance between the two approaches. On the one hand we should not, at least without good reason, try to experiment with any horse that is competing well at some particular distance as long as he does have viable opportunities at that distance. On the other, no horse should repeatedly be asked to run against superior opposition if lesser rivals can be faced by attempting a new trip. Obviously if the horse cannot cope with inferior rivals at the new distance he must revert to Plan A.

It is interesting that British trainers almost invariably increase the distance of their charges, while dramatic improvement might often be made by shortening the trip for many old horses. In Australia it not uncommon for horses to run over a variety of distances and such was also the case in Britain a century ago and in America much more recently. African Chimes was claimed at ten furlongs as a back-end three-year-old; he was then rated 57. Although no world beater he subsequently won 18 races at distances down to five furlongs, and achieved a handicap mark of 96. Forty pounds is a considerable rise in the weights, but this horse was quite unsuited to running long, whether he actually stayed the trip or not. After winning eight races in 1992 he was claimed out of our stable, but he ran so poorly over two unsuccessful seasons that his rating was reduced to the original level before returning to me to win a further five races as a seven- and eight-year-old.

Milk Of The Barley was another versatile horse as regards distance, being quite effective from six furlongs to ten furlongs, as long as he

Milk Of The Barley - an attractive though temperamental horse and an able runner, albeit on his own terms. Tony Ives up.

Provideo and Tony Ives winning at Sandown Park. A blow for the homebreds! Physically unattractive and with a difficult disposition; none of his siblings were any good. (Photo courtesy of Mel Fordham)

was in the mood. He was a very funny-tempered animal and a difficult ride in a race although his owner-breeder would not accept that fact. He also performed consistently poorly after he left the stable due to his owner's displeasure with our stable jockey at the time. He soon regained his form on his return to the fold and he ran second in a Group One race.

In most cases, those horses that run regularly will do their exercise as normal with the rest of the string. Runners should be ridden out for a trot the day after the race and should resume cantering the day after that as long as they are

unscathed. There is a widespread perception that racehorses should do very little except enjoy themselves between races. This theory has several quite successful exponents, although two-year-old winners do not usually figure prominently in the statistics of these stables. The method probably achieves a measure of success by default, in that unfit horses tend to get well-handicapped, and then to run themselves into form from a handicap mark that they may well be capable of far exceeding. Some sore or sulky old horses may actually do more exercise loose in a paddock than they could easily be persuaded to do in a normal training programme. As a rule, the boxing precept that training hard makes fighting easy should always be applied at least to some degree to racehorse training.

It is interesting that Sam Chifney, in his work of almost two centuries ago, remarked, "A horse will change in his two days running very much for the worse if he has been fed and watered too plentifully...from a supposed kindness to the horse, by unskilful people...What is given him is likely to stay with him till after his second race...[and] must at times affect him very much in his second running". Any jockey who has wasted severely will observe the truth of these remarks from his personal experience. When not at his minimum weight he may be relatively unaffected, in the short term, by what he eats or drinks, but once he is already very light any intake will greatly affect his weight and sharpness. Whilst we do not wish to return to the days of severely drawing our horses before they race, we must be sure to maintain their training schedule so as to avoid their becoming stuffy. Both Timeless Times (USA) in 1990 and Provideo in 1984 did a tremendous amount of work when winning 16 races each as two-year-olds, and regularly did three-part speeds between their races. Their extreme fitness stood them in good stead on those occasions when they had to recover quickly from a severe test. Provideo was actually very coarse in his wind for a wiry type of animal, and it was always felt necessary to restrict his hay intake.

Whilst on the subject of Chifney it is worth noting that the anti-rearing bit currently named after him bears no resemblance to his original design, although it does closely resemble another bit used with drawing reins in the early 19th century. The original Chifney pattern was actually a curb bit with a swivel joint where the mouthpiece joined the side bar to attach to the cheeks of the bridle; it would probably have been quite unsuitable for racing purposes as it would have been far too severe. Samuel Sidney remarked in *The Book of the Horse* (published

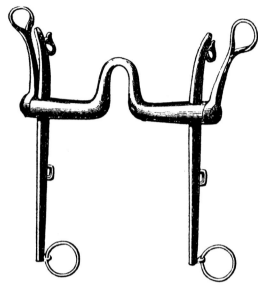

Original Chifney pattern bit.

in the 1880s) that "the leverage is so powerful that if a knife were substituted for the (curb) chain it would cut clean through the lower jaw".

Another bit which seems to have lost its identity is the Rockwell snaffle which is often wrongly referred to in England as a Citation bit. This bit actually appears identical to the Educating Bridle advocated by Professor E.K. Crocker in his book of 1894, and which he may well have borrowed from Rockwell himself who exhibited as a horse-tamer in the 1860s. There was a tremendous amount of cross-pollination between all the various methods of taming, gentling, starting and generally dealing with the problem horse, although each exponent tended to proclaim his own method as the Holy Grail. *The Education Of The Horse* by Crocker is an excellent book on behavioural problems in the horse and is well worthy of study by anyone in everyday working contact with any animals.

A horse racing in the afternoon should be fed earlier than usual in the morning, as he has to travel, but he will receive no hay. In practice he will not eat this feed in many cases. At the track his water is removed three or four hours before the race unless the weather is hot, although he is allowed four or five swallows when the lad gets him ready. In fact, there seems little reason to remove it in most cases as no horse is likely to drink a lot of water suddenly in the last hour or two; if he does wish to drink the full amount he will do so as soon as he is loosed. Horses should not be left with unfixed buckets for fear of accidents, and a tub with no handle should be used instead. Many horses never eat their breakfast promptly anyway, particularly at an unusual hour, and so effectively draw themselves to a certain extent. Horses leaving later in the morning for evening racing should get their breakfast as normal and will eat it as normal, but they may also get a little hay. Care must be taken to ensure inedible bedding at the track, or a muzzle should be fitted four or five hours before the race.

It is essential that any horse that may be required to complete a busy season be a good traveller, and although this is to some degree in the lap of the gods, certain steps should be taken to ensure our horses travel as well as possible. Two of the major causes of unrest are narrow stalls in the transport and erratic driving, both of which we can easily control. Big horses, as well as those that have shown any tendency to be restive, should always have an extra-wide stall, and in bad cases a double stall. Very bad travellers may be happier loose in a mare-and-foal sized section of the lorry. It is advisable if possible always to be the last pick-up on shared transport as this avoids an irritable horse becoming upset whilst waiting for others to load. We should be aware of starting stalls problems possibly leading to a horse becoming a bad travellers and vice versa. The wider the stall and the smoother the ride the less trouble will be encountered. Our lads will report any poor driving, and we can take it up with the transport company. As in the case of the feed man, we must ensure that our relationship with the firm puts us in line for their best drivers. It may be advisable to send the better horses and any very frequent runners on their own, as the extra cost is quite justified for horses that are regular earners. A ramp should always be used for loading and unloading, to avoid upsets which can easily become the basis for bad loading and unloading habits. It is important that horses should never be allowed to get cold in transport, particularly those which initially may sweat; these should travel, particularly in cold weather, with a net cooler under their sheet.

Although they are naturally popular with lads, overnight stays should be avoided whenever possible. Horses naturally rest and eat better in their home surroundings and a very early start is much less wearing for them than a night of nervous anticipation. The extra cost of travelling solo will be justified by results. Although many stables do bandage or otherwise protect the legs for travel, this practice presents more problems than it solves, and most horses will be more comfortable, and safer, barelegged. A wide, heavy-duty tape can be wrappped around the shoe and the clenches in order to guard to a degree against stepping a shoe off.

Elastic girths are to be preferred for racing, although they are rather heavy. Narrow-waisted animals should always wear a breast-girth as we do not want to worry about slipping saddles. As long as a horse looks well in his coat, his being light in his middle is no disgrace.

There is some argument in favour of two-year-olds, and indeed any badly behaved older animals, wearing neckstraps in order, hopefully, to avoid the occasional horse getting loose. It may actually be good policy always to use one, so as not to highlight any bad actors and thus alarm the rider. Any promising horse that has shown signs of excitability at the start, or that seems likely to get loose, should always have one of our lads sent to the start with him. Those horses that do behave badly either loading or when installed can often be rehabilitated by a qualified exponent of Monty Roberts's methods, and this solution should always be considered before the situation becomes desperate. Horses which do wear the so-called Roberts rug in order to prevent their feeling

On Stage was dependent on blinkers but was a talented and versatile performer. He would have been well able to emulate the exploits of Provideo and Timeless Times (USA) had he been asked to do so. Tony Ives up.
(Photo courtesy of Leslie Sampson)

the sides of the stalls cannot obviously be expected to break quite as smartly (even though it is pulled off as the gate opens) as do their unencumbered rivals, although they should do much better than they did previously.

Blinkers, Bits, and Nosebands

"All the armour wherein the trusted." St. Luke 11:21

Blinkers are an extremely important part of our armoury, although their correct use seems to be little understood in England today. There is a strong impression, at least in Newmarket, that their use implies a 'winding up' and that therefore any improvement in performance is

likely to occur on the first occasion that a horse wears them in public. Any improvement wrought by this method relies on the adrenalin rush of fear, and is not a basis for sustained improvement. In many cases the procedure is counter-productive due to the animal having exhausted itself mentally before the race takes place. Those rare horses that are dramatically improved by this method may well have benefited equally had the winding up been administered with or without the blinkers fitted. Happily, this practice is on the wane and at any rate it forms no part of our policy. However, should the raceday use of the whip ever be banned, there is likely to be a resurgence in these very traumatic training procedures.

The majority of working and driving horses wear blinkers of some description as a matter of course and these are not fitted with a view to making these animals excited or keen. Their object is purely to focus a horse's attention on the business in hand by shutting out most distractions and by giving him almost tunnel vision. Far from making horses more apprehensive, blinkers are best employed to settle them down when they are already excited by their surroundings or their regime. The term 'excited' may in this context include nervous, resentful, rebellious and even headstrong behaviour, all of which must benefit from any long-lasting sedative effect we might employ. For long-term success it is important to introduce the blinkers in a sensible manner, and for the horse to become as confident in them as a poor swimmer is in a lifejacket, or a child in a security blanket. If possible he should always associate the blinkers with going quietly and efficiently about his business. When we do achieve this, many sweating maniacs and downright hooligans will greatly improve.

For some reason blinkers are regarded in England as the rogue's badge and many stables neglect to make proper use of them. Although difficult to fit with his blinkers, which was done out on the track at the same moment that Tony Ives mounted, Provideo behaved well once he reached the start. He would have won 17 races at two years had the blinkers been employed one race earlier in his career. His busy schedule forced him to lose once after blinkers were obviously necessary to prevent him waiting for the opposition, as we had no chance to school him in them before declaration time for his next race. Graded stakes winner On Stage had to wear blinkers even to be clipped, and Proud And Keen, a useful but very washy horse, actually wore his blinkers between the racecourse stables and the paddock in order to keep him calm. Irregularities in the vision of horses may be a subject that would repay some

careful study. Unbelievably there were some quite famous Harness racehorses that were completely blind, including Sleepy Tom, one-time holder of the world record for pacers. Such animals must have been extremely well schooled and driven.

The occasional wearing of blinkers is very different to their constant use, and possibly results in some slight disorientation that puts the uncooperative or overconfident horse at a disadvantage. This may account for the improvement in performance of many lazy runners when fitted with blinds on racedays only. Once the blinkers are fitted, horses are obviously unable to anticipate precisely any use of the whip and may also feel inclined to head for what is effectively the light at the end of the tunnel ahead of them. Perhaps, in bull-fighting terms, we take blinkered horses out of their own territory and into ours where, like the bull, they are easier to work with. A blinker with slots in the cup is referred to in Europe as a visor and this can also be useful on idle horses, as they cannot really see what is going on, although they are aware of movement around them. Sometimes, a horse that must wear blinkers to show his form will be helped by regularly changing the type of cup in order to give him something to think about.

It is vital that all blinkered horses do go forward, but an initial tendency to sit back must be regarded in the same way as we those yearlings that won't initially follow the pony. A few minutes extra time will usually ensure good results. If it does not, blinkers will not prove helpful in a race. It may be advisable to do some stalls practice in blinkers as many horses will dwell on their first start as they wait to see the other horses, but we must remember to build confidence and not apprehension.

We should have different kinds of blinkers for various situations as individual horses may have different requirements in this department. Half cups or open blinkers are normally fitted to young horses to race as they allow better vision of the track ahead and will allow the horse to see a challenger before it has passed. Full blinkers restrict vision very much and can be alarming to a young horse in close quarters, particularly in a big field of runners, with unpredictable results.

One-eyed, or extension blinkers, can transform those horses that hang badly to one side or the other. Whether the horse lugs in or bears out, the big cup is fitted on the side he goes toward. Any horse will want to keep away from the unknown and will tend towards the side he can see best, so he usually proves much easier to steer. Fayruz was a decent horse,

winning six races within 26 days at two, but as he was much stronger and hung severely he needed to wear this blinker at three years old. He was then much easier to keep straight, but if he did happen to get a bump on the blind side he would overreact and hang the other way. This tendency is actually quite logical and should always be remembered.

There are bits available for every situation, but unfortunately many prove less than effective in practice. In most cases we should try to address the underlying problem rather than expect a change of equipment to work a miracle. The majority of racehorses will resent a severe bit and

Fayruz as a 3-year-old. The one-eyed blinker is keeping him straight under pressure. Although he was narrowly beaten, this ride (Pat Eddery up) was one of the finest that we ever had.
(Photo courtesy of Leslie Sampson)

[26]

All photos of bits/nosebands courtesy of 'Titch' D. Coombes

This more moderate version works well and is acceptable to most horses. A tongue tie can be used for racing if necessary; again the horse should be schooled in the tongue tie before he runs. The tongue tie should be wrapped two or three times around the tongue rather than tied round it before securing the ends below the jaw.

Dental problems can often be implicated in the case of hard pullers, horses that hang and those which appear to be afraid of the bit and this aspect should be fully investigated at an early stage of any attempt to resolve the issue. A regular dental check-up should take place. It is normally best to remove all wolf teeth as a matter of course.

Hanging to one side or the other is likely to result from a cut on the inside of the cheek caused by the edges of the molars, and this possibility should be investigated; however, a likely cause of this very undesirable habit (and of the cuts!) is that the exercise rider has been accustomed to hold the animal with its head turned round to one side because it is too keen for him, which progressively deadens that side of the mouth. Unfortunately, racehorses are much better at learning bad habits than good ones, and this one can become confirmed in a very short time. A Dexter ring snaffle [27] can be useful on those horses with a tendency to hang moderately and is inoffensive to most animals. Those horses that hang on one rein more severely should have a strong elastic band, such as a jockey's wristband, attaching the ring of the bit to the throat latch on the side they go towards [28]. This tends to keep the bit straight in the mouth and very often resolves the problem as the horse is obliged to accept gentle but inescapable pressure on the side he previously refused to use. It can be left on in the stable as a gentle but inescapable method of curing one-sidedness, although, as with any bit that is left on constantly, care must be taken to avoid a sore mouth due to hay becoming entangled in it. As mentioned elsewhere, a one-eyed blinker can prove effective. A severe case

whilst they may be more controllable in one there is a great danger that they may become jibbers, and at best they are unlikely to leave the gate well in their races. In many cases pulling is associated with having the tongue over the bit, and this habit must be guarded against. In America a tongue tie made of crêpe bandage is used, which is simple and effective, but British horses tend to be out at exercise for an hour or more which makes this method unsuitable for daily use. A figure of eight, or cross, noseband is effective in keeping the mouth shut, which discourages the habit, and is also useful to prevent pulling. Care should be taken to fit the noseband correctly so that the horse breathes normally. An even easier method to control this habit before it becomes confirmed is an ordinary nose band with a flash, a thin strap attached by a loop to the front of the nose band and secured beneath the chin [26].

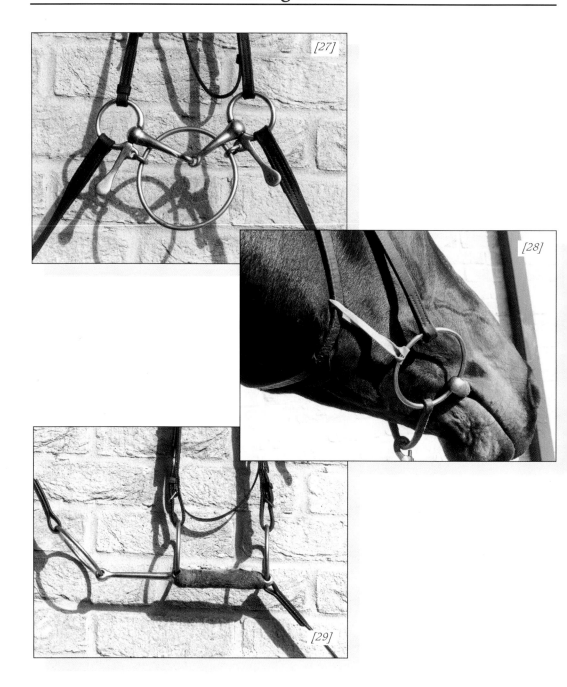

that fails to respond to any of these methods can wear a sidelining bit in his races. In this case it might be better to reserve the special bit for racedays. This bit can be easily made by any local engineering firm from stainless steel rod by utilizing three rings cannibalised from ordinary snaffles. It can be used for horses that hang in either direction by simply reversing the mouthpiece so that the extension bar is on the other side. If necessary the mouthpiece can be covered with leather or vetwrap [29].

Two other useful bits to have are a

combination of the mouthpiece of a regular keyed breaking bridle and the loose rings of an ordinary snaffle [30], and the mouthpiece of a standard pelham or kimblewick, again with snaffle rings [31]. These combinations are easily made up by a local engineering firm. The former can be very useful in giving an irritable or highly strung animal something to think about, and is well worth trying for a variety of mouth and behavioural problems. It has a lot more play than the unaltered version. The latter can be very useful for any animal that would normally be considered a candidate for a rubber bit, or for a horse with cuts on the inside of his cheeks. This bit does not close in on a horse like a snaffle; the port sits on top of the tongue and it seems to be almost as gentle as a rubber bit even though

most racing people would think of it as a severe mouthpiece because of its normal association with a curb chain. It can easily be covered with vetwrap. The main advantage is that although it is easy on a horse's mouth there is more control than with a rubber bit should it be needed. There is less of a problem in changing horses back into the normal steel snaffle from this bit than we often experience when using a rubber one. A curved mouthpiece, which can be covered with leather or vetwrap, is easily adapted from a regular snaffle [32].

A very hard-pulling horse is worth trying in a modification of the harness racer's lip strap. A nylon sock, or something similar, is fitted under the top lip, passed above the bit, pulled fairly tight and tied under the chin [33]. Care should

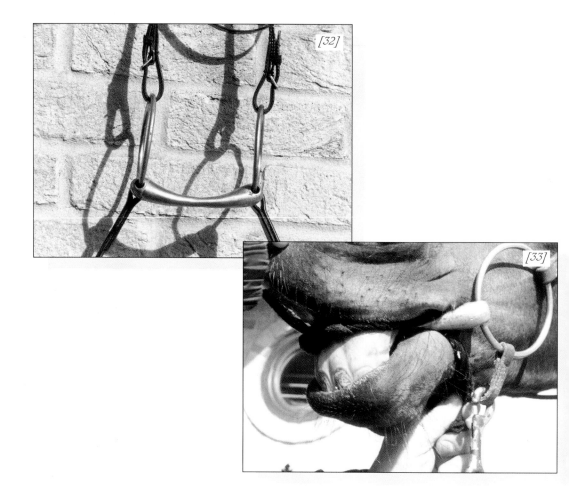

be taken to ensure that the horse is comfortable, but the pressure of the bit will exert some pull on the nerves below the gum. In many cases this produces good results. Great care should be taken not to damage the gum and this method should only be used with a considerate rider. The strap can be easily removed without dismounting once the horse gets used to it, and can be useful in getting headstrong animals to the start but it should normally be removed before the race. If it is retained for the race, most likely on a horse racing longer distances, the rider must be fully aware of the potential severity of this equipment and ride accordingly. This strap can sometimes be useful as a short-term distraction with a particularly nervous or rebellious

animal, but its use in such situations should be undertaken with care.

The 'Australian' rubber modified overchecks are quite fashionable in England, but of little use. When tight enough to keep the bit high in the horse's mouth as intended they tend to pull the bridle forward over his ears. A more effective device can easily be made from a loop of elastic [34], stitched or taped to the centre of the bit [35], which passes around the nose and attaches to a strap running down the face. The bit is held tight to the roof of the mouth and the strap down the face may also prove a slight psychological barrier to a puller [36]. Brondesbury was very headstrong and wore this nose band when winning six out of seven at two years, including breaking the track record at Royal Ascot.

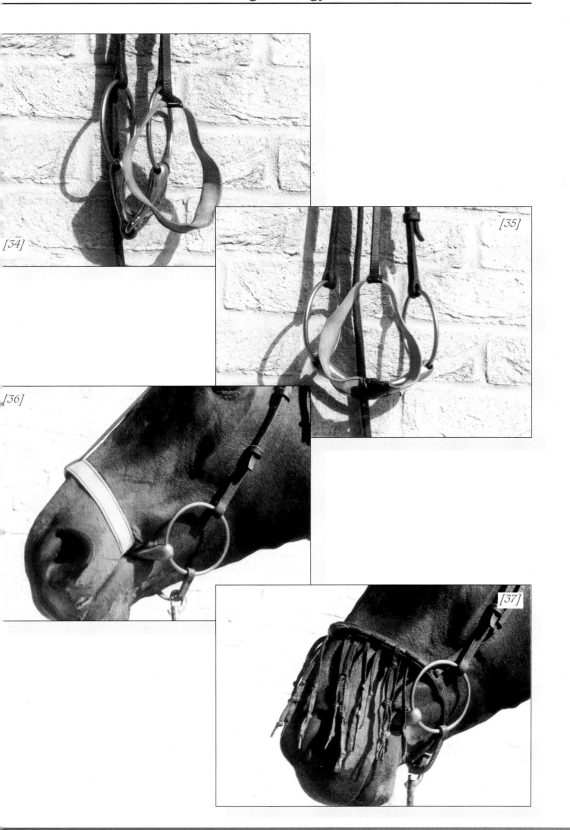

[34]

[35]

[36]

[37]

It is as well to have a very light running martingale amongst the racing equipment as some hard pullers take advantage of its absence on race day. It can be let out at the start once the horse has arrived there quietly. Although most horses do seem to pull far less at the races than in the mornings, care should always be taken to ensure that those horses that are headstrong do go down steadily to the start, with their heads against the rail. We are not interested in trials of strength, only in the result of the race. Obviously there is no problem in America as the horses have a pony to lead them to the gate.

Sheepskin nosebands, or shadow rolls, are borrowed from harness racing, where staying on stride is vital, and are intended to prevent a horse from trying to jump minor irregularities, tracks, footprints, divots, pieces of debris, or shadows when he is racing. The most dramatic demonstration of what can happen may have been when Dayjur threw away the 1990 Breeders' Cup Sprint by hurdling the shadow of the grandstand; the situation may have been saved by fitting this noseband, particularly as he had previously demonstrated similar tendencies at Longchamp. This addition can prove effective in improving the head carriage of some animals with a tendency to stargaze. A horse that seems easily distracted by his surroundings can be tried in blinkers with a shadow roll attached to the bottom edge.

Sometimes we find a horse that, racing on dirt, repeatedly shakes his head as the kickback hits his nose. If he is basically racing well but is just too conscious of anything touching his nose it may be worth fitting a nose band with a fringe which constantly flaps against him to take his mind off the sand hitting him [37]. This problem of head shaking is occasionally noticed at exercise in heavy rain or when snow is falling, but in most cases it will be no more than a nuisance. It seems likely that the effect of the dirt hitting the eyeshields used by some stables may be if anything more distracting than the effect of it hitting the horse's face.

British racing is famous for the variety of its courses. Unfortunately most of them do have undesirable characteristics of one sort or another, and we should give a certain amount of consideration to whether or not a particular animal is likely to handle a particular track. The greatest race in the world, the Epsom Derby, happens to be run on one of the worst courses in the world, with a severe camber throughout the straight. At Royal Ascot, the best horses in the country must actually race across a public highway covered by mats and cut grass in all races on the straight course.

Long-striding and inexperienced horses should not be expected to excel on very sharp or undulating tracks, and nonstayers cannot be guaranteed to get home on stiff, galloping tracks. However, as in the matter of distance, the strength of the opposition is a strong factor in any decision-making. Our efforts are more likely to bear fruit against weak opponents on less than ideal tracks than against better horses on more suitable ones. We must always play the percentages in order to succeed, and a sound knowledge not only of all courses, but also of our horses' preferences is essential.

The statement that a good horse goes on any ground may be simplistic, quite apart from the difficulty of finding a good horse! It is probably true to say however that a decent horse will always go on decent ground, even though he may demonstrate a preference for either top of the ground or for soft ground. Very few horses actually like either heavy ground or rock-hard ground, although some are less inconvenienced than others and so may apparently show great improvement. As mentioned elsewhere, heavy ground should be avoided with two-year-olds unless a golden opportunity presents itself. Horses that interfere are more likely to do so on very soft ground as their front feet cannot breakover quite so fast as on top of the ground.

The Human Element

"Man that is born of woman is of few days, and full of trouble." Job 14:1

The labour situation in British racing is already quite serious and is deteriorating steadily. There are now very few lads left who went through the old apprenticeship system which, for all its disadvantages, did at least produce staff who had some idea of the plot. There is such a shortage of labour nowadays that a lad may be given four horses to look after before he is capable of doing one reasonably well, which is hardly a recipe for successful staff training.

This problem is common to all stables and we will need to work within the framework currently available to produce our horses in the best shape possible. Hopefully we can at the same time instruct our lads in a sound appreciation of what the job should involve, although in an industry with no qualification-based system for advancement this may prove difficult. When the labour pool is so inadequate that even very poor staff may be paid the maximum wage for the job there is obviously little incentive for self-improvement and there is also considerable resentment amongst those older lads who have served their apprenticeship.

The roots of the staff problem trace directly to those old-time trainers, particularly those who trained for the racing Establishment, who for many years shamelessly exploited waifs from the inner cities as apprentice jockeys. In many instances, there was no intention of these boys being anything other than cheap labour in the stableyard during the 5, or even 7, years for which they were inescapably bound to their master. Although the indenture system did produce competent stablemen, most of these apprentices were denied the chance to be jockeys. Unfortunately, the system failed to pay them a living wage when they did come out of their time, because there was always a stream of new apprentices coming in from big families in the slums who were only too pleased to get their offspring off the feed bill. As soon as there were jobs available in factories, the better lads began to leave racing in search of a decent wage; consequently, those apprentices who were still coming in were advanced more quickly and with less instruction into boardwagemen. As there are no longer, thank goodness, virtual starvation conditions in the big cities, the school leavers are now physically bigger and less inclined to seek employment in racing.

The Jockey Club never monitored the abuse of the apprenticeship system by trainers, to ensure that boys indentured as jockeys were either given rides or given early release from their long indentures. Had they done so then the system might have survived. The eventual half-cocked solution of a one-year apprenticeship is impractical because an apprentice can now leave after some time has been wasted on him and go elsewhere, often on full wages. This ridiculous scenario is discouraging both to any trainer genuinely prepared to teach an apprentice and to those older lads who have a lifetime's experience. A proper apprenticeship should imply an agreement in which both parties have clearly defined responsibilities and there are mutual benefits. If a trainer takes the trouble to teach an apprentice then he should expect to have a useful staff member for at least the second half of the apprenticeship term, whilst on the other hand the graduate pupil should expect to be able to earn a decent wage based on the fact he has completed a lengthy course of practical study.

It is only fair to relate that not all the old trainers were so derelict in their duties and that some, though very autocratic by modern standards, did fulfil their side of the bargain. Possibly the greatest producer of both competent jockeys and top class stablemen was the late Fred Armstrong, father of Robert, the present Newmarket trainer, who is remembered with grudging affection by his many graduates as 'Sammy'. His young riders at one time virtually circled the globe as jockeys and the stablemen he produced were the best boardwagemen in the country.

The old racing lad did take a certain pride in his calling even to the extent that he would be outraged at the idea of using a four-pronged fork, which was considered a labourer's tool; a racing lad only used a pitchfork! One such was Don Tilbury, a well-known character in Newmarket and a relic of an even earlier era, as he would have been apprenticed before the Great War. He would only do two horses (in fact, the traditional term to denote a racing lad is 'doing his two'), but he was so meticulous that he even scrubbed the handles of his fork and broom. Don wore a clean stable rubber around his waist as an apron and he always came to work in a suit. Like many of his profession he was inclined to consume all his wages in liquid form and when it was gone he would be obliged to tap his workmates for drinking money before setting out for the bar in the White Hart: "Give us two bob for a Guinness. I only want an entry fee, I'll be all right once I get in!" This was about 1963, with two bob being 10p in new money.

The relationship between a horse and his lad can be pivotal to the success, or otherwise, of his racing career, even if this is not widely appreciated. Although this mainly involves the amount of patience required to deal with a

nervous or irritable animal, there are occasions when almost the reverse may be true. We sometimes see the situation, normally with a very quiet lad, in which the horse gradually takes the upper hand in the relationship and becomes increasingly aggressive and dominant towards his groom. The horse is probably just declaring himself as leader of their two-member herd, but the partnership should be split up before any real problems arise. This tricky situation will need very tactful handling, particularly if they are both highly valued team members. The original lad will not want to give up a useful horse and his successor must not be allowed to make a big thing of the affair, either with the horse or to the other staff. This type of horse should be given to a lad who will be very firm with him but who will otherwise virtually ignore him. If the problem is promptly addressed it should disappear very quickly, but once the horse starts to warm to his theme we may have a real problem. A ticklish horse should never be aggravated by being overgroomed; he can easily be kept looking well by use of one of the showshine-type products. In the old days, many horses became savage due to excessive strapping, and that is one aspect of the old system we are well rid of. It must always be understood that any lad knocking his horses about will be dismissed. Anyone whose horses seem afraid of him in the box is likely to be guilty of spiteful behaviour towards them, and must be kept under close observation. This type of lad can be extremely plausible and so often remains undiscovered. Even though the lad might manage to become quite a teacher's pet, his horses' demeanour is not contrived and will accurately predict his handler's true character. It is noticeable that a lad who might have corrected one of his charges quite severely in the proper circumstances will not obtain the same cowering reaction from his horse whenever he approaches it. Lads will tend never to report even serious misdemeanours by their contemporaries, and we should never assume

Timeless Times (USA), summer 1990 - about the time of his record-equalling sixteenth win. The ideal type of the 'cheap-and-cheerful' runner. Sixteen seems to be a hard number to surpass - both Citation and Cigar also foundered upon it! For some reason, his devoted lad Alan Houston is not in the picture. (Photo courtesy of Laurie Morton)

that we would be informed of transgressions which the staff as a whole know perfectly well are not acceptable in the best interests of the stable. We should take care to remember Darvill's advice that "Lads are tricky".

An old horse may appear to be very sore, particularly in his slower paces, but still race well. It is recommended that the same lad ride him all the time so as to be able to judge whether he is any worse than usual. Although these horses are never part of our master plan, they do occur from time to time and, as we can't sell them, we must do what we can with them.

Some of the old sprinters can be extremely stiff, and may well not appreciate trotting to loosen up, but with care and patience they may still race very effectively. Listed-race winners Gypsy Dancer and Camisite were cripples when they first came out in the morning, but their riders understood their varying degrees of lameness and the rate at which they warmed up, and these horses had long and fruitful careers. Horses carrying chronic unsoundnesses are better ridden by the lad who looks after them, as long as he is capable of handling them at exercise, because naturally he will have more of a vested interest in their welfare.

Adequan injections or an oral supplementation with chondroitin sulphate are likely to help these old horses to cope with their aches and pains, without risking the horrendous breakdowns that often follow the use of anti-inflammatory drugs. It is also well worth experimenting with isoxsuprine in these cases as it will sometimes produce dramatic results almost overnight, especially if arthritis is not their only problem. This is an extremely volatile substance and clearance times are difficult to estimate; great care must be taken when this drug comes anywhere near horses running in the forseeable future.

Both Group One performer Milk Of The Barley and Provideo were horrible horses to do in the box, and their successes might well have been less with different grooms. Group One winner Mac's Imp was also a very uncertain-tempered individual both in and out of the stable and both his lad and his exercise rider deserved great credit for their efforts. Timeless Times was a very kind horse and his excellent lad was devoted to him. Funnily enough, this lad was sometimes dominated by a horse he was too soft with in the box, although he was a good hand breaking yearlings.

Girls as a whole may care more for their charges than males do, and they therefore tend to look after them better with minimum prompting. There was at one time a feeling that girls should not be given colts to care for, but as long as they behave sensibly and professionally towards their horses we should not experience any problems.

All staff should appear as polite and helpful as possible to any visiting owner, but should be instructed to be noncommittal when discussing their horses in order to avoid raising expectations which the horse, and the trainer, might find impossible to deliver. In fact, it is quite remarkable how interested many owners are in the lad's opinion of their animals, very often attributing to them more weight than to those of the trainer. This problem will never disappear and trainers should always keep it in mind. Sometimes we may get the distinct impression that secretive relationships may exist between one of our owners and a particular lad, or even with the stable jockey, which might not be conducive to the best interests of the stable as a whole. Should we suspect such a relationship then we must take care to keep our own counsel with regard to the prospects and programmes for the horses other than discussing them with their individual owners. In this situation no one should become aware of our opinion of any promising animal, and it should be looked after and ridden at exercise by a lad who is not involved in any such mutual admiration society. This might seem a little dramatic, but this situation definitely implies either lack of trust in the trainer or a certain deviousness and if such situations are allowed to flourish unchecked they will invariably end in unpleasantness of some description.

Whilst we cannot return to the good old bad old days, the labour situation does need some sort of a plan to ensure a decent wage is paid for a job well done, but how this can be achieved is difficult to envisage. It is unrealistic to expect the present apprentice training school to produce in a matter of weeks what used to take years, and the prognosis is presently poor on the labour front. We can only hope to attract the best of what is currently available, and to train them in a system that will stand them in good stead when they move on.

Jockeys and Raceriding

"Their strength is to sit still." Isaiah 30:7

The problem of securing a jockey to ride for us deserves careful consideration. Jockeyship is one of the least understood aspects of the whole sport, even by the younger jockeys themselves. This last fact is hardly surprising in view of the previous observations on the apprenticeship system, as even the most elementary technical foundations have never been laid in many cases. This need not imply any less natural ability than the riders of previous generations but merely a shortfall in knowledge of the basic, never mind the finer, points of their profession.

Unfortunately, the majority of what is currently printed on race-riding is so lacking in even the most elementary understanding as to be embarrassing, and we should review a few indisputable facts before considering how best to achieve our aims in this vital area. Many sportsmen share certain fundamental difficulties and, in most sports, addressing these shortcomings has become a growth industry, with household names regularly attending clinics and consulting various gurus. It is not at all necessary that these advisors be top class protagonists themselves in order to have a clear understanding of the many problems involving effective techniques, and we may explore the subject at some length on that basis. For a clear explanation of the basic techniques of jockeyship, John Hislop's works are still as good as any and should still be studied by all apprentices, and by most of the racing press.

In an ideal situation, the horse might be considered simply an extension of the jockey's legs, or the running department, and the jockey the refinement of the partnership's thinking and planning department. If we could organise things on this simple precept, life would be very easy for all concerned. In practice, little attempt

The importance of aerodynamic forces on the racehorse is generally ignored in Britain and the American style is widely criticised. Emma on Mr Yong's Goldfame, our final winner. (Photo courtesy of Proshot)

is made to transform an uneasy coalition into a single entity, rather the reverse being true, with the two components often hampering each other's efforts. Because there are no absolute methods of defining success in a sport where every combination changes from race to race, poor techniques are very likely to become accepted if they are associated with winning performances. This obviously influences the riding of youngsters, as they always seek to imitate the generation before them, and standards of practice may tend to slip even further. The undeniable fact is that very many wins may still be achieved because of the natural ability of one partner, and despite the technically faulty input of the other.

The success in recent years of several at least partial exponents of the much tidier American style may be one positive step. Use of the stick is very contentious at the moment but if dramatic improvement does not very soon take place in this regard there must be a real prospect of the matter being taken out of the hands of the racing authorities, as has already happened in Scandinavia where the use of the whip is banned. Over 100 years ago, Admiral Rous was of the opinion that no more than six jockeys in England were fit to be entrusted with a whip, while Fred Archer, certainly in his latter years, rarely hit his mounts more than two or three times. The present out-and-out reliance on the whip is unprofessional, unneccessary and unacceptable at the threshold of the third millennium.

With a view to determining the actual class of riders currently available in Britain, it seems reasonable to expect any top class rider with regular high class mounts to far outstrip his peers in winning percentage. Although this is true of the various local leaders in America, who may boast win-to-race percentage results in the high twenties, it is not currently true in Britain, where the leaders' figures currently tend towards the high teens or possibly 20%. Fred Archer rode 34% winners in his lifetime, and Lester Piggott

regularly achieved between 25 and 28% when in his prime. This is an extremely crude method of evaluation, but it may confirm the impression that we have little to fear should we decide to appoint a stable jockey and refine their skills as we go, given that the opposition contrive, at best, to get it wrong 80 times out of every 100 attempts on the choicest mounts!

One of the most glaring misapprehensions shared by the racing press and the man in the betting office (the natural successor to that paragon of intelligence, the man on the Clapham omnibus) is that vigour in the saddle has some direct connection to skill in the saddle. It does not. Racing cannot conceivably be the only sport where a skilful performer makes his task appear difficult. In any other discipline involving aerodynamics in any way, the absolute reverse is true. The ultimate objective in every speed-related sport is complete smoothness of action. This is not a matter of opinion, it is a matter of fact. No rider can hope to achieve his maximum potential until he accepts this truth and tries to improve himself aerodynamically, although he may obviously ride very many winners without doing so.

Every horse must have a maximum speed, and by definition he cannot ever exceed that speed. Without doubt, any resistance or additional hindrance he encounters must reduce it. It must follow that a theoretical horse, which had been trained to run to the limit of his speed, would gallop faster with a motionless dead weight than if that weight were moving about. However strong or vigorous the rider might appear, no horse will ever be able to run faster than his true capability in any given situation. The task of the jockey should be seen as trying to engineer that set of circumstances most favourable to his mount's best effort. Some confusion may arise because any animal may well run better for a perceived strong rider, but the horse must still be, by definition, within his physical capabilities. Our aim should be to have our horse run as near as necessary to his ultimate capability with the minimum of abuse so as to prolong his enthusiasm, and hence his career, for as long as possible. It should be apparent by this point that practical common sense is the foundation of this whole training method, and that we cannot ever afford to accept illogical thought processes, however widely accepted.

Whether most horses can ever attain their optimum speed under a punishing ride is difficult to ascertain, although logic would appear to suggest that more efficient, and therefore faster, stride patterns could be expected under different circumstances. There seems no good reason to suppose that a tiring horse can possibly be other than hampered when his cargo shifts violently in the closing stages of his race, although fortunately for him the opposition are sure to be in similar distress. We can very often see horses floundering at the end of a race like drowning men; their need at this point is for encouragement and stability in aid of their extreme effort. Unfortunately, what they very often get instead is 120lbs of struggling burden! Of course, we must realise that any jockey would require considerable *sang froid* to sit still and attempt to nurse a staggering horse home before the present ill-informed audience, and that the situation is unlikely to improve until there is a better understanding of this subject by all watchers of the sport.

In his interesting video on race-riding, Pat Day, an American rider very much in the mould of the legendary Bill Shoemaker, suggests a simple test for those who doubt these precepts. He suggests that anyone experimenting with a small child riding on their shoulders will immediately become aware of the difference between carrying a motionless passenger and an animated one. Whether providing the small child with a whip can regain the momentum lost by the additional drag can obviously be evaluated on an individual basis. If in fact this experiment were to prove the case for vigorous whip riding, then all rowing teams might usefully include a strong cox with a stick rather than the present unobtrusive figure purely encouraging and directing the rowers. However well our horses may have been taught to carry and balance themselves, they cannot be expected to keep the jockey balanced as well.

A good jockey may be observed to alter the course of his mount when it is tending to hang one way or the other by the use of his own bodyweight, and will be rightly praised for his action. There seems no reason to suppose that the shifting weight of many riders in their desperate and vigorous finishing efforts do not similarly influence their mounts' direction. Even the most cursory examination of head-on films will demonstrate the erratic course many jockeys follow, even when they are racing in the clear rather than weaving their way through the field. Few people seem to realise that this demonstates defective riding and that the horse is unbalanced. It follows that less than optimum performance is the inevitable result. If our horses and our jockey can proceed from point A to point B without wandering or becoming unbalanced we must have a slight but indisputable advantage.

There are very definite advantages to the policy of retaining a stable jockey. Most victories are won at home to a great extent, due to careful preparation in the stable and on the gallops. Most defeats are also engineered at home by ineffective training or inefficient identification of suitable opportunities. Consistent and often unobtrusive riding by a committed team member should always win more races, or at least lose fewer, than dramatic moves and 'Garrison finishes' by riders unfamiliar with our horses. Those riders who do demonstrate sporadic brilliant efforts invariably produce at least equal numbers of horrifyingly incompetent ones. They seem rather like Longfellow's little girl with the curl in the middle of her forehead: "When she was good, she was very, very good, but when she was bad, she was horrid!"

The simple continuity that a retainer allows is a tremendous advantage, and it often means

Superlative, Tony Ives, just defeats Keen, Lester Piggott, in a desperate struggle at Kempton - the third horse was beaten 25 lengths, and the result of the photo took several minutes to come!
(Photo courtesy of Mel Fordham)

that the horses in the team may survive a longer, more productive season due to the more considerate handling. The contract rider obviously has a vested interest in the season as a whole, whereas a rider with no guarantee of keeping the mount is apt to subscribe to the 'bird in the hand' theory, with no thought of the future prospects of the horse. This can be particularly galling when our horse gets narrowly beaten after he has been subjected to a gruelling race to overcome a bad initial position caused by pilot error. A good retained rider in the same position should remember that two wrongs don't make a right and should accept the situation. We are obliged to keep faith with the retained rider in these circumstances if we expect him to protect our investment in this way. Most trainers, unfortunately, are not prepared to do this nowadays and will automatically blame the rider for any disaster as this gets them off the hook themselves. Although happy to accept all the credit for winners, regardless of the jockey, most trainers are very quick to blame the rider for beaten horses. They seem to deny, even to themselves, their own responsibility for the many races that may be lost due to prerace factors quite beyond the control of the rider.

The two chief assets of any race rider are judgement of pace and traffic sense, both of which are far more honoured in the breach rather than in the observance. Judgement of pace is often understood, particularly by racing scribes, only in its most basic sense, which involves a horse in the lead. In this instance it does not require genius to slow the early fractions as far as possible and then to try to steal a march on the opposition for a dash home. Making strong running in a race is much more complicated in that a jockey must set a pace testing enough to expose any nonstayers amongst his opponents without completely exhausting his own mount. Our stable jockey Tony Ives was an able exponent of this method, and was extremely good at keeping a fading horse balanced at the end. True judgement of pace is when the jockey evaluates the pace of the race when he is back in the field and uses his own horse accordingly, and this skill is often unobtrusive rather than dramatic to watch. An early appreciation of the pace of any race and the ability to predict the likely effect on the final result as far as his own mount is concerned enables the opportunist rider to win races he should have lost.

The knack of consistently finding clear sailing through the field is a rare gift in a jockey. Luck in running is always to be hoped for but, although hope springs eternal in the racing world, common sense also plays a major part and many disastrous hold-ups can be easily anticipated simply through awareness of the strengths and weaknesses of the other runners and riders. Both Alan Munro and Emma O'Gorman showed great natural ability in these two areas of their profession at an early age. Actually there might be said to be a third vital attribute a rider should have, which is the ability to instinctively abandon a preconceived plan should circumstances change. A front-runner cannot be expected to lead if he misses the break, nor can any horse that does not settle be subjected to a wrestling match with any great expectation of winning the race. When things do go wrong our jockey must be able to assume that

we will support any improvisations he may have to make; on the other hand, should departures from the plot become commonplace then they are unlikely to prove constructive and we might be thought to have a communication problem.

Any rider who is not making the running should be alert to the leader attempting to slow things down, and should then either move up to force the pace or should at least be prepared, with his mount already in gear and running, to anticipate the moment when the leader does decide to set sail for home. In a slowly run race he cannot expect to wait until after the leader has moved before calling on his own mount and still expect to succeed, unless of course he is on by far the best horse. In that case he may well prevail, but only after giving his horse an unnecessarily hard race, for which, ironically, the pundits may well congratulate him. If another runner can be induced to challenge the leader and force him to quicken the pace so much the better; but if no one challenges an easy lead the chances are that the leader will hold on and win the race.

If the stable should decide to provide a pacemaker for one of its runners it is essential that intelligent use is made of this aid. There is no sense sitting far back and ignoring the leader; rather, the two riders should have decided before they start just how far and how fast the pacemaker will or can go and the fancied horse should keep fairly close to him.

In a very fast run race, the reverse tactic is indicated and it is correct procedure never to get involved in speed duels if they are avoidable, as even when the first battle is won there is grave danger of defeat by a relatively fresh opponent from the rear. The faster the early fractions, the farther back it is safe to be. As long as he knows that his own mount is sailing along at a good pace, a jockey need not worry if he is even 15 lengths behind. After extremely brisk early fractions the speed in front will usually collapse by more than three seconds over the final three furlongs and the trailing horse will run the leaders down by merely maintaining his gallop, although he may appear to the uninitiated to be flying at the finish. This is one occasion when doing the right thing actually does look exciting. The main danger when attempting to make up ground is the great risk of being impeded by already-beaten horses as they drop away. Any horse that does have a lot of ground to gain can ill afford to get stopped in his run, and it is normally safer to go to the outside and to make one long run at the leaders. Although not so exciting to the onlooker, this smooth progress is far less tiring for the horse. When obliged to lay out of his ground and give his opponents too much start due to events beyond his control, a jockey is usually far safer to lose a couple of extra lengths in order to guarantee one clear run, than to hope to fight his way through the field. Horses making up considerable ground should always be ridden to lead near the line and not a furlong from home as this wastes energy and very often leads to needless defeat.

Many experienced race-watchers fail to weigh up accurately the pros and cons of racing wide or of going the shortest way on the inside rail. Although a smooth run on the inside would obviously be the preferred choice, it is unrealistic to expect to achieve this on a regular basis and many times a far better result would be obtained by concentrating on getting a clear run rather than on saving ground. It is relatively easy to quantify the amount of extra ground covered by racing wide around a turn. The number of horse widths out from the rail, around a 180° turn, will be roughly equal to the number of extra lengths added to the trip. If we take a horse as being one yard wide and roughly three times as long, and calculate the difference in diameter of two half-circles (which represent the two tracks of the inside and the outside horses around one 180° turn) as being 3.14 multiplied by the difference in the two radii, we see that in a six furlong race around one turn the disadvantage of racing four wide is about twelve yards, or about 1% of the distance of the race. This handicap is considerable but it is quantifiable and acceptable. In the unlikely event of a horse remaining hung up four wide for a complete circuit the extra distance would be doubled, although of course a race around two turns would certainly be considerably longer than six furlongs, unless it took place at a bullring in America, and so the disadvantage might be similar in percentage terms. It is highly likely, though not so easy to quantify, that the energy cost of stopping and starting whilst racing in the bunch on the rail will be considerably more than that small percentage. Racing moderately wide effectively eliminates the considerable risk of not being able to move at a critical stage due to traffic problems, which in itself must be more energy efficient. The widely available difference in fuel performance figures for all cars between urban and motorway driving give a clue as to the true cost in energy of acceleration and deceleration as opposed to constant speed. That difference will be seen to be rather more than 1 or 2%.

The only way to be sure of a clear passage whilst taking the shortest route is to make the running, but that plan in itself is fraught with various dangers. The degree of disadvantage due to wind resistance suffered by the leader, which all wheeled sports take very seriously, must be considered. Another serious problem may result from the rider sending a horse away from the gate at high speed in order to gain the lead, and then finding that his mount is always doing too much and wasting energy because he cannot get him to relax again. A horse that has good racing manners will obviously be more likely to execute this strategy successfully, as his rider can dash to the front and then slow the pace down at will, and will thus be able to control the running of the race.

The task of any jockey is made simpler if the horses are properly schooled to race, and a rider who is able to assist in their education is a great asset. This precept is increasingly well understood in the many jump racing yards that now adopt schooling techniques borrowed from other disciplines. It seems less popular in flat stables where jockeys tend to ride fast work on those horses that have identified themselves as being ready to race, but contribute nothing else. If we can find a rider who is prepared to absorb our philosophy towards the business and to become involved on a daily basis, it should be a considerable help. We must aim to produce racehorses that have been trained to race in every sense of those words if we are to enjoy better than average success.

As previously stated, we cannot expect our rider to respect our best interests unless he receives some consideration in return in the form of loyalty. The childish practice of blaming jockeys regardless of what actually happens in a race is not conducive to a lasting relationship. As there is a finite number of riders available, even the most rabid critics are obliged to use the sacked rider again eventually. They should bear in mind that the rider always has the last word on how any horse actually performs and that a jockey may well choose an inconvenient occasion to repay a grievance! The trainer should always decide riding arrangements and riding instructions, and should naturally then accept the responsibility for the performance of the horses. If he is not capable of doing so then he can hardly be capable of making the many other decisions involved in the training process. In 1870, when Mat Dawson heard that Lord Falmouth had given Tom French additional instructions as to riding Wheatear before winning at Newmarket, he requested that his Lordship remove the whole string forthwith "as the confidence which ought to exist between them was evidently gone". Fortunately, matters were resolved, and the partnership was subsequently successful in 12 Classic races.

Whilst on the subject of loyalty, we might wonder how Mr Dawson would have reacted to the all too common scenario of some owners checking on the progess of their (and, very often, other people's!) horses in evening telephone conversations with lads in the yard. As this can hardly be regarded as other than a similar lack of confidence, and as it is sure to lead to trouble, one or both parties should probably be removed from the stable at the earliest convenient opportunity.

There is little fundamental difference between a racehorse and a racing car as far as the actual race is concerned. If all else is equal, the victor will be either the best mounted or whichever one makes most efficient use of the energy available. The one that makes most efficient use of energy is the one whose driver or rider squanders the least energy in acceleration, deceleration and general manoeuvring. In both sports the supply of energy is finite, and once it's gone, it really has gone. Dramatic moves during a race are always expensive in terms of energy expenditure and should be avoided, unless they are made explicitly to take advantage of some difficulty a rival has experienced, and to thereby poach an unassailable lead before he can recover himself sufficiently to mount an effective counterchallenge.

The other reason for avoiding dramatic acceleration is difficult to explain but may involve the collapse of the rhythm that must always be associated with physical effort for best results. Anyone who has ridden a bicycle with the chain slightly loose will recognise that any sudden and violent increase in pedalling will bring the chain off, whereas the pace can certainly be gradually and carefully increased. A brick can be carefully pushed across a shiny surface using only a drinking straw, as long as we don't suddenly increase the pressure, but if we do the straw immediately crumples and everything stops. An angler with a big fish on a light line is in the same position, and must be careful not to overplay his hand. Situations that threaten to disrupt to some degree the smooth tempo of a horse's running arise in most races. The loss of momentum, when these minor crises are clumsily handled, is often dramatic and irreversible.

The importance of maintaining rhythm for

the efficient use of energy is demonstrated when any horse that is apparently travelling well folds up in two or three strides simply because his rider has failed to build some momentum gradually before demanding extra effort, or has failed to allow his mount an opportunity to recover his composure following some sudden disruption to their progress. In these cases the horse is often labelled dishonest because he found nothing when asked to quicken. Although the jockey may well be at fault, he will probably avoid censure because to most people it looks as if he is trying hard. The fact that he is trying hard to do the wrong thing is not generally appreciated! In shorter races, particularly juvenile events, it is very common to see horses being completely bustled off their legs and running deplorably. In many cases, losing another two or three lengths in the early stages would allow them to hit their best stride and therefore to run much better. It will always prove difficult to convict a competent rider of deliberately stopping a horse by utilising this plan simply because to all intents and purposes he appears to have ridden an aggressive race. A variation on this situation often occurs with a horse that runs much too freely in the early stages of his race, only apparently to stop to nothing because his jockey wrongly expects that power to remain instantly at his disposal – despite the fact that he has spent sometimes several furlongs trying to reduce it. In cases where the horse may still have some energy reserves it seems only reasonable to inform him of the change of plan before hitting the panic button. An automobile is unable to accelerate quickly without being informed of the driver's intentions by means of a gear-change, and, in this respect at least, a horse is not dissimilar. The jockey must always be sure he has his mount 'in his hands', ready for the instruction to accelerate, before calling on him for that acceleration. He cannot expect to change instantly from pulling to pushing. However, as remarked by Eddie Delahoussaye below, it is

unreasonable to expect the younger jockeys to learn the finer points of their craft never having been instructed on those points.

Many horses will run extremely impressively if the race goes fast and they are allowed to drop out of early contention in the race and settle into their own rhythm in the early stages. These horses are further examples of the above delicate balance between success and absolute disaster, and they are often quite incapable of making their own pace in a slower run race. Fortunately, they are often best served by the furious pace of big fields in valuable handicaps, but they are always extremely vulnerable against even lesser opposition in a small field, and we should always appreciate the problem that they present for the rider. This lack of tactical speed will always be a serious drawback and these horses should be sold if, as often happens after a valuable handicap, a good price can be obtained. Mac's Fighter was a prime example of this. Although not as good in smaller fields with a more moderate pace, he did win the Wokingham Handicap at Royal Ascot with 9st 12lbs on his back, and he was beaten a nose by Steinlen in the Laurel Dash, because in both of those races the pace was very strong. Unfortunately, he was subsequently faced with impossible tasks by the handicapper, we kept him too long, and he was eventually sold for a tiny fraction of his one-time value.

Varying styles of jockeyship can be equally effective, subject to certain basic rules, and the only method of comparing one rider with another objectively may be by computer comparison between the speed figures allotted to all horses after all races. The London School of Economics, which presumably has some experience of data collation, seemed to view this exercise (by Computerform) as the only realistic method of comparison. Many of the racing press were outraged at the variations with their own perceptions of relative riding skills, but the premise seems to be sound and might well be used as a starting point in our search for a stable jockey. This method of rating jockeys might be regarded as similar to using the Comparative Earnings Index for more accurate evaluation of stallions. It will afford a more reliable guide to the actual contribution that can be anticipated from the jockey in any horse/rider combination than will the simpler percentage of winning rides. The winning percentage figure can be compared to the Average Earnings Index because it is similarly distorted by the contribution made by the racehorse, in the case of jockeys, and by the mare in the case of stallions. If this theory has a weakness it is that, possibly, unfashionable riders might tend to persevere more with beaten horses than do those more in demand. This fact might distort up or down the value of figures earned by those beaten horses and so account for some of the apparent anomalies. The definitive comparison might be one involving the ratings of only horses that finish in the money.

Once a stable jockey has been appointed and is riding work daily, we should ensure that they play their part in educating our young horses. This does not mean purely in their fast work because when they are cantering, and even whilst they are walking, their earlier lessons can always be practiced and reinforced. Making our horses handier and more responsive to the signals they will receive in a race must, at the very least, make them more tactically efficient in that race. We should ideally like to achieve a situation where some horses could sense where to go next purely by following the body language of their rider and so always remain ahead of the game. This may sound far-fetched, but something like this does happen for example with cutting horses when working cattle, with good polo ponies and with the horses ridden by huntsmen and whippers-in. This skill certainly would be an interesting tool for any jockey to develop. In fact the very best riders, when right at the top of their game, may be practising something like this unconsciously. Certainly they do at times seem instinctively and effortlessly to extricate themselves from the field, with the horse weaving his way through just as if he were following a map.

Particularly in two-year-old races, although we never wish to give a horse an unnecessarily hard race, it is as well to guard against any idling or greenness. If our horse is leading he should be sent about his business between the three and two furlong markers so as to forestall any challengers, and to put the race beyond doubt. Failure to do this often results in a hard race between our horse, which is now getting slightly bored in front, and a rival that may have taken time to get the hang of things. The outcome very often favours the one closing, and riding to avoid this situation should always be stable policy.

There is something to be said for the rider always being alert to the possibility of stealing a march on his rivals whenever he thinks he has a good chance of lasting home. Although it seems rather drastic, this policy should always be considered on a confirmed short runner, a horse that seems to have difficulty lasting out even the minimum trip. Waiting in front in the hope of conserving their energy almost always results in these animals dying in their rider's hands and fading out of contention. Short runners that do get into the habit of waiting in front and then weakening dramatically tend to get progressively worse. This is always a potential problem with a very fast two-year-old, and we may inadvertently confirm this disastrous habit even in his work.

Brondesbury almost went round again when he won his first race, and he almost went to the top of the town after his second win at Newmarket, so presumably did not have a congenital stamina problem at a sprinting level. Once his racing career started he was so much faster off the mark than his workmates that he was soon in grave danger of becoming a confirmed short runner purely because he had settled the work very quickly and then lost interest. As he was extremely headstrong, it was not advisable to fire him up further in those circumstances by trying to make him work out to the end and the whole thing became very worrying. He did in fact just last home over the very stiff Ascot track, and actually broke the track record, but had he not been sent about his business by Tony Ives when he already held a clear advantage there would have been a very different result. This type of horse should be kept in regular competition if at all possible in order to avoid compounding these difficulties in his home work.

Should the situation be reversed, and the leader make an early dash for home, our jockey must never attempt to overhaul an early departed rival anywhere but in the shadow of the winning post, as too hasty a pursuit will use our horse up. It is vital not to compound the mistake of getting too far behind by trying to regain the ground too quickly. To the uneducated eye a dramatic challenge,even though faltering into defeat after regaining the lost ground too quickly, may appear to be dynamic riding, but for best results the lost ground should always be regained as gradually and unobtrusively as possible.

The easiest race for any horse is a waiting race, as he is benefiting from the horses ahead of him taking the brunt of the air resistance, and he may only actually be racing for a short distance. Unfortunately, many horses lack any meaningful natural acceleration and connections often feel forced into more aggressive and energy-depleting tactics. For some reason, not enough attention is given to the fact that very few horses can maintain their maximum speed for more than one and a half or two furlongs whether they are racing in front or behind. Many more races might be won, without the necessity of quickening, if more conservative tactics were used to ensure mounting a challenge only after the opposition had exhausted itself and was slowing down. To experiment with this form of riding a jockey requires a strong nerve but, as the strain on our

horses is obviously appreciably lessened we should encourage the practice.

There are no longer any riders in Britain like Scobie Breasley who would repeatedly get up to win on the line, with no one except himself knowing what, if anything, he had in hand. A famous story relates that a senior member of the Jockey Club congratulated Mrs Mae Breasley on a great victory during Scobie's subsequent training career. The worthy gentleman reportedly said, "Well done! I hope Scobie had a good bet?" Mrs Breasley, slightly surprised, replied, "Oh no, Scobie hasn't had a bet since he gave up riding!" (Jockeys, of course, are forbidden to bet.) Fortunately, this delicate skill is not completely a thing of the past. In a *Racing Post* interview, Bill Shoemaker recently said, regarding fellow Hall of Fame member Eddie Delahoussaye: "He knows how much horse he has, and he knows how not to show it. That's something you learn as you get older." In the same piece by Dan Farley, Delahoussaye remarks that little instruction, or criticism, is given to young riders nowadays, so "How can a young rider learn any respect? How can they learn to ride?"

Jockeys might often bluff their way through races they should have lost if they paid more attention to this theory of disguising just how much horse they have, or with what reserve of energy their mount has to finish, instead of telegraphing their every intention to their rivals. George Fordham was the bane of the great Fred Archer's life, especially on the straight course at Newmarket, and apparently took great pleasure in outwitting his younger rival, who was the darling of the racing world, not to mention the country as a whole. Flinging his saddle to the ground after a tactical defeat by his older adversary, Archer exclaimed, "I can't beat that kidding bastard!"

The finer points of race-riding were, of course, far more appreciated in Fordham's heyday when match racing was popular. A match, from the original challenge, through the weighting of the horses, to the actual race, was based on disguising one's strengths and weaknesses from one's opponents, and prompting them to make mistakes. Heat racing also called for much more tactical riding, particularly as the odds would vary as the contest progressed, and decisions had to be made as to whether to try for an early victory or merely to save your distance to continue in the hope of winning in the end. The longest recorded harness race took 12 one mile heats over 2 days to resolve at Independence, Iowa, in 1891. Birchwood, a two-year-old, finished third! An accurate estimation of how much horse was left, both in your own case and amongst the opposition, must have been essential for success in those days. The winners of such long contests tended to be those, both equine and human, with the best racing technique.

It is essential that all jockeys be able to change both their hands on the reins and their whip hand without even thinking about it. Both these skills should be practised day in and day out so that their implementation needs no thought at all. A piano player, for instance, does not need to look at the keys and he could not play anything remotely difficult if he did so. On a more mundane level, a master bricklayer barely looks at each brick, yet lays great numbers with amazing precision. If, by constant practice, our rider does make his technical skills similarly automatic he becomes more effectively part of his mount, and has much more time to watch the race unfold.

There are two basic reasons for a jockey to change his hands and they should involve very different techniques. In the first case the rider may feel that he needs a slightly shorter hold of a horse that is taking a strong hold of the bridle, and in this situation he should achieve his aim as quietly as possible to avoid further exciting his mount. The reins should always be held in a double rather than a single bridge to enable him to pick up a couple of inches virtually unnoticed by the horse. In the second case he does wish to convey some urgency to his mount and he

changes his hold more aggressively as a signal to a lazy horse that he should extend himself. However, unless the horse is exceptionally idle, and he really wishes to threaten it with dire consequences unless it wakes its ideas up, he should never take his hands away from his mount's neck when changing his hands for fear of unbalancing him. The untidy practice of ostentatious hand-changing may currently be widely accepted, but except in the specific case of attempting to frighten a bone idle horse to greater efforts without resort to the whip, it is incorrect. It must tend to unbalance the animal and thus to create a further drain on energy. Most horses that have been properly schooled using the method described will usually do very nearly all that they are capable of for a rider that they respect without any resort to the whip. The problem is that many horses, particularly older or lazier ones, very soon realise that they need not respect their riders, and the jockey then is obliged to attempt to establish his authority with the whip. The horse can still only achieve a finite degree of speed whether under the whip for an incomplete rider for whom he may have little regard or voluntarily for a rider whom he respects. Frankie Durr was a great exponent of this form of hand-riding, and although a very strong jockey, he was not obliged to rely upon his whip, simply because he was enough of a horseman that his mounts believed him when he indicated to them that more effort was required.

Changing the whip from one hand to the other is also a vital accomplishment, as failure to do so can easily lead to the disqualification of the horse and to the suspension of the jockey. The whip must be immediately either put away or preferably transferred to the other hand as soon as any horse leaves a straight line. The only permissible exception to this rule is when the horse has no opponents anywhere near him on the side to which he is hanging, and he is running on strongly, with the outcome of the struggle so close as to be possibly affected by

It was hard to think of a sensible reply when the Stewards asked whether African Chimes was suitable for an apprentice! (Photo courtesy of Leslie Sampson)

making the switch. When involved in a Steward's Enquiry, the jockey who has changed his whip as promptly as possible will normally be given the benefit of any doubt. As mentioned elsewhere, hand-riding is always to be preferred, from every point of view, whenever possible.

The ability to speak clearly when involved in an enquiry is another useful skill for a jockey. In Britain, because of the the lack of daily and practical experience on the part of many of the amateur stewards, a clever presentation of the jockey's case, especially if reinforced by just the right amount of injured innocence, can often carry the day. It is preferable that our jockey always maintains good relations with the authorities, as we have no wish for our horses to be penalised on his account.

One very amusing incident in a Steward's Enquiry, which might give a clue as to the proficiency or otherwise to be encountered in such meetings, took place when an old horse was involved in a minor scrimmage with another unplaced animal. As is quite usual in an instance where neither stood to get the race, both riders virtually denied ever having seen each other during the contest and were eventually dismissed. After the enquiry the trainer was called back before the bench, and the following interview occurred. Chairperson of Stewards, slightly exasperated by failure to secure a conviction: "Mr Trainer, do you really think this horse is a suitable mount for an apprentice?" Trainer, slightly puzzled: "Well, she has ridden him to 10 wins so far, and six others have only managed one between them!" In fact, 17 different riders eventually tried unsuccessfully to win on African Chimes, including the very best, although he did eventually win 18 races for his apprentice partner.

The opinions of even the most successful jockeys are rarely of much help to us as long as we are truly aware of the abilities of our horses, and in fact can be very misleading. In all aspects of this business we must be guided by what we see with our own two eyes, both every morning and in the race. The owner of Reesh was informed by an excellent senior rider, following his only ride on the horse, that this horse would be better suited by a mile, as he lacked speed. Reesh proceeded subsequently to win four consecutive stakes, three of them Group races, over five and six furlongs. An equally common mistake is the supposition that any horse that is run out of the money in the final furlong has failed to stay the trip; in many cases he has been defeated because he could not quicken, and he actually needs further.

There are many similar cases, for jockeys very often say the first thing that comes into their heads. To be fair, there is a widespread expectation on the part of many owners and trainers of some explanation, however bizarre,

Reesh won four major sprints at three - despite a senior rider's opinion that he needed much further. Here he comfortably wins the Palace House Stakes. Taffy Thomas up. (Photo courtesy of Leslie Sampson)

of their animal's running. Lester Piggott was the great exception among jockeys, and it was often amusing to see those hoping for a lengthy postmortem to be rewarded with a just a wry smile, although the trainer might well be given an insightful comment later in the day. Piggott was without doubt the most talented European rider of the second half of the 20th century.

An apprentice can be a useful addition to any stable, if properly trained and managed, but there will be a great deal of aggravation involved unless we are very careful. It is extremely expensive to run horses purely to instruct young riders, and any horses kept for that purpose must not only be competitive in their own class, but should also be useful in leading work at home. Old horses that are suitable can be picked up quite cheaply from claiming races or from the sales.

The technical schooling given to any apprentice should be very thorough, with particular attention paid to stylish riding, including on the way to the start as this often attracts notice by other trainers. Obviously all variations of changing hands and whip-riding should be practised until they could be done blindfolded before our embryonic jockey is loosed upon an unsuspecting public. The first few rides should be regarded as sighting missions to allow beginners to play themselves in without any pressure and without getting in anyone's way. Once they do know what they are doing they should not be booked for horses without ability as although good horses may make good jockeys, the reverse is also definitely true. We aim to mould a useful member of our team, not a defeatist resigned merely to going down and coming back.

It is extremely unusual for any apprentice regularly to achieve the same level of performance with idle horses as would a senior rider, hence the riding allowance, and deplorable runs by horses in apparently suitable races are very common even with some highly praised youngsters at the controls. If any apprentice can

already ride big sprawling horses at the start of their career then their future should be considered bright as long as they are given the right opportunities.

Weight is a problem for many riders and it is essential that our apprentice approach this aspect of their life sensibly. Excessive wasting is very debilitating to young riders and it should be avoided, with their weight being constantly maintained, by a sensible diet, at within a couple of pounds of their realistic minimum. If this plan is strictly followed, those last two pounds can be relatively easily lost when required. "The youth that trains to ride or run a race, must bear privation with unruffled face," as Byron remarked. All apprentices must also frequently bear the frustration of being jocked off by a senior rider with similarly unruffled face.

We may often hear heart-rending tales of riders who are obliged to spend long hours sweating to make the weight; however, common sense leads us to suspect that in most cases the same few pounds are going on and coming off daily. Tony Ives may have been the prime example of this, as he regularly reduced by 6 or 7lbs in the mornings, which often led to his being unavailable to ride work. The theory of roughly maintaining the weight of his last ride of the afternoon held few attractions for Tony! The methods of sweating and taking strong purgatives to waste used by Fred Archer have always been so widely described as to become a part of our heritage without much thought being given to this aspect of the matter. A contemporary of Archer at Heath House, lightweight rider Harry Morgan, tells us, in E. M. Humphris' *Life of Fred Archer*: "Archer wasted by taking medicine and Turkish baths. Fred did like sweet stuff. He was a one for jam and cakes. In fact, for anything sweet."

Mention of Fred Archer raises an interesting point regarding jockeys, which is their vulnerabilty to accusations of malpractice in the form of stopping horses. Even Archer (whose reputation stood so high that the contemporary phrase 'Archer's up' signified that all was well with any endeavour) was accused by mischief-makers of stopping Gaillard in the 1883 Derby so that his brother might win with second-placed Highland Chief. Following her St Leger victory in 1882 there was also much ill-informed comment on Dutch Oven's previous beaten races. The fact that Gaillard was only beaten in what we would call a three-way photo finish, and that Archer had been furious at being claimed to ride Dutch Oven, as he had agreed upon a fee of a thousand pounds to ride the favourite Geheimmiss, were overlooked. This demonstrates just how easily the jockey can be accused by trouble-makers who talk through their pockets. Most horses that could have won their race are defeated through lack of peak fitness, lack of ability, bad luck in running or simple human error. Unfortunately, under the present British system, a great many horses which are not perhaps quite able to win are certainly prevented from finishing anywhere near the placed horses with a view to influencing their handicap rating.

The influence that the Turf formerly exerted on Society generally is exemplified by the number of its phrases which, like 'Archer's up!', entered the language, although their origins are no longer acknowledged. The phrases 'to put one's best foot forward' and 'to wrap in cotton wool' refer, respectively, to the change of leads by a racehorse in the closing stages of his race and to the American system of heavily bandaging racehorses to protect their delicate and valuable legs. 'To keep under wraps' and 'to catch on the hop' have also descended from racing practices. The first derives from the former (pre-rubber reins) practice of jockeys wrapping the reins around their hands, thereby not allowing their mount to show his full speed, and the second to the ability of a trotting driver to catch his horse in its attempt to break its gait before it managed to do so. In Cockney rhyming slang to be alone is to be 'on your Tod (Sloan)'. Pool rooms were initially the places where the original form of pool betting took place, and where the Faces presumably amused themselves by playing the game which later took the name of the venue.

To retain a rider we need only be concerned with our own opinion of their riding performance as that will invariably be more accurate than that of disgruntled bettors. We should always be aware that there may be occasions even when using the best jockeys in which the easiest way to placate the irate owner will be to blame the rider for the defeat.

In many respects, the same theories apply to apprentice training as to breaking the yearlings and they are as set out in the Book of Proverbs, 22:6: "Train up a child in the way he should go: and when he is old he will not depart from it." To this end, all apprentices should be made aware of the importance of presenting themselves as smart and polite. They must be especially aware of the necessity of keeping their own counsel as regards the horses in the stable if they do expect us to advance their career. Some owners may attempt to cultivate relationships with the work riders to obtain information regarding horses other than their own. These people would certainly not appreciate their personal string being discussed with others and this practice should be discouraged, as it invariably leads to bad feeling.

Commercial Considerations

"A good name is rather to be chosen than great riches." Proverbs 32:16

he success or otherwise of the whole enterprise will depend on the turnover generated by the sales of our horses, and although it might be foolish to think of the operation as profitable there is every reason to anticipate a long innings as long as we remain focused on this fact. If the total of sales can, over an extended period, be made to equal the total purchase price, then the actual cost will be the difference between the training expense and any prize money. Obviously in Britain that shortfall may be large, but the expense must be set against the pleasure of competing regularly at a respectable level in the Sport of Kings. In other racing jurisdictions it may well be possible to make this particular system work financially as well as from a sporting angle, due to the healthier prize money available.

We may frequently be obliged to sell horses that we would rather retain to race, as their export value very often far outstrips any earning potential on the racecourses of Britain. This might be seen as a drawback to the system as a whole, but as long as the same tried and tested procedures are religiously followed there is no reason to suppose we cannot regularly find replacements to repeat the process next year.

There is no sense in continuing to shoulder the expense of those horses that do not give hope of a successful outcome unless we really do expect them to improve for some reason, possibly over a longer trip, or when they get a little stronger or more experienced. A filly with a very promising sibling in another stable might also sometimes be retained whilst we monitor his progress, as the sister of a top performer is always saleable. All marginal animals that do not hold out realistic hopes of considerable improvement must always be sold if any reasonable offer is available. The continuing wear and tear of racing tends to diminish whatever charm they do possess for the next purchaser, and their expenses mount steadily if they continue to race unproductively. Those horses that do promise to improve are naturally to be very sparingly raced until they can begin to show some form. The winter racing on the all-weather tracks has provided an excellent showcase for these horses, and their prices are enhanced by their ability to handle the dirt.

Young horses that have been unlucky enough to have been defeated by a debutant talking horse should not be exposed again until the possibility of an advantageous sale has been fully explored. Fortunately, there is a steady supply of overhyped newcomers. In Newmarket we say, "The dogs are barking this one's name!" It is sometimes relatively easy to sell one of their victims at an inflated price. It is obviously essential that we are able to judge correctly the true ability of our own horse if we are occasionally to turn such a racecourse defeat into a commercial success. Once it is generally accepted that we are always genuine sellers we may do very well in this particular situation.

The reverse of the situation described above should also be borne in mind. We may occasionally find one of our string, which we have tried quite highly at home, is defeated or hard-pressed in his race by an unconsidered rival. As long as we have no reason to suppose there to be anything amiss with our horse, and particularly should the rival hail from a stable with few two-year-olds, we should attempt to buy the other animal. It is quite common for small stables that do not specialise in youngsters to be entertaining to some degree an angel unawares.

Our general rule should be to sell all our stock whenever we think that their full sale potential has been realised. At the same time, we hope that the horse may still prove to be relatively successful for the new owner. Always to leave something for the next man has proved a sound maxim for generations of professional horse dealers, and we must remember this in order to dispose of our animals to best advantage over an extended period. Repeat business is definitely the key to this area of operations and buyers will always tend to return to a fruitful scource, even at high prices.

We may very occasionally sell a horse that subsequently does exceptionally well for his new connections and when this happens it must be accepted with good grace. We never give refunds on those horses which don't improve, so our regular clients are entitled to an unwitting bargain now and again. The people to whom we sell presumably buy all the horses thinking that they will do well. If we pay strict attention to our guidelines there will be very few such occasions for regret, and any such can be regarded as good publicity and should be weighed against the many ordinary horses sold at inflated prices. Unfortunately this concept can prove difficult for owners, although they are normally quite delighted when the money comes in for any oversold day-to-day horses. Although it is essential to sell regularly, it is as well to make sure the various scenarios are fully discussed with owners before each and every sale in order to eliminate recriminations at a later date.

Those horses with defects should be sold as well as can be arranged without normally involving our regular clients. Once we have established a close rapport with regular purchasers, then they may take certain horses with fully disclosed defects at a price that reflects the extra risk involved. If this situation is to develop and is to continue, it is essential that the client be accurately informed of any problem, and that he receives no unpleasant surprises. We must never risk losing our credibility with regular contacts for the short-term advantage of selling one animal, and our owners must be made aware of the vital importance of this fact.

Horses with moderately serious physical problems and those that prove incorrigible in their behaviour are best sold at public auction, without reserve and without warranty. When asked to recommend these animals we should be aware of the implications of dropping them on the toes of any existing, or future, clients and of causing bad feeling for no great gain. It is better to make some such remark as "He's not for you" in answer to any enquiries about doubtful cast-offs. Anyone who does bid for our culls without asking about their history and prospects is fair game! When our sales at auction fail to attract good prices we can accept this as a backhanded compliment, since it implies that people are wary of trying to improve the records of what are known to be our rejects. Horses from stables that realise long prices for their sale drafts, often far above the animals' apparent worth based on their current form, may be regarded as likely to be improved upon by another trainer.

We should be at pains to ensure that those horses claimed from us will rarely show anything of note for their new connections. Once this has been established by the subsequent failure of those we do lose then we may occasionally take the liberty of running an old horse with some problems well below his correct grade without much fear of losing him. If our horses were to regularly run for a price well below their value we would deserve to have some of them taken. Any trainer's annoyance at losing horses out of claiming races is unprofessional, and demonstrates a lack of self-belief.

Very seriously or terminally damaged

horses, and complete lunatics, should be destroyed in the yard, as that at least spares them the trauma they will otherwise endure. Although we will normally not be involved in horses at the bottom end of the market the problem of the steady decline in value, and therefore in circumstances, of many ageing racehorses is a distressing one with no apparent solution. The racing authorities could perhaps address the problem through a charge of, say £2,000 per initial registration, redeemable on destruction by the authority's official agency. This plan would prove universally unpopular because of the cost, but something along those lines would at least spare racehorses a distressing descent through the equine ranks; it is once they have left the racing scene that their real troubles tend to commence.

The Chinese poet Tu Fu wrote in the 8th century of the pitiful cavalry horses abandoned by the roadside once they were no longer needed. Although this book is not really intended to be a compendium of poetry, the words seemed to describe graphically the underbelly of our sport.

"The thin horse in the Eastern Wasteland distresses me,
His bones stand out like the pillars on a wall.
Hitched up, he tries to move, but staggers and keels over
Yet how he still longs to prance and step high!

If you examine the six brands, he bears the official stamp,
He was left at the roadside by the three armies.
His skin is dry and flaking, encrusted with mud,
His coat dull, he stands desolate in frost and snow."

This emotive little poem can be found in Olwen Way's comprehensive anthology *The Poetry of Horses*. With her late husband Robert, Olwen bred the brilliant two mile chaser Flyingbolt at Borough Green near Newmarket.

Gambling
"A horse is counted but a vain thing to save a man."
Psalms 32:16

Whilst on the subject of underbellies(!), betting seems to hold a fatal fascination for many people. The majority of those who regularly bet on horses do not seem to realise that a professional gambler should be content to show a percentage return greater than that he would receive were his money in something like unit trusts, although that speculation would obviously be less time-consuming. As that degree of profitability over an extended period, which might easily involve lengthy barren spells, is the best-case scenario, it is difficult to see any purpose in gambling forming part of our plan. There is no reason, however, not to support our runners to a moderate degree when we feel that they are competitive and, most importantly, the odds against them represent value.

In practical terms, the training of horses to maximise their potential earnings and value could very often be compromised by gambling considerations. If we wish to run our horses initially so as to make sure they are favourably handicapped we must necessarily devalue them. Suppose an animal we adjudge to be capable of running to a rating of 85 receives one of 50 or 60 after a few quiet runs, then he should certainly have an excellent chance of winning a handicap whenever he is turned loose. The often-overlooked downside to this plan is that the animal's capital value has been greatly reduced, whilst his cost in the form of training and racing expenses has been increased by possibly several thousand pounds. We have still to go out and win the race! In practice, there can be no guarantee that even the best-handicapped horse in the world will have racing luck on any particular day, or that he may not encounter an even better animal which has also been "just practising" (in the words of trainer and gambler Barney Curley). If he is unlucky, the expenses will have taken another dramatic leap in the form of the unsuccessful wager. If by any chance we should have it off and should happen to win a substantial sum on one or two occasions there will subsequently be great difficulty getting our wagers accepted at a rewarding price, if at all. Generally speaking nowadays, all those who recount their massive gambles are overall losers in a big way. The bookmakers are only interested in taking sizeable bets from major losers, or possibly from those whom they have identified as potential major losers.

A sound maiden that has reasonable placed form in England is always a saleable item on the American market, and to concentrate upon preserving the capital value of the horse makes more sense than lining up a bet. There does seem to exist amongst racing enthusiasts a definite syndrome in which the true bottom line may seem, in the short term at least, less important than being thought to be clever. As we have tried hard to implement a code of practice based upon common sense, this self-delusion is not an attractive proposition. We hope to survive in the harsh environment of racing due to correct practices and applied knowledge rather than to create the illusion of success by winning handicaps, whilst at the same time having regularly to refinance the whole operation due to our having so devalued the majority of our string.

From time to time there may occur an opportunity to bet with above-average hope of success on a smart two-year-old with as yet unexposed ability and these chances may be seized eagerly. Obviously, any betting transaction carries the risk of failure, but as long as we have not intentionally decreased the value of the horse in setting them up, nor incurred the extra expense of training and running a nontryer, there is every hope that selective betting on the better class team members may show some profit. The total enterprise of a racing stable may be said to be one enormous wager, and great care must be taken not to tip

the scales further against us. To this end, we should always be aware of the statistical probability of success or failure of betting generally, and to restrict betting to those occasions when we feel that the price offered about our runner is generous based on our particular estimation of his talent. We should never bet on an odds-on shot, however big a certainty he might appear.

One of the best trials we ever had of a two-year-old was a horse called Ayoub that worked with a four-year-old, Jawhara, getting a stone, and again at level weights. The old horse, in between the two works, easily won a competitive handicap with 9st 5lb on her back. Needless to say, the bold Ayoub failed. This horse should have been a certainty, as his trial had been duplicated and in fact he had also worked with the very smart three-year-old, Abdu, getting a stone. The fact of this reversal emphasises the folly of allowing betting to complicate our already difficult task. On the other hand, Brondesbury was beating the useful four-year-old Tamdown Flyer at level weights in early March before his two-year-old debut, and he did win by half the track. When Que Sera made her first start, the weather was so bad that there was an inspection of the track and the continuation of racing after the feature race was in some doubt. This filly's work with Camisite, an old horse and a stakes winner, had been so good that abandonment of the meeting was the only worry. She duly won with her head on her chest, although her owner was so unnerved by the track conditions that he failed to maximise his opportunity. He said after the race that he had waited all his life to be told, "This will win", and when it happened he had gone to pieces because of the weather! To any student of trial form the defeat of Ayoub would have been an impossibility, and his name should always be borne in mind as a warning that wagering can be detrimental to financial health even in seemingly cast-iron circumstances.

Interpretation of statistics does seem to be a closed book to the racing world, and their lack of

Abdu and Tommy Hardman. This was another who might have equalled the record number of wins at two; as it was he won nine times. Unfortunately, he won only one of his first five starts, and at the end of the year he was elevated to the highest level of competition. This picture was taken at the end of his juvenile year. Despite being so small, he was regularly placed in all the best sprints at three and four - in an era of good sprinters.
(Photo courtesy of Rouch & Co.)

regard for this subject appears to ignore the fact that the real world makes all its forecasts and predictions based on careful analysis of previous events. There is a great deal of information available to us should we care to avail ourselves of it, but this information may need some closer examination before we act upon it. The figures relating to success in many areas of the sport will be found to be relatively easy to obtain, but are of little use without some interpretation. An insurance company decides on the level of premium to be charged in different cases by considering what the statistical probabilities are, based on past experience; all our decisions should be similarly based on the balance of probability. The late Eddie Magner was certainly one of racing's eccentrics, although he could speak at first hand of Pretty Polly (and her dam!), but in his saner moments he often remarked (to then young trainers!) that, "Experience teaches fools, but a wise man learns by the experience of others." It is easier to appreciate now his advice on the wisdom of properly examining all available data in a very high-risk business; Magner would have greatly appreciated this last remark, as his other stock truism to us was that "Youth is wasted on the young."

It is a well-known fact, as they say, that approximately one in three betting favourites win. However, there are also figures available to inform us what percentage of horses actually races, wins a race at two, wins a race ever, wins first time out, wins a stakes race, wins a Group race, becomes a stallion prospect and so on. In examining statistics in Britain it might make sense to in some way disregard the purported successes of lowly rated animals, purely because their resale value will in most cases be proportional to their rating. If our personal results do not, after allowing ourselves time to get up and running, at the very least match the industry's overall success rates then we cannot hope to continue without constant injections of fresh capital. On the other hand, if our stable statistics do happen to well exceed what might be termed the statistical norm, we may anticipate some chance of survival, as long as the same system continues to be applied.

As long as the results appear to confirm the soundness of our system over a period of time, taking account of the standard of the stock we are working with, we should certainly not change any aspect of it too hastily in the case of the inevitable periodic slump. Panic-stricken alterations to feeding and exercise regimes are common in these circumstances, but are not to be recommended when a proven system is already in place. If we remain calm and relatively cheerful, most slumps go away as quickly as they arrive and often no real explanation may ever emerge. It is important, however, not to become too resigned to bad results and the number of stable runners should always be reduced until things start to improve. We should keep Mr Kipling's advice before us at all times: "If you can meet with Triumph and Disaster and treat those two impostors just the same…you'll be a man my son!" Sometimes it is more difficult to be a good winner than a good loser and this is equally worth bearing in mind should we get on

a roll, as several consecutive victories will inevitably precede a proportional run of defeats.

Any deviation that may be made from the tried and tested, particularly in the case of the purchasing strategy, which is vitally important, must be very carefully monitored and it should be abandoned immediately it appears less effective than the old method. Should any other factors, such as the progeny of certain sires or recruits from certain farms, specific pinhookers, or even breeders, seem to predispose towards poor performance in a racing environment, we should examine the matter closely and deal with it clinically, so as not to compromise the results of the whole stable. Even with no clear scientific explanation for declining results in the wake of any change in the sources of young stock, we would be wise to revert to our original strategy as far as recruiting is concerned. In the unlikely event that suspect sources should subsequently provide our rivals with a succession of classy performers, we may be proved to have acted hastily; however, missing occasional able runners is far less serious than condemning ourselves to being saddled with persistent underachievers. Obviously an ability to interpret and compare statistics and the laws of reasonable probability with some degree of common sense is necessary when attempting to identify areas of increased risk, so as to avoid wrongly attributing the blame for any fall in success.

Systemic Disease
"Do men gather grapes of thorns, or figs of thistles?"
St. Matthew 7:16

Any suspicion that the inmates of the stable are not performing as they ought, and specifically that they are not responding to the training regime in a normal progressive manner, needs urgent and thorough investigation. There will always be unexplained slumps in the performance of any stable, but if the inmates do seem constantly to suffer a succession of minor ills, and temperament problems do increase, there is every prospect of some systemic disease in the stable. Several former major league flat race trainers have suffered virtually complete collapse of their stables in recent years, with no explanation other than 'The Virus'. This universal excuse has become as widely accepted as evidence that the modern racehorse is too delicate to be trained, and whilst it would be foolish to underestimate the devastating effects of many viral episodes, it seems unreasonable to believe that horses escape other career-compromising illnesses. Any repeated unusual symptoms, even if they seem to be insignificant, in a racing yard should be examined as a matter of urgency. Good trainers do not forget how to train, although they may certainly lose confidence if their established and successful practices no longer seem to obtain results.

The true potential of systemic disease to derail a racehorse's career may not be fully appreciated currently simply because most victims will never demonstrate particularly serious symptoms that cannot be attributed to something else. Both equine protozoal myeloencephalitis (EPM) and Lyme disease have proved to be implicated in disastrous decline in many animals, but may well have passed undiagnosed in many others. Although unrelated diseases, they may cause some similar symptoms to each other and to other infections. If one or more of these problems does get into any group of horses, and particularly if there may be a whirlpool effect due to the constant exchange of animals between the racing stable and implicated studs, there is every likelihood of a steady decline in results. Repeated episodes of slight fever, slight laminitis, chronic sore heels in the front legs of males, set fast, stumbling, interfering, occasional bolting, poor behaviour in starting stalls and entering or leaving the stable, mimicking of soft tissue injuries, muscle loss, obsessive behaviour such as babyish chewing in older horses, constant licking, box-walking,

severe bed-scraping and so on, are not normal. None of these afflictions could be said to be particularly serious, and so they might easily be dismissed; however, they should not occur regularly in a well-run stable of healthy horses and for that reason are very likely to be indicative of a more sinister scenario.

As more work is done on these infections and as the pool of knowledge steadily increases it is very possible that they will be found to be both more serious and more widespread than is currently thought. Some of them will almost certainly be proved to be vertically transmissible, and the possibility of cross-species infection may not be completely understood at present. It should be noted that it is extremely rare actually to see an engorged tick on a horse in training in Britain, even on one of the many animals clinically proven to be infected. Conceivably, the not uncommon insect bites, which often have runners coming from them, or the small (1 cm square) patches that appear to have had the hair removed and which occur behind the elbows, on the withers and particularly on the hocks, are the result of an attack on the horse by the tiny larval tick.

A fit and healthy racehorse is not a particularly neurotic animal, nor is it continually prey to minor ailments. If our organisation is to fulfil its objectives, it must be confident of exploiting each animal to its fullest potential. Achieving the degree of success commonly accepted throughout the sport will be relatively simple even with unhealthy horses, but we must consistently produce better than average runners for resale in order to generate cash flow, and this simply cannot be done with unhealthy horses. Our veterinary adviser should accept that inability to cope with and respond to a rigorous training regime is evidence of a problem. If he simply implicates a viral infection, in spite of there being no concrete evidence of one, without considering other causes of uncharacteristic failure in the team then we should urgently enlist help elsewhere, or the whole set-up will grind to a halt.

As there is very likely to be in some way or other a degree of rodent involvement in the spread of any general stable sickness problem, that situation must be addressed as vigorously as possible. Long-term antibiotic treatment of the whole string is advisable, as the life cycle of some infectious agents may be quite long. Every horse should probably have his own bridle and his own sponge, as all bodily fluids may also be implicated in the spread of such diseases. New arrivals must always be treated once we have attempted to eradicate any infection in the existing team, in order to avoid the possibility of fresh infection. There may well be no risk of reinfection, but at the moment, because of lack of interest in these illnesses, no one really knows. With some diseases it is perfectly conceivable that animals which are themselves racing relatively successfully might still be a source of infection to others. The prognosis for complete recovery in horses which showed signs of their central nervous system having been affected by demonstrating neurosis, minor coordination problems, or learning difficulties, is very questionable. Unless those individuals undergo rigorous antibiotic treatment, the outlook for their stud career may also be far from rosy. The English Rules of Racing have recently allowed the racing of horses that are receiving antibiotic treatment and it may prove necessary to maintain treatment throughout much of the career of certain animals purely to enable them to be trained. Obviously, should such horses ever hit a high spot in their form they should be sold immediately.

These thoughts have proved quite entertaining to set down on paper, but have deepened my regrets at not paying more attention to the Old Man whilst I still had the chance to discuss and more completely absorb the theory and practice of horsemanship he had adapted from 'Professor' Jesse Beery's system, published in pamphlet form in 1908. Nevertheless this effort may now, I hope, furnish some interest and insight for those who have never been associated with the practical side of racing, nor had the opportunity to find out what makes a racehorse tick. If they should be read by any who have already felt the heat of racing competition then those readers might compare the content with their own experiences. Should anyone discover a useful hint on the practical aspects of running a successful training operation, or be stimulated to expand successfully on any of the matters raised, the project might be thought to have been worthwhile. All the practices described have been followed and refined over 30 years, and the results achieved might be said to have given them some validity. There may be instances of repetition of certain points, but certain basic truths recur in many situations. The reverse will hopefully not be found to be the case, and there should not be any occasions where the text contains in different places an opposing view on anything stated elsewhere, which might lead to confusion in the reader. The frequent statements that certain actions tend to result in specific reactions might be thought half-hearted or unconvincing, but in life as a whole there may be said to be exceptions to every rule. The intention here was to recommend following only those courses most likely, in the majority of cases and if properly applied, to be successful in diminishing the physical and financial dangers inherent in the horse business. Practice makes perfect for horses and humans alike. Those terms referring to conformation that are felt to be sufficiently explained and illustrated in specific sections of the text have not had that explanation repeated in the glossary. The exercise charts have been added in an attempt to illustrate the theory of systematic progression of work described in the text, and do not specifically relate to any particular animal.

We have throughout adopted various watchwords and one more motto may serve as a footnote: *Every Horse Teaches!*

The Old Man. Paddy O'Gorman on Northumberland Plate and Cesarewitch winner Utrillo chats with Clive Graham, 'The Scout', on The Severals at Newmarket in 1962. (Photo courtesy of Albert McCabe, Daily Express)

Tables

Write the vision, and make it plain upon tables, that he may run that readeth it. Habakkuk 2;2

PROGRAMME FOR OLDER HORSES STARTING FROM SCRATCH, NEW ARRIVALS OR RECOVERING AFTER INJURY

Day 1–3	Ridden and led 30 min. Use ACP. if necessary
Day 4	Ridden loose in enclosed area 1 hour, including 3 x 5 minute jogs
Day 5	As above, including 4 jogs
Day 6–8	As above, including 3 x 10 min jogs
Day 9–11	Assess whether safe to go outside, 1 hour including 3 x 15 min trots. Be careful.
Day 12–16	Trot 20 min walk 10 min, trot 25 min
Day 17	Trot 2 x 15 min walk 2 x 5 min, canter 1 x 2 fur @ 20 secs/fur
Day 18–19	Same, plus canter 3 fur @ 20 sec/fur
Day 20–21	Trot 15 min, walk 2 x 3 fur @ 20 sec/fur
Day 22–23	Trot 15 min, walk, canter 2 x 4 fur @ 20 sec/fur
Day 24–25	Trot 15 min, walk, canter 3 x 4 fur @ 20 sec/fur
Day 26–27	Trot 15 min, canter 3 x 5 fur @ 20 sec/ fur
Day 28–31*	Trot 10 min, canter 2 x 5 fur @ 20 sec/fur, 1x 5 fur @ 18 sec/fur
Day 32–35	Trot 10 min, canter 2 x 5 fur @ 18 sec/fur, 1x 6 fur @ 18 sec/fur
Day 36–39	Trot 5 min, canter 2 x 6 fur @ 18 sec/fur 1 x 7 fur @ 18 sec/fur
Day 40–43	2 x 7 fur @ 18 sec/fur, 1 x 5 fur @ 16 sec/fur
Day 44–47	3 x 6 fur @ 16 sec/fur
Day 48–49	2 x 6 fur @ 16 sec/fur, 1 x 6 fur @ 15 sec/fur
Day 50–51	1 x 6 fur @ 16 sec/fur, 2 x 6 fur @ 15 sec/fur
Day 52–53	1 x 6 fur @ 16 sec/fur, 1 x 6 fur @ 14 sec/fur
Day 54	1 x 6 fur @ 16 sec fur, 1 x 4 fur @ 13 sec/fur
Day 55	1 x 7 fur @ 18 sec/fur [Easy day after first speed]
Day 56–57*	1 x 6 fur @ 16 sec/fur, 1 x 6 fur @ 15 sec/fur
Day 58	1 x 6 fur @ 16 sec/fur, 1 x 5 fur @ 13 sec/fur
Day 59–60	1 x 6 fur @ 16 sec/fur, 1 x 6 fur @ 15 sec/fur
Day 61	1 x 6 fur @ 16 sec/fur, 1 x 4 fur @ 12 sec/fur
Day 62–64	1 x 7 fur @ 16 sec/fur, 1 x 6 fur @ 15 sec/fur
Day 65	1 x 7 fur @ 16 sec/fur, 2 x 3 fur @ 12 sec/fur
Day 66–69	1 x 7 fur @ 16 sec/fur, 1 x 7 fur @ 15 sec/fur
Day 70	1 x 7 fur @ 16 sec/fur, 2 x 4 fur @ 13 sec/fur

Should be ready to resume normal regime for older horses; again, all increases assume easy completion of previous tasks. Sundays off. Any section can be expanded, but should not be shortened. Always walk 5/10 min between canters. Fresh horses should wear boots and should be kept as calm as possible to avoid further delays due to accidents.

*See *Training Programme For 2-Year-Olds* (page 158/9) for explanation of asterisks.

PROGRAMME FOR SORE SHINS REHABILITATION

Programme assumes sore shins are discovered before horse works with them.

Day 1	Walk 1 hour.	Hosepipe 2 x 15 mins [a.m. and p.m.]
Day 2	As above	
Day 3	As above	
Day 4	As above. Assess whether sound to jog.	Hosepipe as above
Day 5	If sound, jog 3 x 5 mins, walk 3 x 15 mins.	Hosepipe as above
Day 6	If sound, trot 3 x 10 mins, walk 3 x 10 mins.	Hosepipe as above
Days 7–17	Trot 3 x 15 mins, walk 3 x 5 mins.	Hosepipe as above
Day 18	Trot 2 x 15 mins, walk 2 x 5 mins, canter 1x 3 fur @ 20 sec/fur.	
		Hosepipe as above
Day 19	If sound, trot 15 mins, 2 x 3 fur @ 20 sec/fur.	Hosepipe as above
Day 20	Trot 10 mins, 2 x 4 fur @ 20 sec/fur.	Hosepipe as above
Day 21	Trot 10 mins, 2 x 5 fur @ 20 sec/ fur.	Hosepipe as above
Day 22	Trot 10 mins, 2 x 5 fur @ 18 sec/fur.	Hosepipe as above
Day 23	As above	
Day 24	Trot 5 mins, 2 x 5 fur @ 16 sec/fur.	Hosepipe as above
Day 25	As above	
Day 26	1 x 5 fur @ 16 sec/fur, 1 x 5 fur @ 15 sec/fur.	Hosepipe as above
Day 27	As above	
Day 28	1 x 6 fur @ 16 sec/fur, 1 x 6 fur @ 15 sec/fur.	Hosepipe as above
Day 29	1 x 6 fur @ 16 sec/fur, 1 x 4 fur @ 14 sec/fur.	Hosepipe as above
Day 30	Back to normal.	

As in all aspects of training, every increase assumes the previous stage was completed satisfactorily.

WEIGHT-FOR-AGE TABLE: FOR HOME TRIAL GALLOPS

A: 3-y-o, weight advantage (lbs) received from 4-y-o
B: 2-y-o, weight advantage (lbs) received from 3-y-o   [Receives A+B from a-4-y-o]

	Jan	Feb	Mar	Apr	May	Jun	Jul	Aug	Sep	Oct	Nov	Dec
5 furlongs												
A:	9	8	7	6	5	4	3	2	1	0	0	0
B:	-	35*	30*	27*	25	23	21	19	17	15	13	11
6 furlongs												
A:	11	10	9	8	7	6	5	4	3	2	1	0
B:	-	-	-	-	-	25	23	21	19	17	15	13
7 furlongs												
A:	13	12	11	10	9	8	7	6	5	4	3	2
B:	-	-	-	-	-	-	25	23	21	19	17	15

This scale is based on the official scale but has been slightly amended so as to appear more logical. As the young horse matures, he requires less of a weight concession, although obviously the longer trip is more difficult for him, hence the increased allowance. The example given on page 70 implies that, if a 2-y-o can work with a 70-rated 3-y-o, receiving only 7lbs instead of the 25 as shown here, then he will need to work to a rating of 88.

*It is not recommended to work 2-year-olds further than 3 furlongs with an older horse in February or 4 furlongs with an older horse in March.

TRAINING PROGRAMME FOR 2-YEAR-OLDS, STARTS JAN 4, EVERY DAY, SUNDAYS OFF

WORKLOAD →

WEEK	20 sec/fur	18 sec/fur	16 sec/fur	15 sec/fur	14 sec/fur	13 sec/fur	12 sec/fur	<12 sec/fur
Wk 1	2 x 4 fur							
Wk 2	2 x 5 fur							
Wk 3	3 x 5 fur							
Wk 4	2 x 5 fur	1 x 4 fur						
Wk 5*	1 x 5 fur	2 x 4 fur						

From now on WORKDAYS twice per week, Tues/Fri or Wed/Sat.

*This programme is too demanding for the more backward 2-year-olds. Once they have learnt to canter properly, by about Week 5, they should adopt a more gradual approach. If they are allowed 3 or 4 months to complete the work suggested between Days 28 and 58 of the *Programme For Older Horses Starting From Scratch* (page 156), then they will be ready to resume this programme at Week 12 (*), although they will have taken around 20 or 22 weeks to reach that point.

WEEK	20 sec/fur	18 sec/fur	16 sec/fur	15 sec/fur	14 sec/fur	13 sec/fur	12 sec/fur	<12 sec/fur
Wk 6 daily	1 x 5 fur	2 x 4 fur						
Workdays	1 x 5 fur							
Wk 7 daily	1 x 5 fur	1 x 5 fur						
Workdays	1 x 5 fur	1 x 5 fur	1 x 4 fur					
Wk 8 daily		1 x 5 fur	1 x 5 fur					
Workdays		1 x 5 fur			1 x 3 fur			
Wk 9 daily		1 x 5 fur		1 x 5 fur				
Workdays		1 x 5 fur			1 x 4 fur			
Wk 10 daily		1 x 5 fur		1 x 5 fur				
Workdays		1 x 5 fur				1 x 3 fur		
Wk 11 daily		1 x 5 fur		1 x 5 fur				
Workdays		1 x 5 fur				1 x 4 fur		
Wk 12 daily*		1 x 5 fur		1 x 5 fur				
Workday 1		1 x 5 fur				1 x 4 fur		
Workday 2		1 x 5 fur					1 x 2½ fur	
Wk 13 daily		1 x 5 fur		1 x 5 fur				
Workday 1		1 x 5 fur				1 x 4 fur		

Day / Session				
Wk 14 daily		1 x 5 fur	1 x 5 fur	
Workday 1	1 x 5 fur	1 x 5 fur	1 x 5 fur	1 x 4 fur
Workday 2	1 x 5 fur	1 x 5 fur		
Wk15 daily		1 x 6 fur	1 x 6 fur	
Workday 1	1 x 6 fur	1 x 6 fur	1 x 5 fur	1 x 4 fur
Workday 2	1 x 6 fur			
Wk 16 daily		1 x 6 fur	1 x 6 fur	
Workday 1	1 x 6 fur	1 x 6 fur	1 x 5 fur	1 x 5 fur
Workday 2	1 x 6 fur			1 x 2½ fur

Wk 17 Barring accidents – ready for a race, although not 100% tight yet.

Sunday	2 x 6 fur		
Monday	1 x 6 fur		
Tuesday	1 x 6 fur [Easy day – busy week]		1 x 5 fur
Wednesday	2 x 6 fur		1 x 5 fur
Thursday	2 x 6 fur		
Friday	1 x 3 fur	1 x 2½ fur	
Saturday	Race 5 furlongs in 1 min 03 sec [standing start]		RACE

Wk 18

Sunday	Walk and trot 20 mins	
Monday	1 x 5 fur	
Tuesday	1 x 5 fur	
Wednesday	2 x 6 fur	
Thursday	1 x 6 fur	
Friday work	1 x 6 fur	1 x 4 fur
Saturday	1 x 6 fur	

Wk 19

Sunday	Walk and trot 20 mins	
Monday	1 x 6 fur	1 x 2½ fur
Tuesday		RACE

Should improve 7lbs [2 or 3 lengths] from first start

This programme is intended to demonstrate the steady progression of the training process. In practice, there will be several holdups due to weather, ground conditions, sickness and sore shins. Every effort should always be made to ensure that there are no irrational leaps in the programme and that each step is completed satisfactorily before proceeding to the next. From this point onwards, the routine canter can, within reason, be the same as for the older horses; however, 2-year-olds should normally never be expected to work further than 6 furlongs at the 12 second rate.

Everyday Training

(See Programme For Older Horses, page 156)

(See Programme For Older Horses, page 156)

*T*he initial groundwork programme should be carefully set out so as to steadily increase fitness whilst building a strong foundation for the season ahead, and should not involve improvisation. Progress is monitored by careful observation of the horse's wind fitness, muscle tone, weight and general attitude. Once the horse has reached competition level, it is extremely difficult to be too specific or regimented about his requirements if the best possible results are to be obtained.

Basic training methods in Newmarket involve 2 daily canters. The first should be at a 'normal' cantering rate of around 17 or 18 sec/fur, followed by a second at around 15 sec/fur. In most cases, three canters are no longer used, probably reduced largely due to time constraints. Tuesday and Friday, or Wednesday and Saturday, are regarded as work days and the second trip will either be three parts speed at around 13 sec/fur or serious work involving 25 or 24 second quarters, usually in company. Any horse's work tends to reflect, to some extent, the distance he will compete at; however, it is extremely difficult to organise long-distance work satisfactorily and a race will often greatly benefit a staying horse. Pure sprinters can also be difficult to work satisfactorily over the full five furlongs and alternatives should be explored so as to lessen the dangers of creating short runners, and of making these animals too keen.

Various factors such as the geography of the ground being used, the state of the going and the availability, or otherwise, of working companions, will tend to influence daily training routines. Charts may tend to show as many variables as constants once the basic training is

completed and actual racing has begun, and would therefore prove confusing. It may be easier to think of the established racehorse's training programme as being based loosely on a points system, in which the important issue is that the weekly target points are actually earned rather than the manner in which they are earned.

In order to demonstrate the rationale behind the recommended flexible system, every rate of speed may be allotted a value. The number of yards covered per second (based on 220 yards divided by the sec/fur rate, rounded up) is for 16 sec/fur - 14 yards, for 15 sec/fur - 15, for 14 sec/fur - 16, for 13 sec/fur - 17 and for 12 sec/fur - 18. The practical relationship of one rate to another for the purpose of calculating work may be said to correspond to that between the number of yards in excess of 10 per second at each rate. For example 16 sec/fur is 4, 15 is 5, 14 is 6, 13 is 7 and 12 sec/fur is 8. If these rough values are borne in mind, it is easy to calculate a very flexible programme without the constraints of a rigid two workday system. It is apparent that if an animal is doing regular swinging canters and half speeds on his second trip daily then, in most cases, he will not require a full programme of really fast work, as long as he races regularly. These figures are intended to illustrate the theory, and do not imply that exact calculations have been made in terms of miles/hour.

If we take the first daily canter as being much the same whether the traditional two workday method is used or a more flexible one, then it need form no part of the calculation. There are many ways of achieving a similar total workload on the second trips throughout the week. A horse completing his first canters as normal and doing a 6 furlong second canter at a 15 second rate on

Monday, Tuesday, Thursday and Friday, with 5 furlong works at a 12 second rate on Wednesday and Saturday, may be said to have delivered (4 x 6 x 5) + (2 x 5 x 8), or 200 units of training in addition to his regular first canters. This is only an example; a clear-winded animal may not require as much and a gross horse might require more. If, however, this were felt to be an appropriate work schedule, then a weekly total of second trips comprising five x 7 fur at a 15 sec rate and one 3 furlong brush at a 12 sec rate would give a similar benefit to an already fit horse. There are virtually untold other ways in which he could deliver roughly the same weekly amount of meaningful training by various combinations which would, quite possibly, be more suited to his temperament and inclinations than the twice weekly workday ritual.

As a very general rule, the physical type of the horse will provide an idea of whether he is likely to require a great deal of work. However, physique can sometimes prove misleading as a guide and close attention should always be paid to how much the individual blows after his exercise, as described in the main text. Those horses which unexpectedly blow very hard, relative to their work and fitness, should be monitored as they may be unwell.

Accomplishing a similar amount of exercise in a less structured way may also tie in better with the work being done by other team members, giving a double benefit to a more flexible approach. The important thing is to keep in view just what a particular horse's overall schedule calls for, rather than become too regimented. The more work that any horse does whilst doing it cheerfully the better, but considerable ingenuity is often required to get, and keep, older and more cunning horses fit without making them sour. The use of times throughout this training schedule has been adopted in order simply to illustrate more clearly the principles advocated.

Any uncalled-for and unplanned increases should be avoided if possible but, if they do occur, they must not be ignored and should be compensated for.

A race should always be regarded as part of the training programme, and the horse should be returned to the training programme very quickly, as long as he has suffered no ill effects, in order to benefit from the effort.

Horses racing over longer trips should regularly go further, say 8 or 10 furlongs on some of their 15 sec rate trips; they can increase their speed a little over the last two furlongs on these occasions, but their fast work can normally be restricted to 6 or 7 furlongs.

It must be emphasised that the times referred to throughout these schedules are purely used in an attempt to clarify the principles involved; in effect, it is extremely difficult to accurately monitor time in a setting such as Newmarket Heath. The method of counting strides per half furlong as described in the text can be a useful aid, but is obviously dependent on correctly identifying the relationship between stride pattern and time for at least some of the horses in the string. An average horse will tend to take around 30 strides to the furlong when he is just barely still on the bridle (at around 12 sec/fur). This equates to a stride of around 22 feet.

As a general rule, more benefit will be derived from short repeats of 3 or 4 furlongs than from one longer trip at the same pace; however, this method can prove unsettling to many horses, particularly in a wide open environment, and it should be practised with caution. It can prove extremely useful in the case of an old horse which has become rather blasé, as he will only benefit by being slightly 'revved-up'.

All exercise is presumed to take place under the safest conditions possible; that is to say, fast work can always be postponed if the underfoot conditions are particularly bad in the short term. All riders must be instructed to use the freshest ground, which on a very wet day may be yesterday's ground once the fresh has been destroyed, and to pull their mounts up with extreme care at the end of work

Glossary

ACP Acepromazine: Mild oral or injected sedative.

Adequan Intramuscular injectable aid to joint wear and tear. Oral equivalent is chondroitin sulphate. Seek veterinary advice.

Back up, or down State of muscular tension, or relaxation. Indicates whether young horse is, or is not, likely to misbehave.

Balancer Proprietary pelletted feed with high protein content.

Bandage bow Visible tendon irregularity caused by ill-fitted leg protection.

Blinkers Prevent most lateral vision, also called blinds.

Blow up Weaken in closing stages of race, specifically due to lack of fitness.

Blue spray Antibiotic topical spray, universal 'heal all' in racing stable. Stings violently.

Boardwageman Stableman who has done an apprenticeship.

Boots Equine leg protectors.

Breakover Point [in time] of foot leaving ground to commence next stride.

Breastgirth Girth around chest to prevent roller from slipping back on yearlings and to prevent saddle slipping on light-framed horses in training and races.

Brush Exercise - short burst.

Bullring American, slang for very tight track, as at county fair.

B******* Comes out of the back end of bulls. Very common both in racing and the military because "B******* Always Baffles Brain".

Canter Routine exercise gait for racehorse, should be qualified by further description. The ground where such exercise takes place.

Cheap speed Ability to run one or two furlongs fast, not very useful in Thoroughbreds as minimum race distance is much further.

Cheeky See *Coltish*.

Clock in head Rider's [supposed] ability to accurately assess pace.

Closer Finishes well.

Cold elements Unregistered ancestors in a pedigree, unlikely to have been completely racing bred.

Coltish Male horse's over-awareness of his sexuality, too amorous or too aggressive.

Comealong Correctional rope halter for impressing 'Follow Me' lesson. See *War bridle*.

Crooked knees Blanket term for knee deformity. See text.

Cut Castrate, geld, make a gelding.

Curb Unsightly blemish below rear of hock, rarely a problem once established.

Curb chain Flat linked chain fitting below chin on more severe bridles from nonracing disciplines. Only seen on racehorses in South America.

Dermobion Antibiotic cream. Seek veterinary advice.

Desensitise Remove nervousness by systematic and inescapable exposure to cause.

Die in his rider's hands Horse - To weaken after giving erroneous impression that he was travelling reasonably comfortably. See *Find nothing*.

Dishonest Horse - Unwilling to try his best, a rogue, a thief, a villain, a pig [male], a cow [female]. Normally strengthened by expletive.

DMSO Excellent circulatory stimulator. Seek veterinary advice.

Double handful:

    Jockey Mount travelling very comfortably.

    Feeder Along with 'a dirty manger', the amount of their feed horses are reported as leaving. Check it for yourself!

Draw Withdraw feed and water for extended period prior to race.

Drop out Jockey - allow mount to fall well behind in early stages in order to reserve energy for finish. Also hold up, give a chance [to relax].

Easy lead The leader is allowed to set his own pace without being pressured by opponents.

EPM Equine Protozoal Myeloencephalitis: Infection by ingested parasite compromises horse's system and in severe cases leads to loss of co-ordination. Supposedly limited to American-breds.

Faces Habitual racecourse visitors. See *Punters*. Implies, not necessarily accurately, some informed knowledge of the game. Can be very reliable sources of very unreliable information!

False-run race Irregular, or very slow early, fractions. Often results in upset result.

Farmer's race Informal work, horses of mixed ability in a bunch at catch weights.

Fever rings Raised horizontal rings on hoof surface, indicating sickness or violent diet change.

Find nothing See *Die in hands*.

Foot/pastern axis [or hoof/pastern] The relationship between the angle of the hoof and that of the pastern, ideally they should agree.

Foot, to have [or lack] a turn of To have [or lack] acceleration. Sometimes referred to as having plenty of toe.

Fractions Sectional times of race or work. Fast early fractions the most costly in terms of energy.

Free Handicap Year end official assessment of the better runners, now integrated with Europe and America.

Free runner Difficult to restrain in early stages of race. In America, rank. See *Take hold*.

Free sweater Inclined to sweat without much exertion, implies nervous, excitable. In America, washy.

Gallop Technically fastest racehorse gait. Denotes strong work in Europe, but cantering exercise in America. Also ground where such exercise takes place.

Galloping track With more emphasis on stamina, suited to long-striding animals.

Garrison finish Vigorous last-ditch effort, after Edward 'Snapper' Garrison, 19th century American jockey.

Get out of system Violent but not sustained reaction provoked, often deliberately, by incautious application of breaking tackle. See *Have a go*.

Green Inexperienced, unable to concentrate on putting maximum effort into a race because of that.

Hack canter Just out of a trot.

Half speed Around 27 or 28 seconds per quarter mile.

Handicap mark Official assessment of horses ability which dictates weight to be allotted.

Hands [to keep his mount in his] Jockey - to have his mount prepared to accelerate on demand.

Hang Horse - tend to deviate from straight line. In America, tend not to go through with his effort in closing stages of race, be ungenuine.

Hard-knocking Horse - gives his all in a race.

Have a go See *Get out of system*.

Have it off Gamble successfully. By implication not really a gamble, due to advance knowledge of likely outcome.

Headcollar Halter.

Hold, to take Horse - to pull for his head, try to accelerate.

Hold of, to catch or grab Jockey - to take, more or less roughly, a shorter hold of his mount as a signal to accelerate. See *Pick up*.

Horseman One able to get a living by hands-on work with horses.

Horseman's Word Formerly associated with secret society of elite horsemen.

Horse sense What horsemen have. Also what prevents horses from betting on people.

Humane twitch Kinder version of the rope loop twisted around the nose to subdue rebellious subjects, this one more like a weak nutcracker. Fairly painless but still effective.

In soak Left standing in breaking tackle.

Isoxsuprine Circulatory stimulator, particularly effective in some foot problems. Extremely difficult to judge clearance times. Seek veterinary advice.

Jarred up Loss of normal fluency of action following training or racing on firm ground. 'Shouldery'.

Jibber Specifically horse which is inclined to refuse to go on to the exercise ground. Many actually do their work as normal once they have jumped off, but the starting problem normally gets worse.

Jocked off Jockey - replaced by another.

Jointy Specifically showing wear and tear in fetlock joints.

Join-up Successful theory of bonding with nervous or unco-operative animals. Can achieve very quick results in getting horses ridden for the first time, but mouthing, traffic practice etc. needs to be done afterwards.

Keys Small pieces of metal loosely attached to breaking bit to encourage salivation, a moist mouth is thought to be more responsive.

Laminitis Internal inflammation of the foot, traditionally associated with over-rich diet, but also symptomatic of more general challenges to the animal's system by systemic disease. Mild cases may not cause lameness, and so not be diagnosed. Very acute and often fatal version known as 'founder'.

Lay out of ground Jockey - intentionally or otherwise, lag far behind leaders during running.

Leary Unreliable, likely to take advantage of the unwary. Common acquired failing amongst, especially older, racehorses and their associates.

Leg [noun] Specifically injury to tendon in foreleg. [adj.] Leg trouble, leg problems - not specific, any limb infirmity.

Long toe, low heel Regrettably a common form of racehorse shoeing, minimises lost shoes, maximises leg injuries.

Lot or **Set** Those horses taken out to exercise at the same time, older horses were traditionally first lot, younger ones second lot, spares third lot.

Look of eagles Superior expression in outlook of racehorse, quite often indicates a superior runner.

Lug in Tend to hang towards the rail, the opposite of bear out.

Lunge rein Long rein used in early training from the ground, preferably with a swivel at the buckle to avoid twisting.

Lyme disease Infection by spirochete resulting in total undermining of system, although manifestations may not be correctly attributed because they are so varied, in fact often referred to as 'the great imitator'. Quite possibly inherited, and certainly appears to be rife on certain properties. A very serious, though under-diagnosed, illness in humans.

Monty Roberts Horseman/showman. Join-up specialist and inventor of reinforced rug for horses unhappy with feel of starting stalls against their sides.

Mouth Horse's - good, bad, light, hard, one-sided etc., responsiveness, or lack of it, to bit.

Naked oat Hybrid variety with no husk, hence more weight of oats in less volume.

Need the race Not yet fit.

Non-trier euphemisms Having a run [round], practising.

No fut, no 'oss Horseman's saying.

Normal canter First daily trip for horses in regular work programme, about 17 or 18 seconds per furlong.

OCD lesion Flaw in bone due to its irregular development. The significance of it is not absolutely clear.

Odds on The bettor has effectively become the bookmaker, in that the winnings will be less than the amount risked due to the horse's perceived outstanding prospect of victory. A certain recipe for disaster.

Offset knee Structurally incorrect, see text.

Pet Make a fuss of, show kindness to - and by implication to reward for current behaviour.

Pick up [his mount] Jockey - See *Hold of, to catch or grab*.

Pick up [his whip] Jockey - Turn whip into forehand position.

Pigeon toes Turn in.

Plater Low grade racehorse, originally selling plate standard but competitive in low grade handicaps introduced recently.

Poling Touching young horse all over with a light pole in order to accustom to handling without risk of handler being kicked.

Pony Horse of any size used for leading or accompanying young or rebellious team members. Not a female in the case of male followers.

Port The raised portion of the mouthpiece in some bar bits.

Punishment Consequence of misbehaviour. To be effective it must be seen as the immediate and guaranteed consequence - stupidly a racehorse is frequently punished for doing his best.

Punters Bettors. More specifically, bettors in the confidence of a lad or jockey who, directly or indirectly, are payed for stable information. Unfortunately, often found amongst the stable's owners.

Quarter mark Decorative markings on horse's coat, to emphasise its gloss.

Races, basic types of:

Maiden Nonwinners. Can be restricted to animals bought at auction below a stated price, or to the produce of stallions whose median yearling price is stated.

Condition race/Allowance race/Weight for Age race Eligibility requirements and weights to be carried are stipulated in conditions at time of entry.

Stakes race/Listed race In Britain, 3% of all races. A prestige category, winning confers heavier black type in sales catalogues.

Group race/Graded race In Britain, the top 2.5% of all races. Very prestigious, particularly Group One, winning them confers major black type.

Classic race The very best races for three-year-olds, run over distances from one mile to almost two miles in Britain, nine furlongs to a mile and a half in America. Five races in European countries, three in America. A winner of three classics is a Triple Crown Winner.

Handicap Weights allotted theoretically give all runners an equal chance, based on previous performance. Obviously open to abuse.

Claiming race More logical system where connections effectively handicap their own animal. The class of competition is relative to the claiming price. All horses can be claimed by qualified persons, an obvious disincentive to running a horse below his class. Unfortunately, British system includes a friendly claim so that abusers of the system can hope to get their horses back if they run them in too cheap a grade.

Selling race Theoretically the lowest grade. The winner is offered for sale by auction after the race, all other runners can be claimed. Useful two-year-olds can occasionally be found amongst selling race winners.

Racing manners Horse's acquired ability to conduct himself to best advantage during a race.

Rein around Placing second lunge rein on off side so as to first commence using the bit as a steering device.

"Revenons a ces moutons!" "Let us get back to the sheep [to business]".

Rogue's badge Unjustified slang for blinkers.

Rolled toe Rounding of the ground surface of the foot or shoe at the toe to facilitate breakover.

Roller Heavy surcingle with breastgirth attached and buckles for sidereins.

Rubber Traditionally a linen cloth for grooming; the groom himself.

Run down Abrasion to underside of fetlock joint caused by lack of strength in suspensory apparatus. Protected by run down bandages and/or patches, or by painting on rubber-like skin [Zinnegard].

Run in all shapes and sizes Excuse used for purchase of poor individuals.

Saturday horse High class performer, stakes races tend to be at the weekend.

Scalping Injury inflicted by forefoot on lower hind leg. Often difficult to protect with bandage because of angle of blow. Harness horses wear specific boot to protect themselves.

Scope Physical frame showing likelihood of considerable development and hence a racing career lasting beyond the juvenile season.

Scope Veterinary endoscopic examination of the horse's airway by portable machine.

See speed Ability of experienced horsemen to identify likely successful runners on first quick inspection.

Set fair Symmetrical arrangement of bedding in stable, flat middle, banked sides.

Setfast Azoturia, in America 'Tied-up'. Acute muscular cramp after exercise, call vet.

Sharp Physically precocious, likely to come to hand early as a two-year-old runner.

Sharp Canter. See swinging canter, two minute rate.

Sharp track With tight turns or undulations, unsuited to long-striding animals.

Short hip Measured from hip to furthest point of buttock. A long hip is more likely to indicate speed.

Sidereins Reins fixed to saddle to keep head moderately raised during driving and initial riding, attached to saddle by keepers fixed to girth straps.

Slack Long weak pasterns.

Something about him See *Look of eagles*.

Spares Newly arrived or lowly regarded horses not allocated to a particular lad.

Speed crazy Over-excited once fast work regime commences, unable to relax at exercise.

Splay feet Turn out. 'Charlie Chaplin'.

Splint Bony enlargement on [usually] foreleg below knee.

Splint Strap of material incorporated between up and down runs of exercise bandage and passed under the fetlock to increase support to suspensory system.

Standing martingale Runs from head to girth and prevents young horses adopting high head carriage. Fix to noseband or headcollar - not on to bit, which is too severe.

Stargazer Carries his head much too high.

Strapping Vigorous and prolonged grooming, previously a great annoyance to many horses. No longer practised.

Stuffy Thick in wind, by implication due to insufficient work.

Sucked along An inexplicably good effort, usually in a small field or a false-run race, and usually not repeated.

Sweetfeed Proprietary feed, a mix of grains in a molasses binding.

Sweet mouth Iron rather than stainless steel bit, promotes salivation.

Swinging canter About 15 seconds per furlong. See *Two minute rate*.

Systemic disease Any disease undermining the system generally.

Taken off his feet, or legs Unable to keep up, unbalanced because of this. Outpaced.

Talking horse His reputation precedes him, often unjustified!

Three parts [or three quarter, speed] About 25 or 26 seconds per quarter mile.

Toe See *Foot, to have [or lack] a turn of*.

Toe grab Banned in Britain. Flange of about 1/4 inch on the ground surface of the toe of a racing plate.

Tongue tie or strap Means of securing tongue in order to avoid breathing or steering problems caused by its getting over the bit.

Trial Formal work, at predetermined weights, in which there is at least one horse with known capabilities.

Trip Distance of race, or work.

Trip The race itself, as in 'horse had a rough trip.'

Trot out Safe transition from working to walking.

Two minute gallop [or rate (per mile)] See swinging canter, sharp canter.

Unbalanced Unable to initially attain a rhythmic stride through being outpaced, or having lost it through exhaustion. Often involves a degree of poor riding.

Ungenuine, ungenerous Horse unwilling to do his best at finish.

Use up Jockey - exhaust, implicitly through faulty tactics, his mount's energy.

Vetrap Proprietary self-adhesive bandage.

Virus Coverall excuse for poor performance, although viral infections are common.

War bridle See *Comealong*. May actually predate any Native American contact with horses.

Washy See *Free sweater*.

Waste Jockey - To reduce weight severely.

Weight for age Scale of weights designed to neutralise difference in maturity and strength between age groups. Must always be considered in a trial.

Whoa Common usage for all slow down and desist commands for racehorses.

Windgall Soft swelling above of fetlock indicating some trauma in the area, quite common but requires constant monitoring. In America, windpuff.

Winding up Thrashing.

Wipe over A quick grooming.

Work for benefit of the two-year-old Older horse not to try to defeat younger work companion.

Working blister Irritation induced to improve blood supply to injured limb, in order to promote healing. Not severe enough to completely stop training.

Index

Index